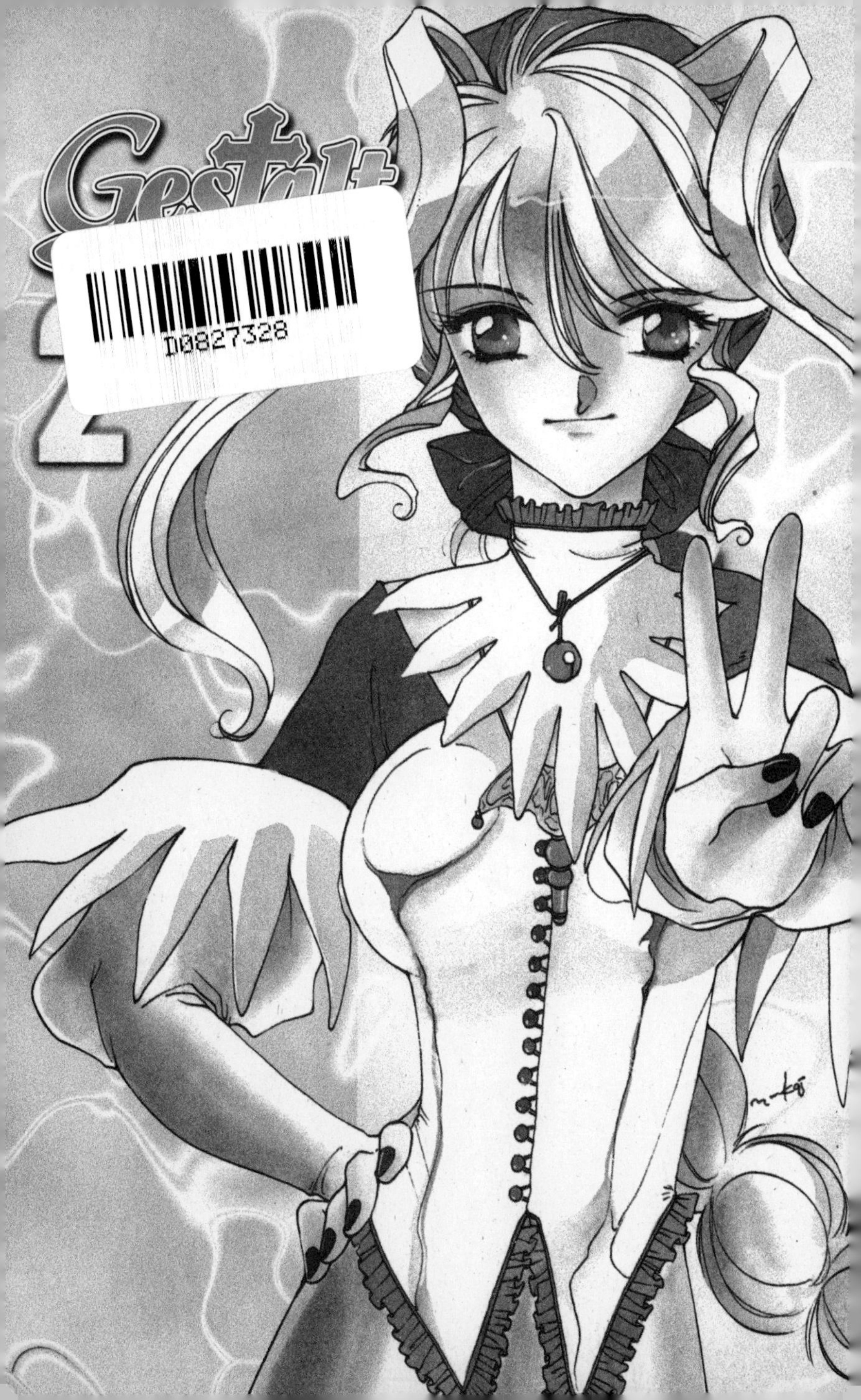
Gestalt
2

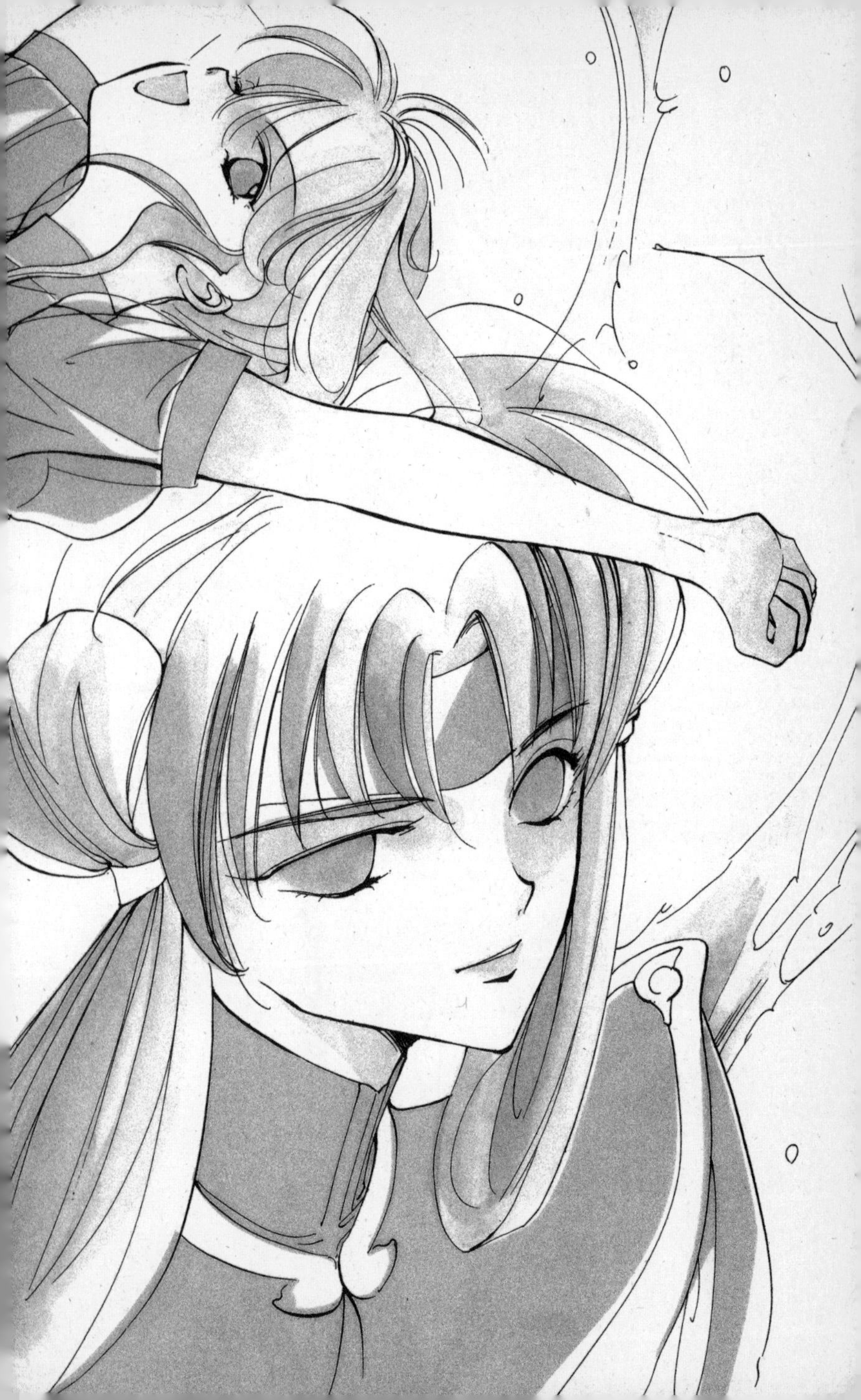

Illust Gallery

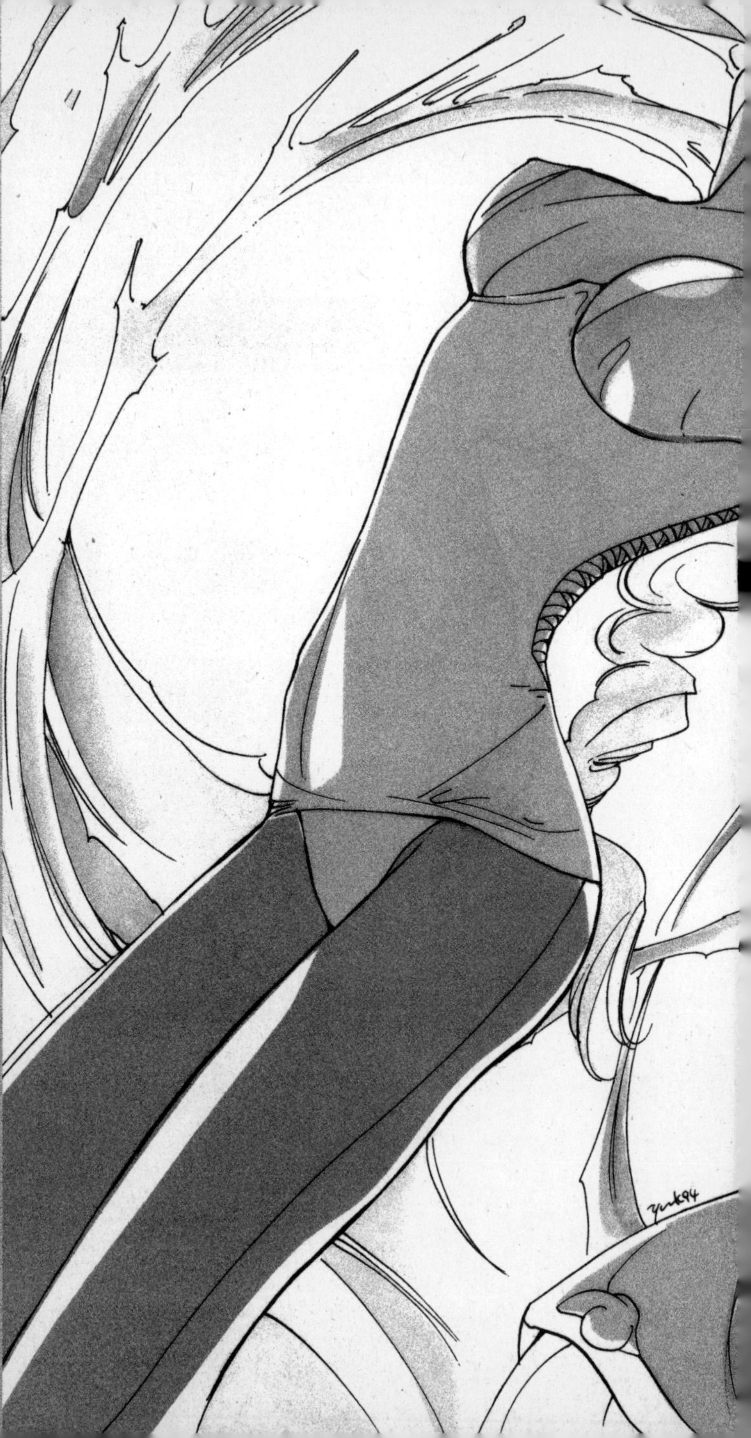

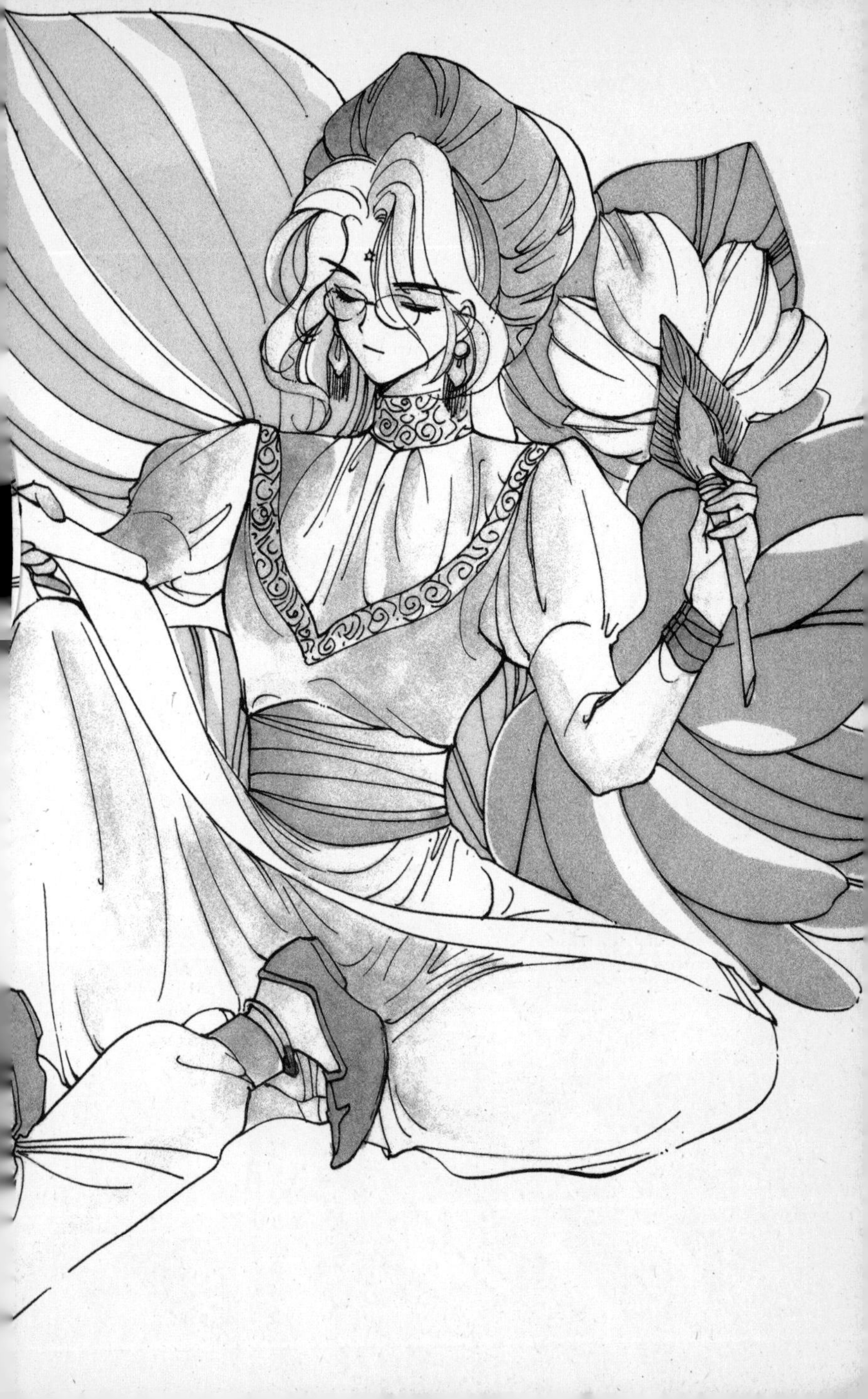

Illust Gallery

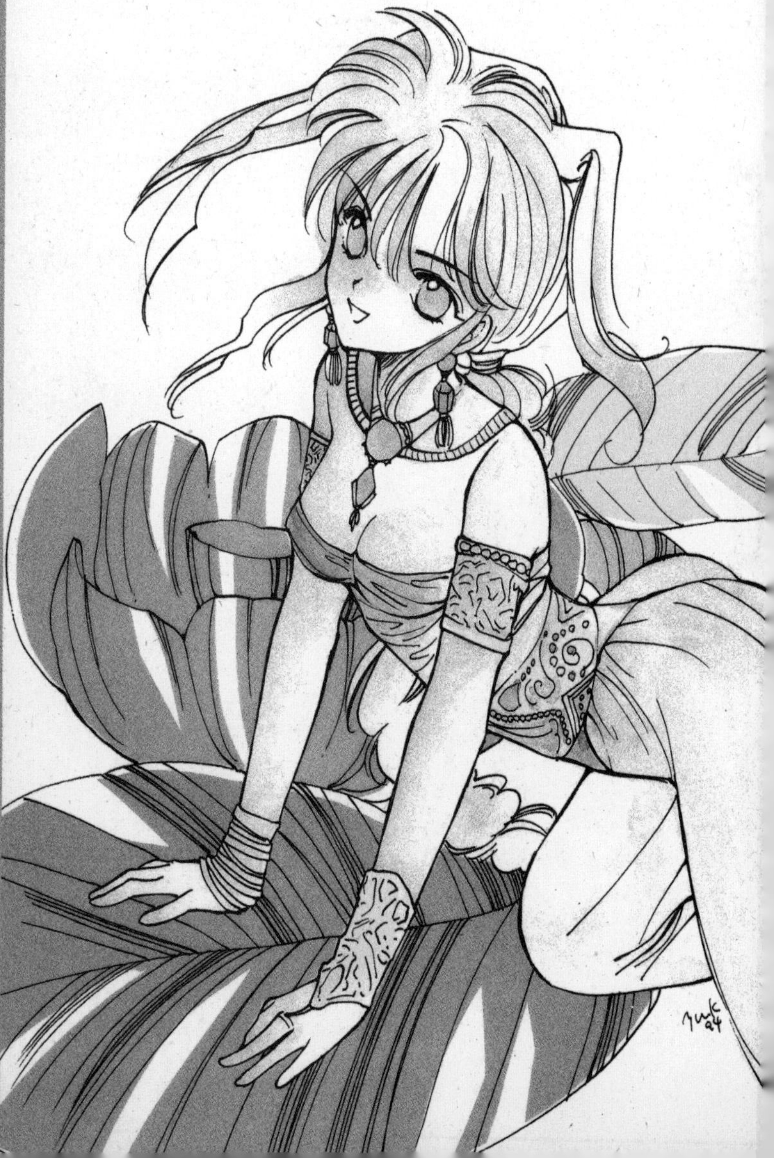

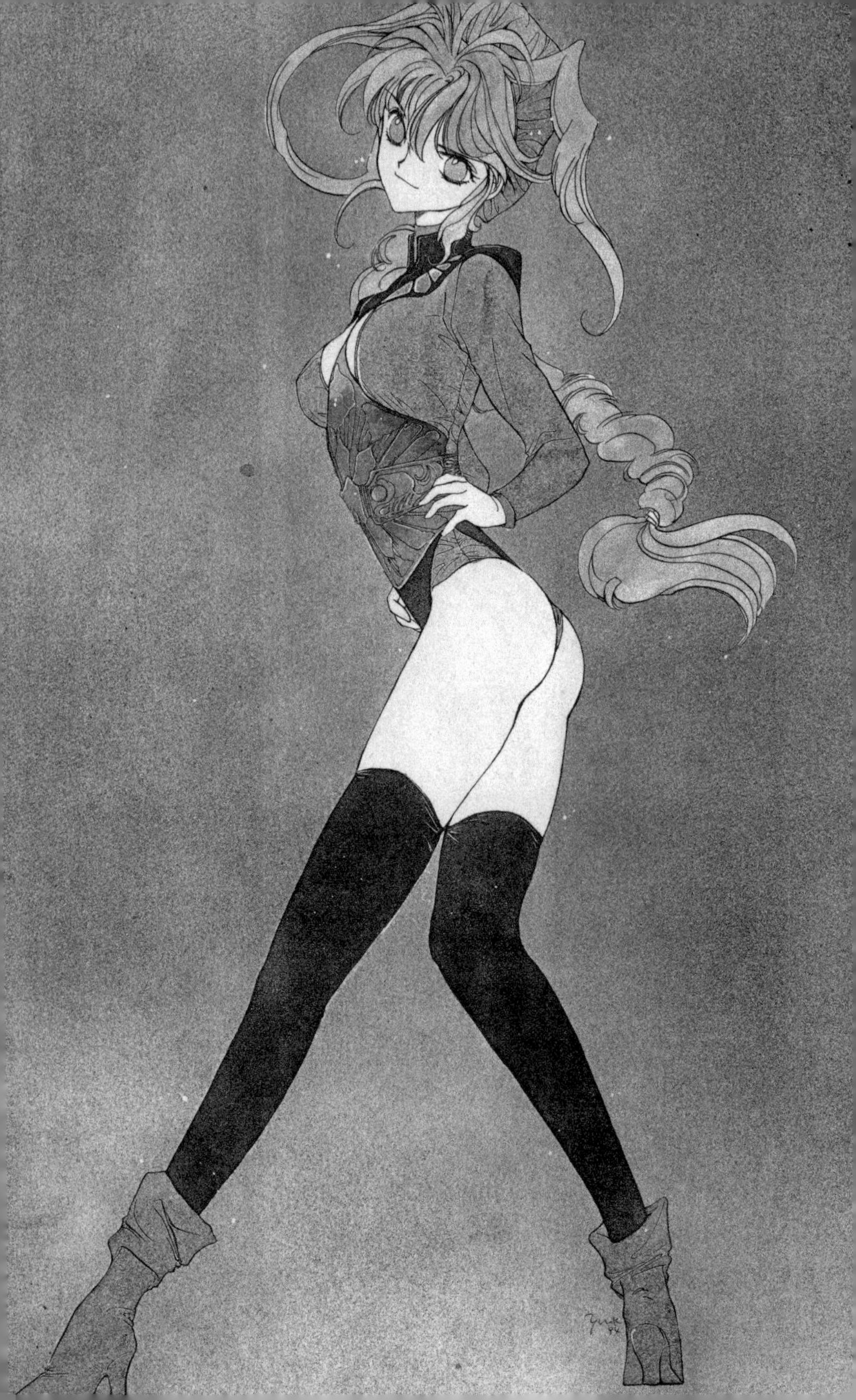

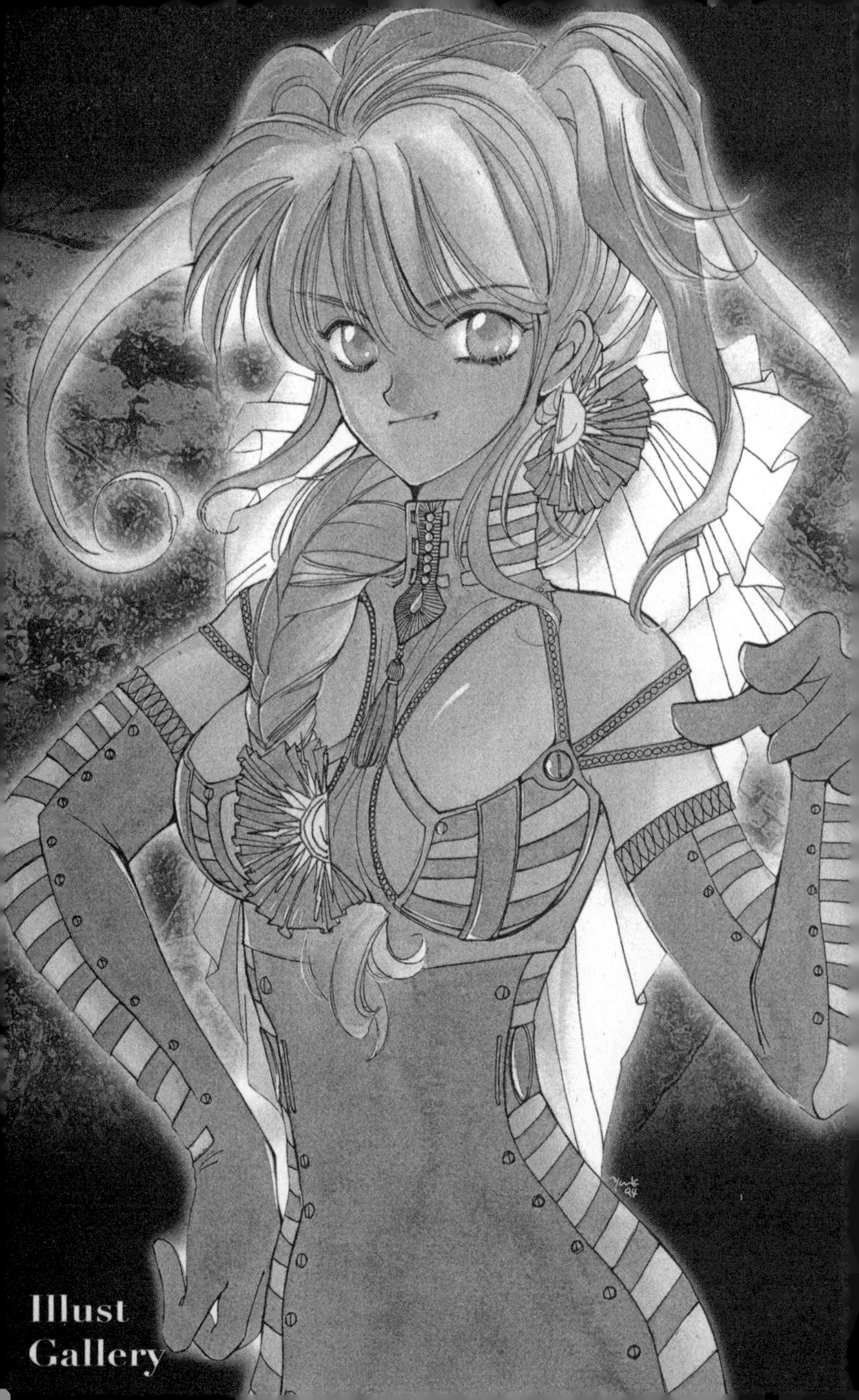
Illust
Gallery

CONTENTS

2

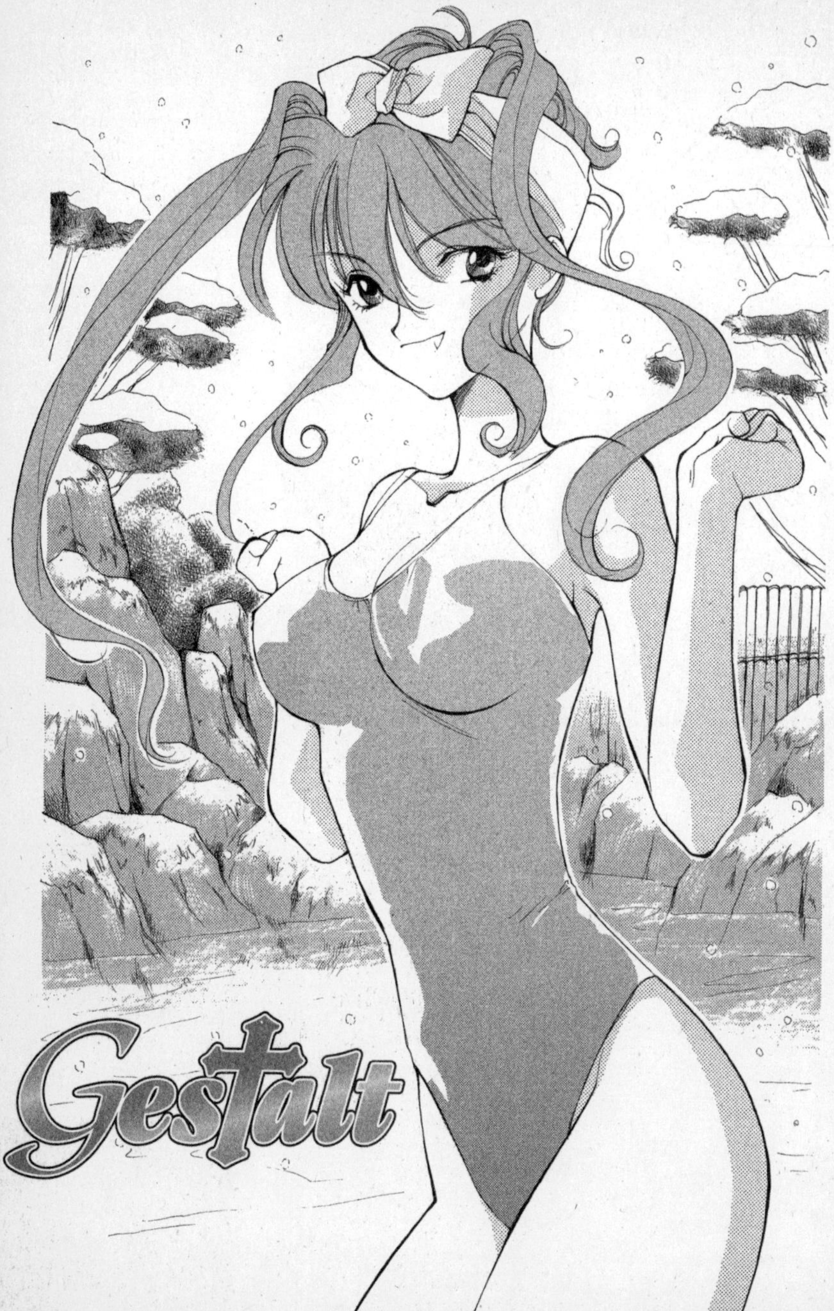
Gestalt

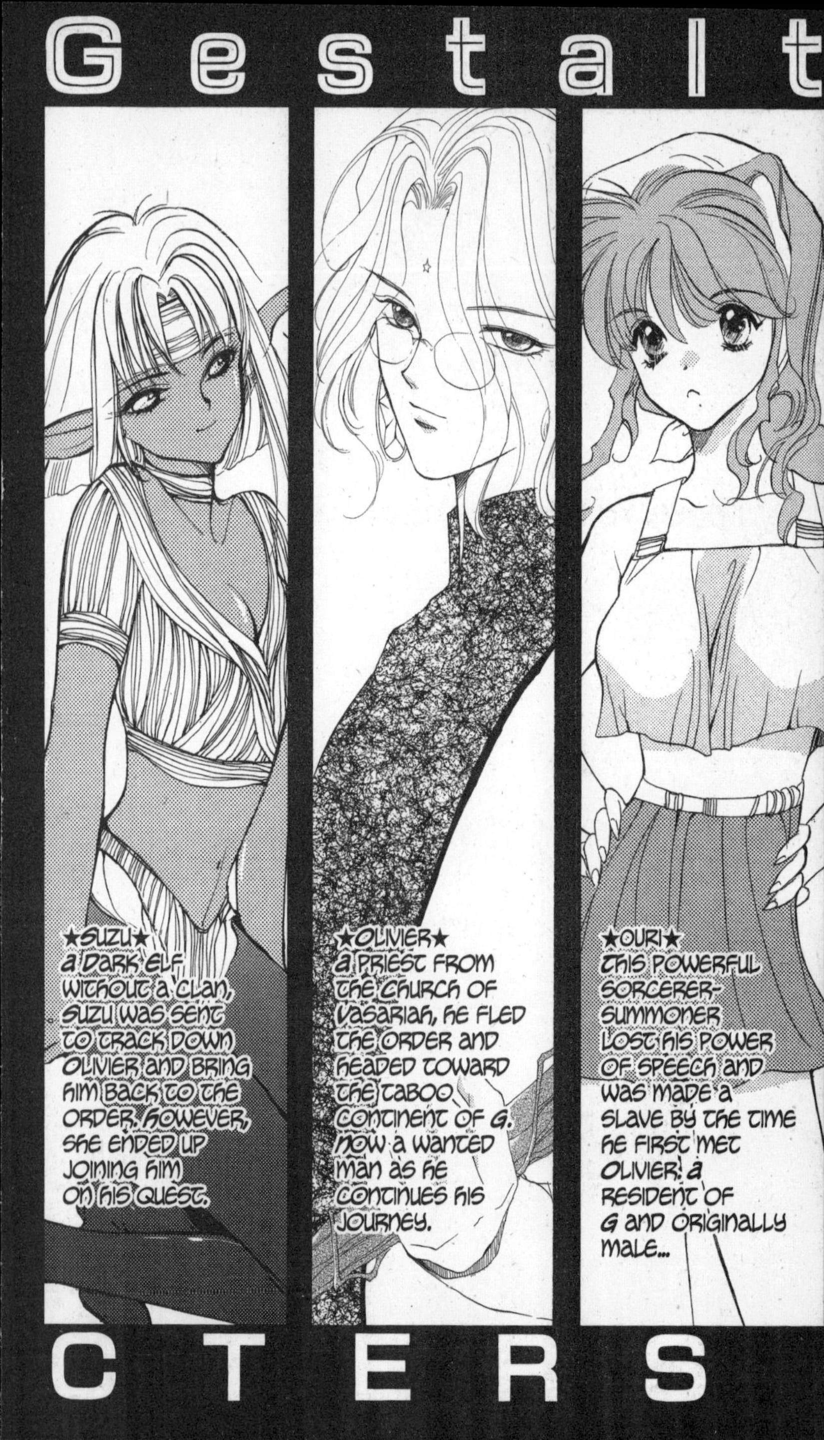
Gestalt
★OURI★
THIS POWERFUL SORCERER-SUMMONER LOST HIS POWER OF SPEECH AND WAS MADE A SLAVE BY THE TIME HE FIRST MET OLIVIER. A RESIDENT OF G AND ORIGINALLY MALE...
★OLIVIER★
A PRIEST FROM THE CHURCH OF VASARIAH, HE FLED THE ORDER AND HEADED TOWARD THE TABOO CONTINENT OF G. NOW A WANTED MAN AS HE CONTINUES HIS JOURNEY.
★SUZU★
A DARK ELF WITHOUT A CLAN, SUZU WAS SENT TO TRACK DOWN OLIVIER AND BRING HIM BACK TO THE ORDER. HOWEVER, SHE ENDED UP JOINING HIM ON HIS QUEST.
CTERS

Legend of the Great Beast

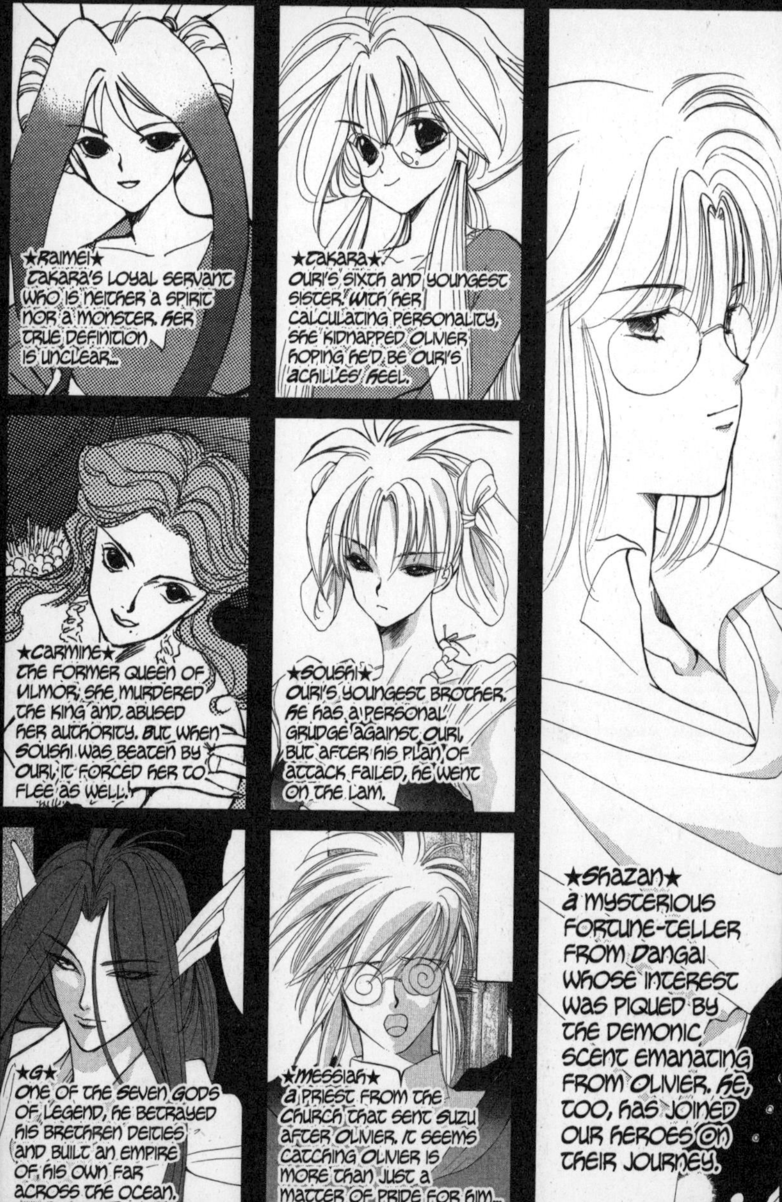
★Shazan★
A MYSTERIOUS FORTUNE-TELLER FROM DANGAI WHOSE INTEREST WAS PIQUED BY THE DEMONIC SCENT EMANATING FROM OLIVIER. HE, TOO, HAS JOINED OUR HEROES ON THEIR JOURNEY.
★Takara★
OURI'S SIXTH AND YOUNGEST SISTER. WITH HER CALCULATING PERSONALITY, SHE KIDNAPPED OLIVIER HOPING HE'D BE OURI'S ACHILLES' HEEL.
★Raimei★
TAKARA'S LOYAL SERVANT WHO IS NEITHER A SPIRIT NOR A MONSTER. HER TRUE DEFINITION IS UNCLEAR...
★Soushi★
OURI'S YOUNGEST BROTHER. HE HAS A PERSONAL GRUDGE AGAINST OURI, BUT AFTER HIS PLAN OF ATTACK FAILED, HE WENT ON THE LAM.
★Carmine★
THE FORMER QUEEN OF ULMOR, SHE MURDERED THE KING AND ABUSED HER AUTHORITY. BUT WHEN SOUSHI WAS BEATEN BY OURI, IT FORCED HER TO FLEE AS WELL.
★Messiah★
A PRIEST FROM THE CHURCH THAT SENT SUZU AFTER OLIVIER. IT SEEMS CATCHING OLIVIER IS MORE THAN JUST A MATTER OF PRIDE FOR HIM...
★G★
ONE OF THE SEVEN GODS OF LEGEND, HE BETRAYED HIS BRETHREN DEITIES AND BUILT AN EMPIRE OF HIS OWN FAR ACROSS THE OCEAN.

CHARA

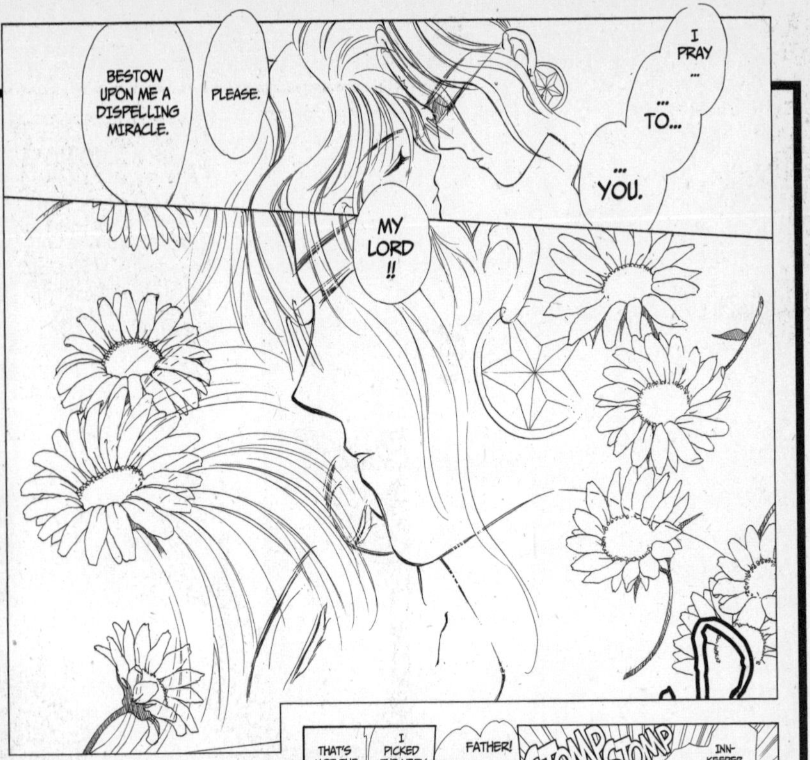
I PRAY ...
... TO...
... YOU.
PLEASE.
BESTOW UPON ME A DISPELLING MIRACLE.
MY LORD !!

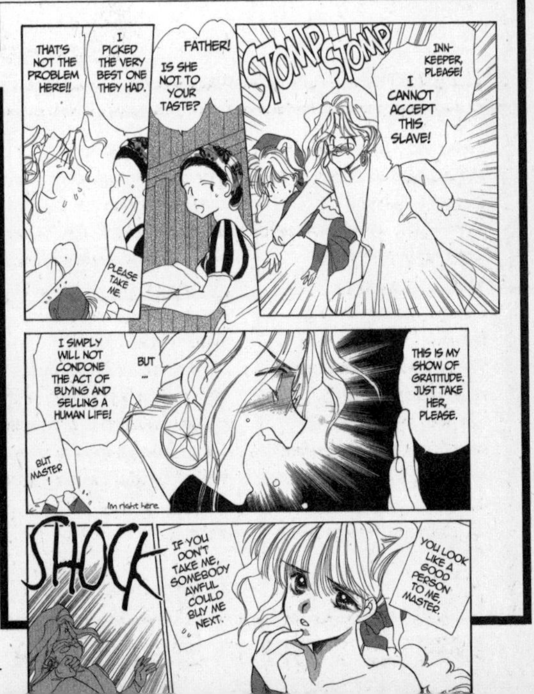
STOMP STOMP
INN-KEEPER, PLEASE!
I CANNOT ACCEPT THIS SLAVE!
FATHER!
IS SHE NOT TO YOUR TASTE?
I PICKED THE VERY BEST ONE THEY HAD.
THAT'S NOT THE PROBLEM HERE!!
PLEASE TAKE ME.
THIS IS MY SHOW OF GRATITUDE. JUST TAKE HER, PLEASE.
BUT ...
I SIMPLY WILL NOT CONDONE THE ACT OF BUYING AND SELLING A HUMAN LIFE!
BUT MASTER !
I'm right here
YOU LOOK LIKE A GOOD PERSON TO ME, MASTER.
IF YOU DON'T TAKE ME, SOMEBODY AWFUL COULD BUY ME NEXT.
SHOCK

In an attempt to gain even more power, Takara kidnapped Olivier and tried to offer him as a sacrifice to the Gods. However, when Olivier awoke on the altar, he was no longer the chaste priest we all know; this new opponent gave off the smell of pure evil! Takara quickly realized she was in over her head, and her life was in danger. Out to get Olivier back, Ouri picked up the unmistakable scent as she neared Takara's headquarters...

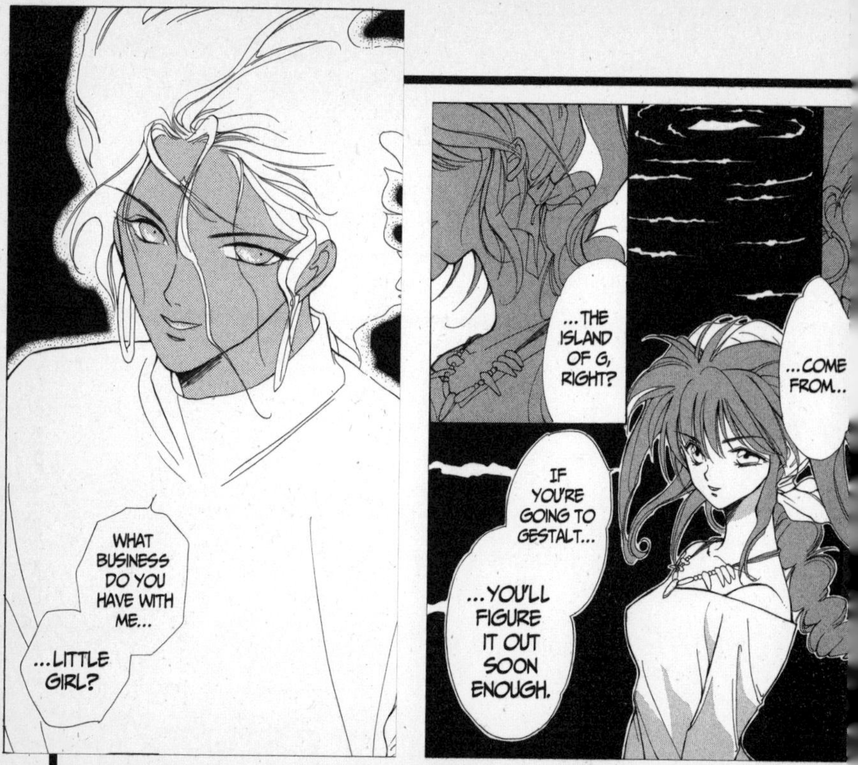
...COME FROM...
...THE ISLAND OF G, RIGHT?
IF YOU'RE GOING TO GESTALT...
...YOU'LL FIGURE IT OUT SOON ENOUGH.
WHAT BUSINESS DO YOU HAVE WITH ME...
...LITTLE GIRL?

THE STORY SO FAR

Olivier was a priest of the Church of Vasariah until the day he fled his post to pursue a mythological beast from legend. In the city of Barbaros, he became the owner of a mute slave girl named Ouri who turned out to be a sorcerer whose power of speech and magic were suppressed.

Not long after, a Dark Elf named Suzu appeared before our heroes, sent by the Order's very own Father Messiah to bring back the runaway priest. Some quick spell-breaking on Olivier's part returned Ouri to his usual formidable self, and saved them from a tight spot. Through some surprising happenstance, Olivier ended up accepting both Ouri and Suzu as his official travel companions.

In the town of Dangai, Ouri's little brother Soushi appeared and forced Ouri to partake in the Game he'd attempted to leave behind; a game that pits him in battle against each of his many siblings. Ouri defeated Soushi, but failed to stop him before he fled with the kingdom's queen.

It was also in Dangai that the mysterious fortune-teller, Shazan, joined our heroes as they continued on their quest. Their next stop, Jinga, brought Ouri's youngest sister, Takara, and her mysterious servant, Raimei, to the main stage as they came after our heroes with everything they had!

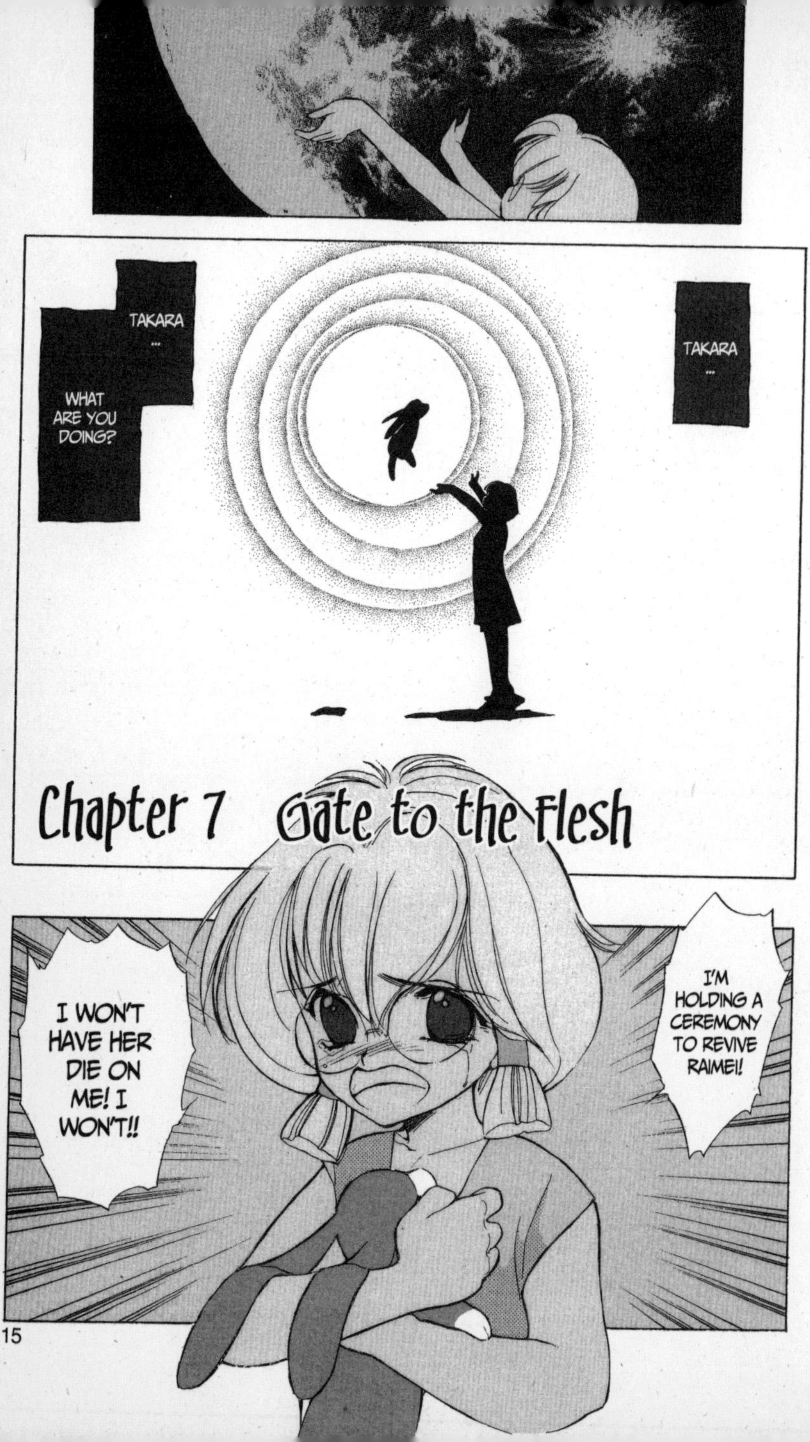
TAKARA ...
TAKARA ...
WHAT ARE YOU DOING?
Chapter 7 Gate to the Flesh
I'M HOLDING A CEREMONY TO REVIVE RAIMEI!
I WON'T HAVE HER DIE ON ME! I WON'T!!

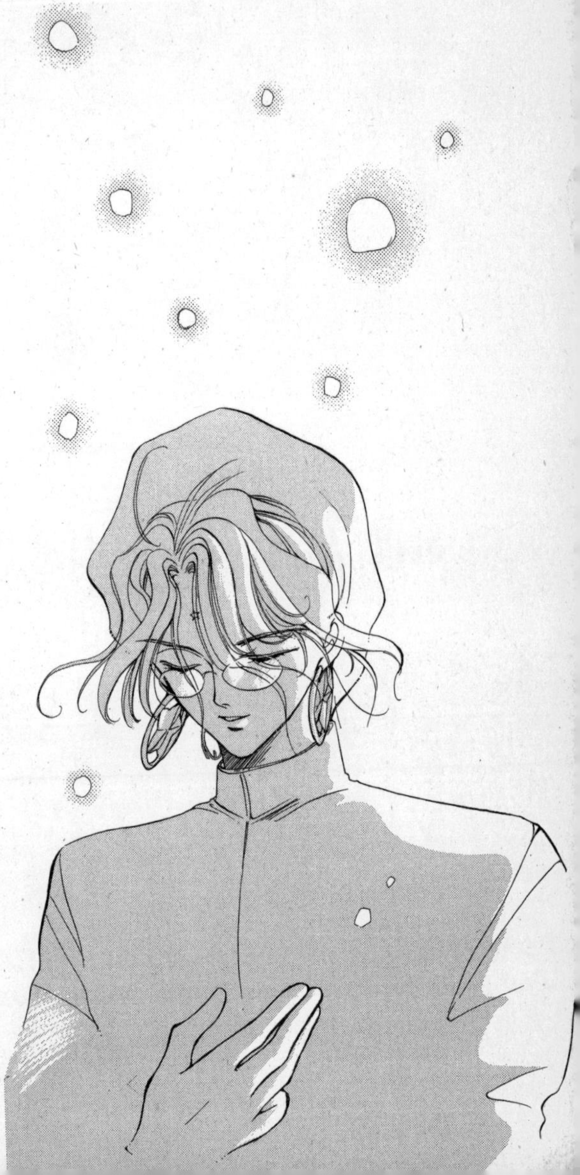

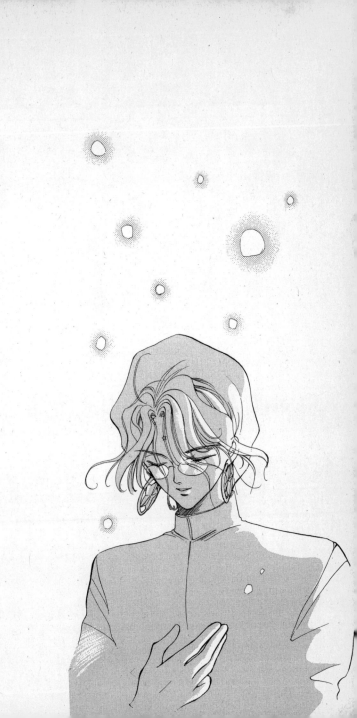

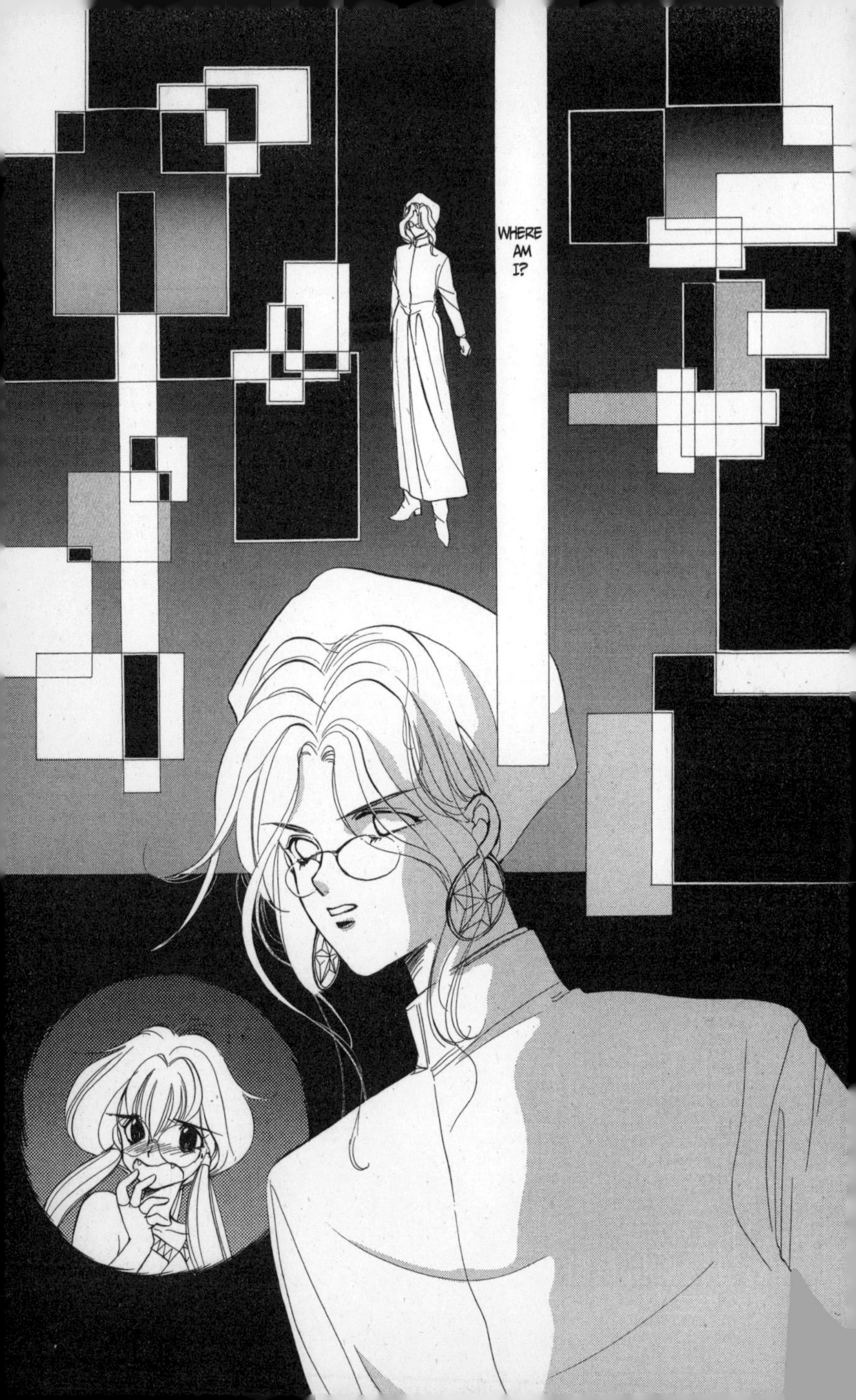
WHERE AM I?

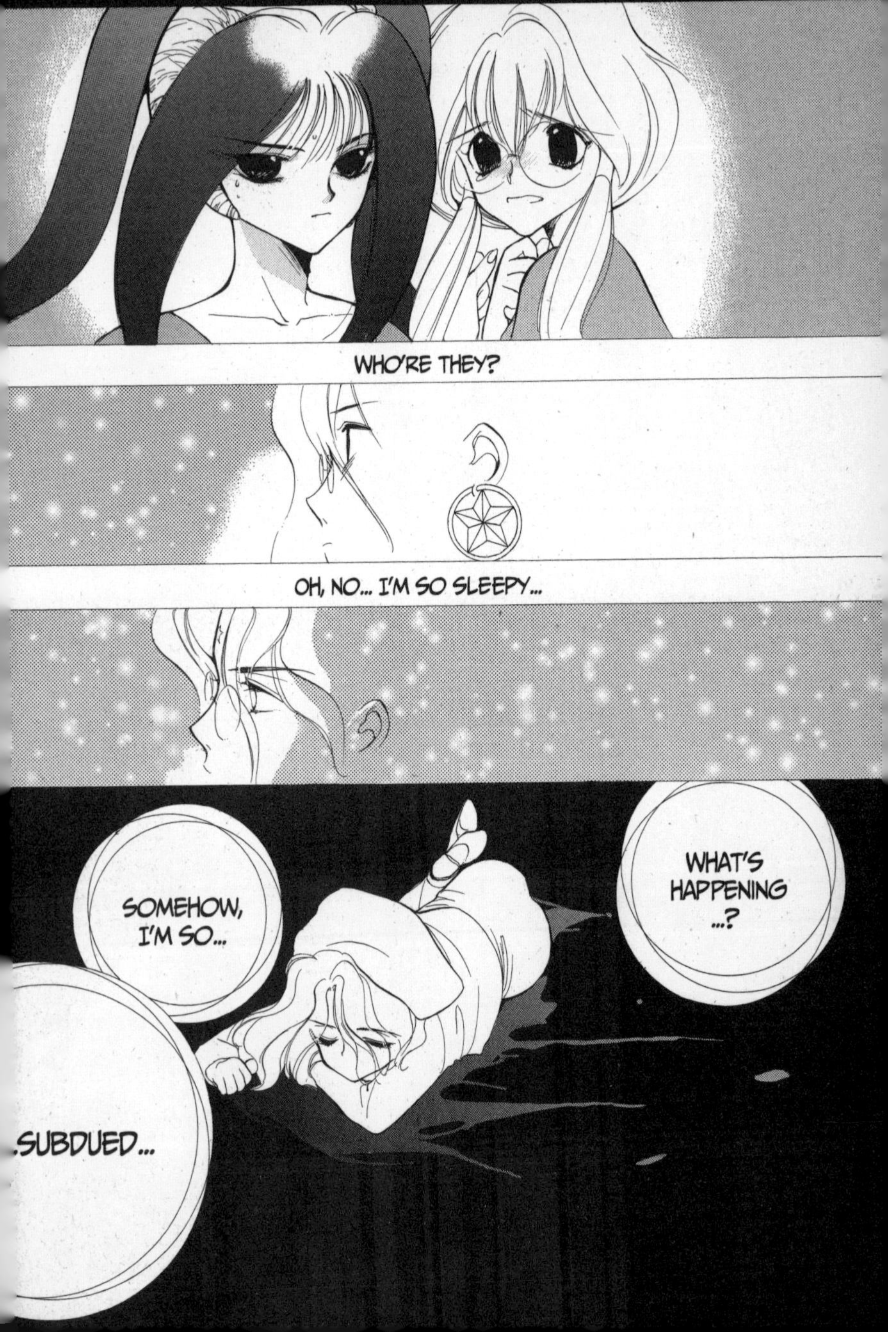
WHO'RE THEY?
OH, NO... I'M SO SLEEPY...
WHAT'S HAPPENING ...?
SOMEHOW, I'M SO...
.SUBDUED...

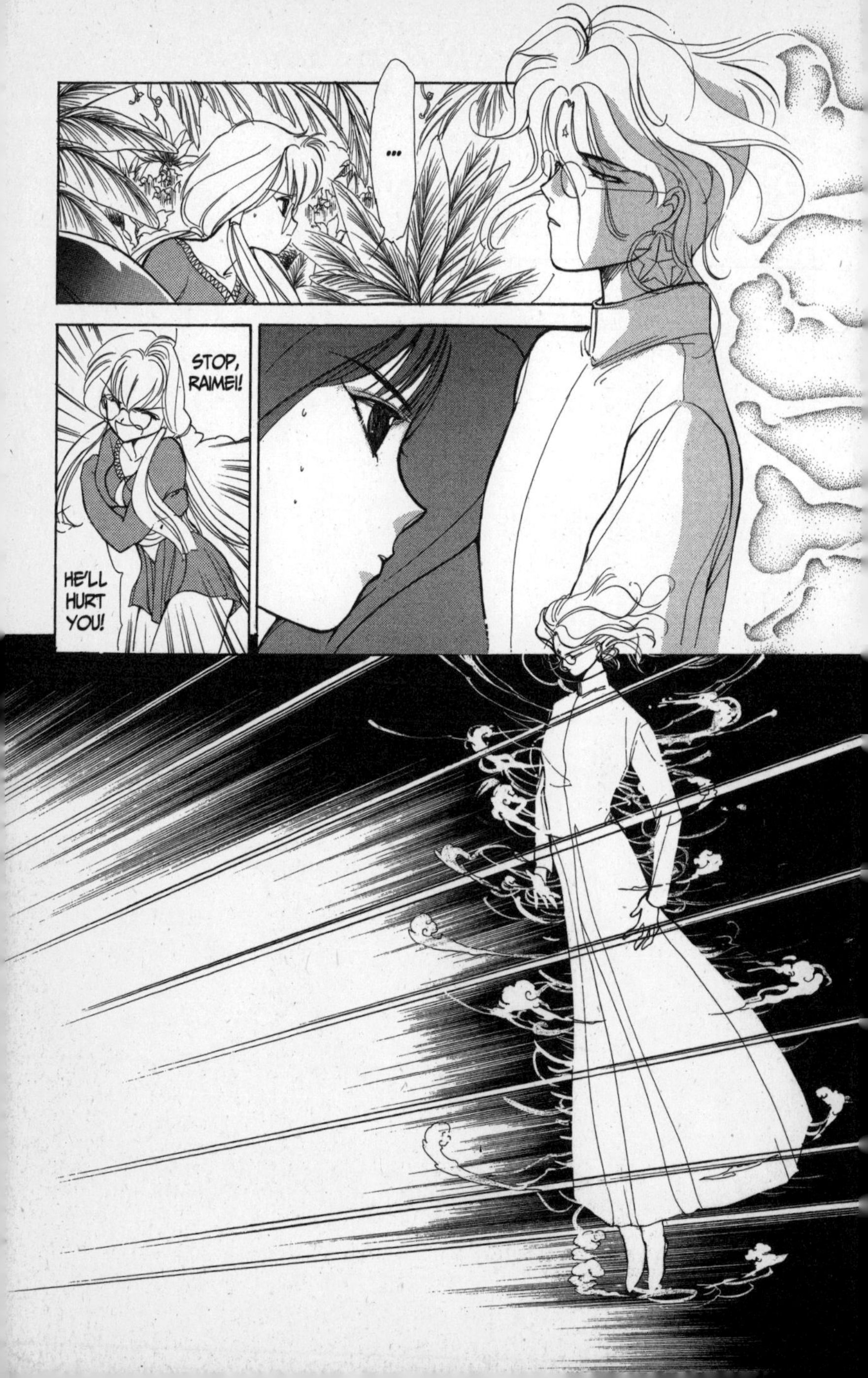
...
STOP, RAIMEI!
HE'LL HURT YOU!

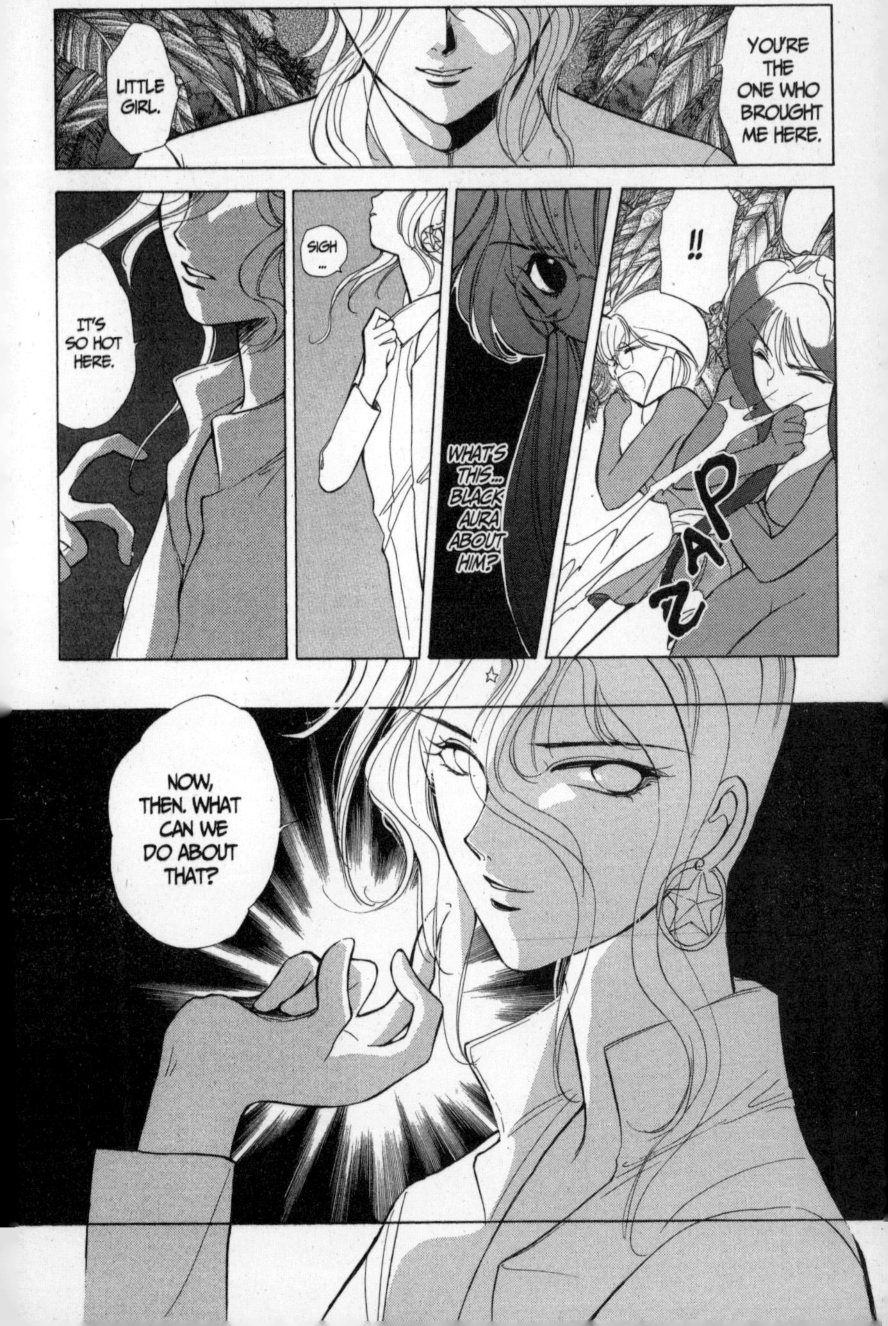
YOU'RE THE ONE WHO BROUGHT ME HERE.
LITTLE GIRL.
!!
ZAP
WHAT'S THIS... BLACK AURA ABOUT HIM?
SIGH...
IT'S SO HOT HERE.
NOW, THEN. WHAT CAN WE DO ABOUT THAT?

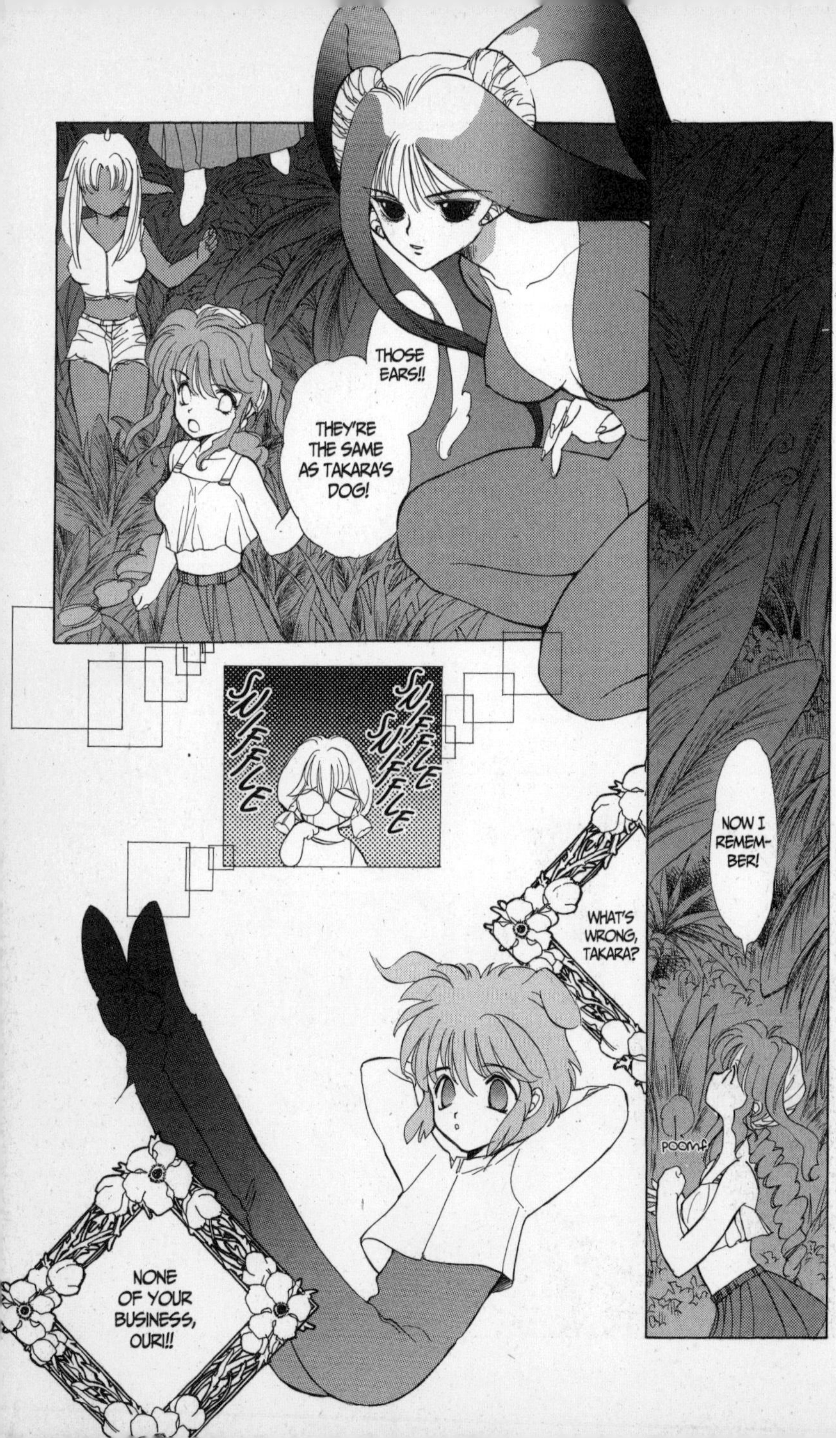
NOW I REMEMBER!
POOMF
THOSE EARS!!
THEY'RE THE SAME AS TAKARA'S DOG!
SNIFFLE SNIFFLE SNIFFLE
WHAT'S WRONG, TAKARA?
NONE OF YOUR BUSINESS, OURI!!

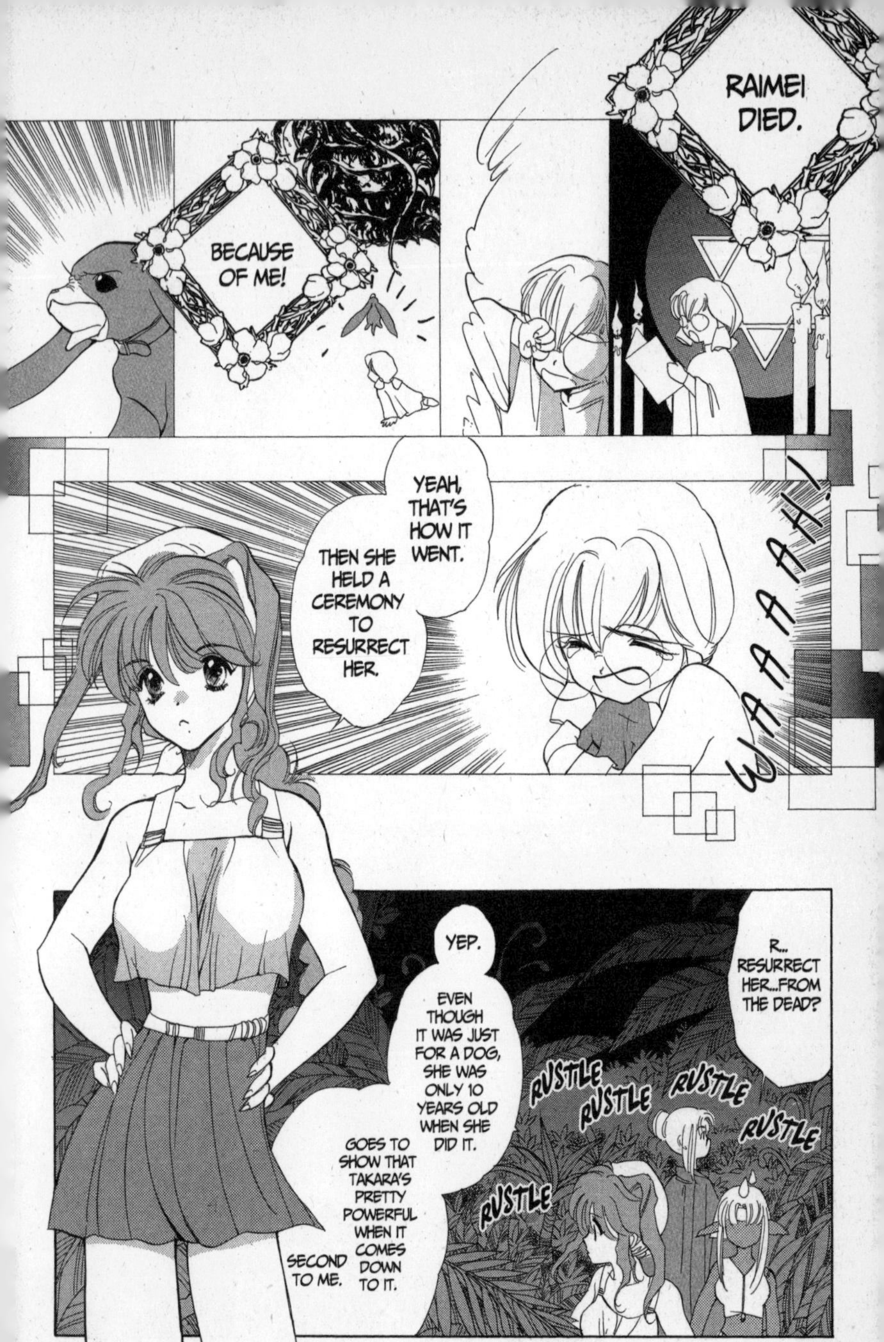
RAIMEI DIED.
BECAUSE OF ME!
WAAAAH!
YEAH, THAT'S HOW IT WENT.
THEN SHE HELD A CEREMONY TO RESURRECT HER.
R... RESURRECT HER...FROM THE DEAD?
RUSTLE
RUSTLE
RUSTLE
RUSTLE
RUSTLE
YEP.
EVEN THOUGH IT WAS JUST FOR A DOG, SHE WAS ONLY 10 YEARS OLD WHEN SHE DID IT.
GOES TO SHOW THAT TAKARA'S PRETTY POWERFUL WHEN IT COMES DOWN TO IT.
SECOND TO ME.

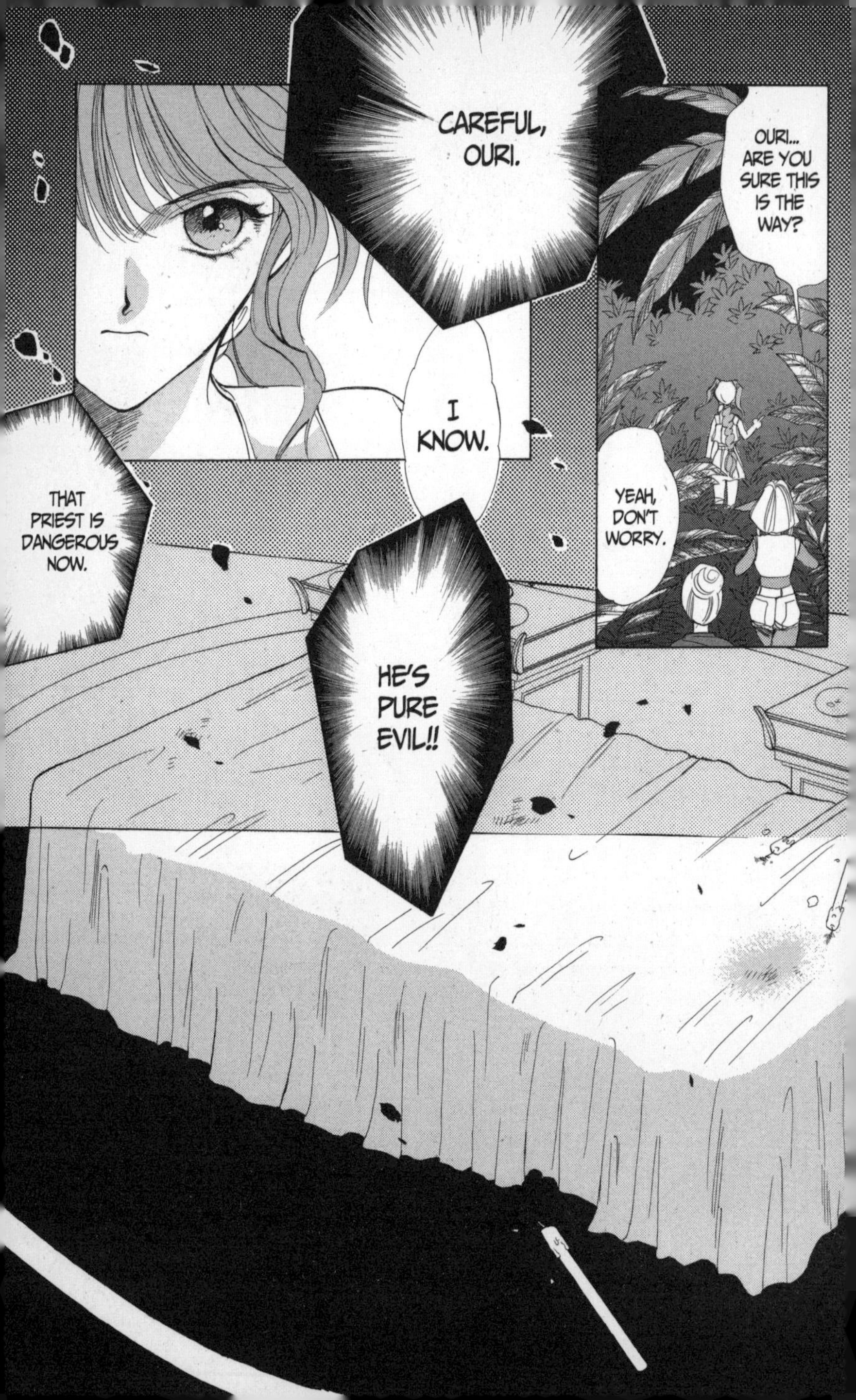
OURI... ARE YOU SURE THIS IS THE WAY?
YEAH, DON'T WORRY.
CAREFUL, OURI.
I KNOW.
THAT PRIEST IS DANGEROUS NOW.
HE'S PURE EVIL!!

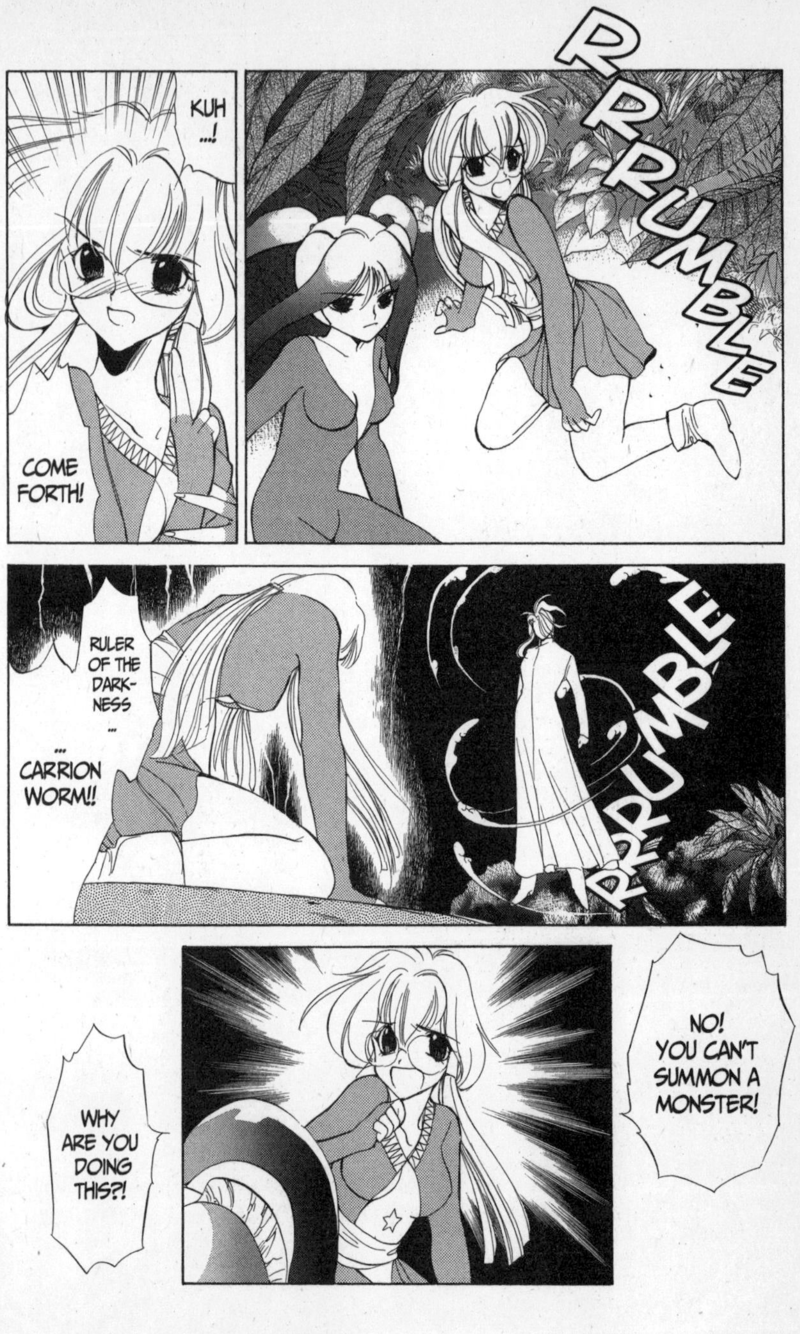
RRRUMBLE
KUH ...!
COME FORTH!
RRRUMBLE
RULER OF THE DARK-NESS ...
... CARRION WORM!!
NO! YOU CAN'T SUMMON A MONSTER!
WHY ARE YOU DOING THIS?!

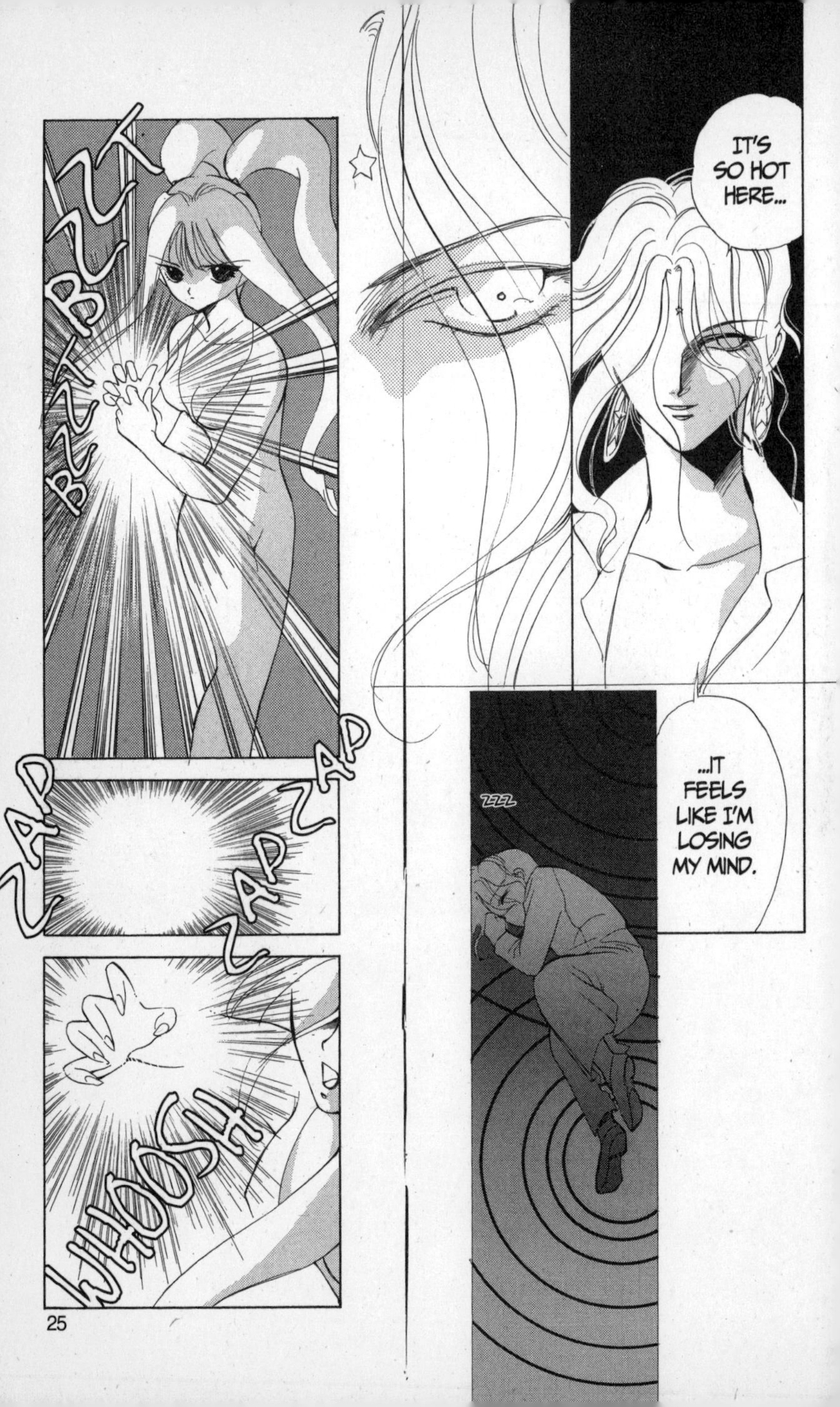
IT'S SO HOT HERE...
...IT FEELS LIKE I'M LOSING MY MIND.
ZZZ
BZZZT BZZZT
ZAP ZAP ZAP
WHOOSH

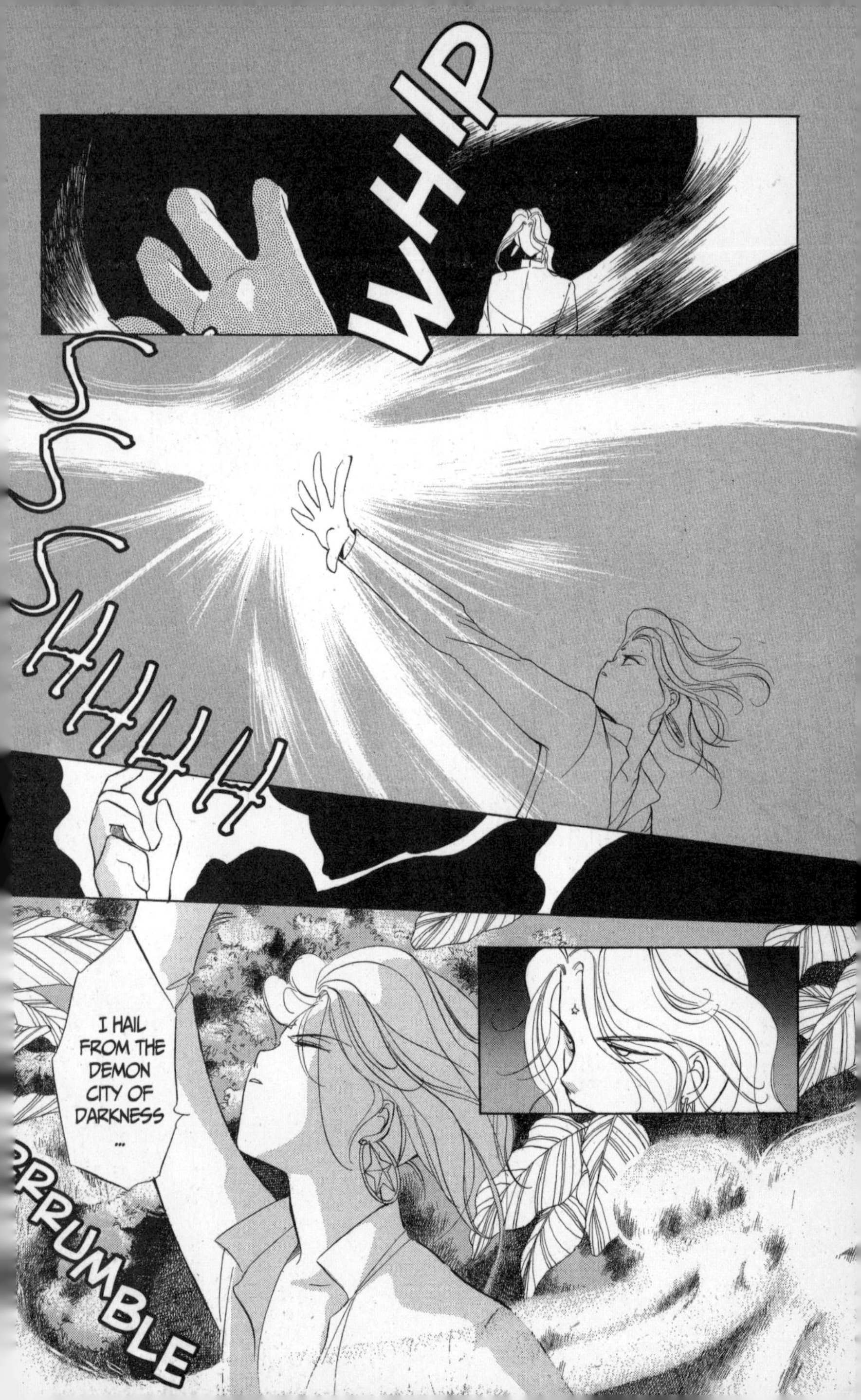
WHIP
SSSHHHHH
I HAIL FROM THE DEMON CITY OF DARKNESS ...
RRRUMBLE

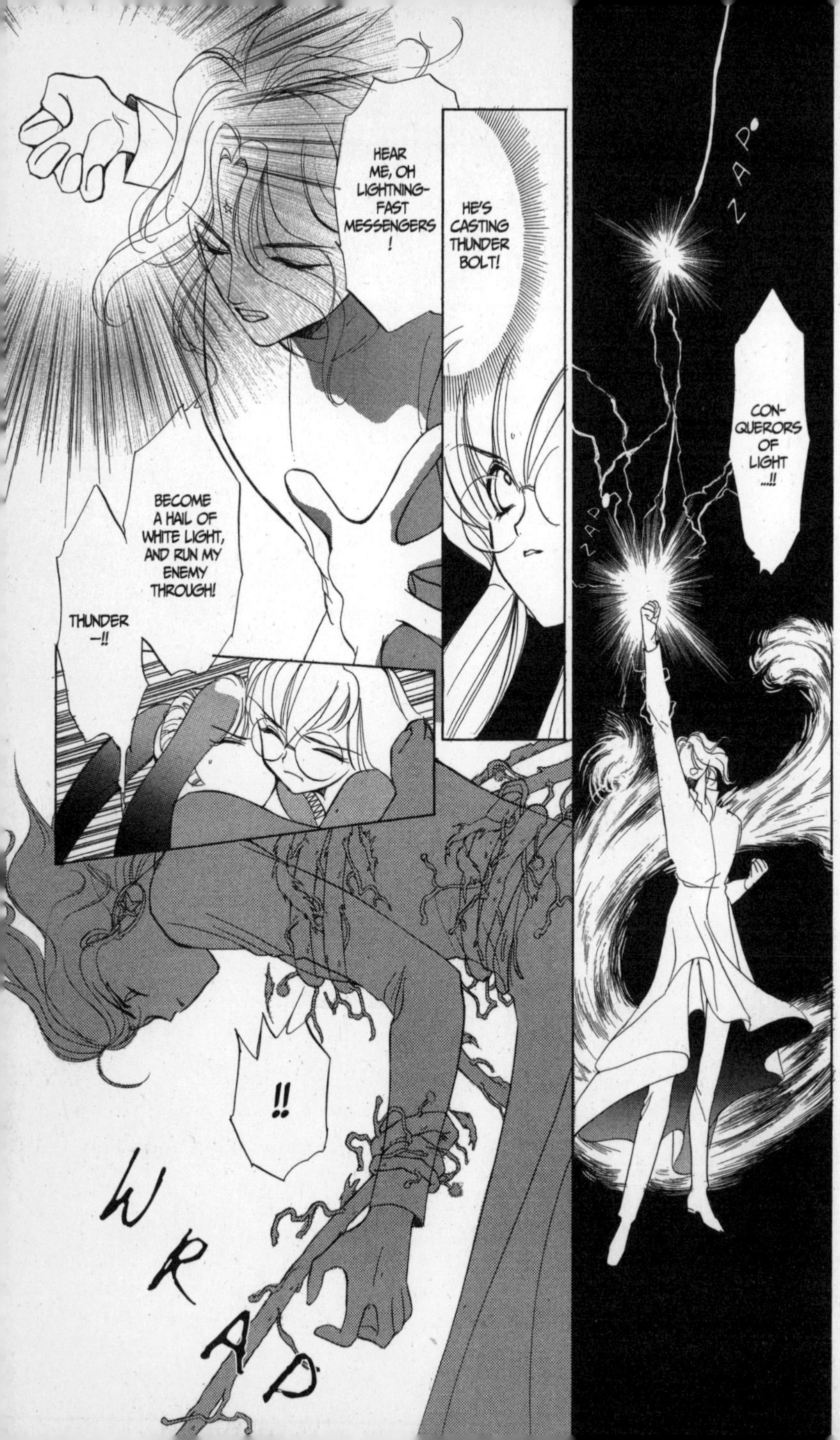
ZAP
CON-QUERORS OF LIGHT ...!!
ZAP
HE'S CASTING THUNDER BOLT!
HEAR ME, OH LIGHTNING-FAST MESSENGERS!
BECOME A HAIL OF WHITE LIGHT, AND RUN MY ENEMY THROUGH!
THUNDER—!!
!!
WRAP

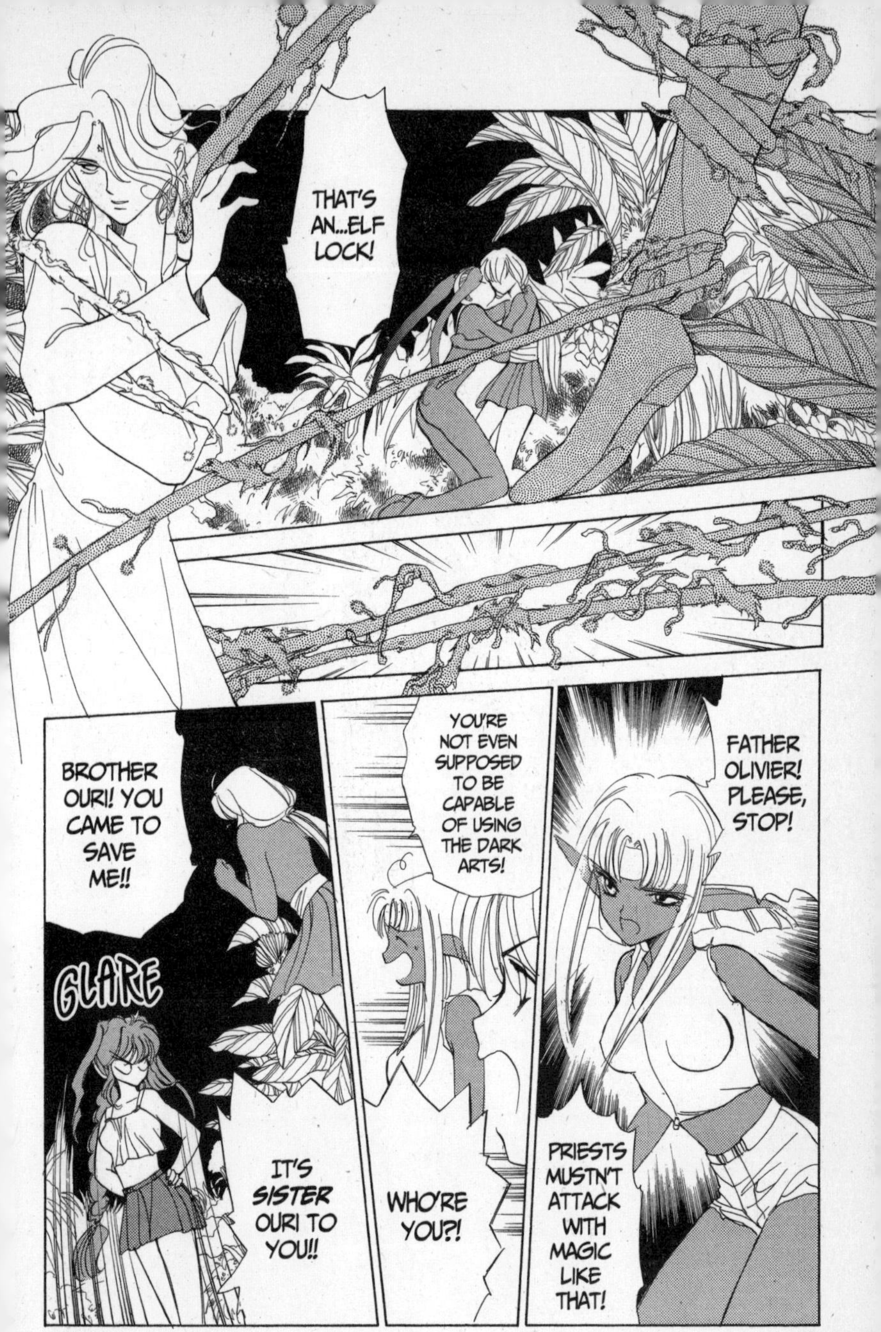
THAT'S AN...ELF LOCK!
FATHER OLIVIER! PLEASE, STOP!
PRIESTS MUSTN'T ATTACK WITH MAGIC LIKE THAT!
YOU'RE NOT EVEN SUPPOSED TO BE CAPABLE OF USING THE DARK ARTS!
WHO'RE YOU?!
BROTHER OURI! YOU CAME TO SAVE ME!!
GLARE
IT'S SISTER OURI TO YOU!!

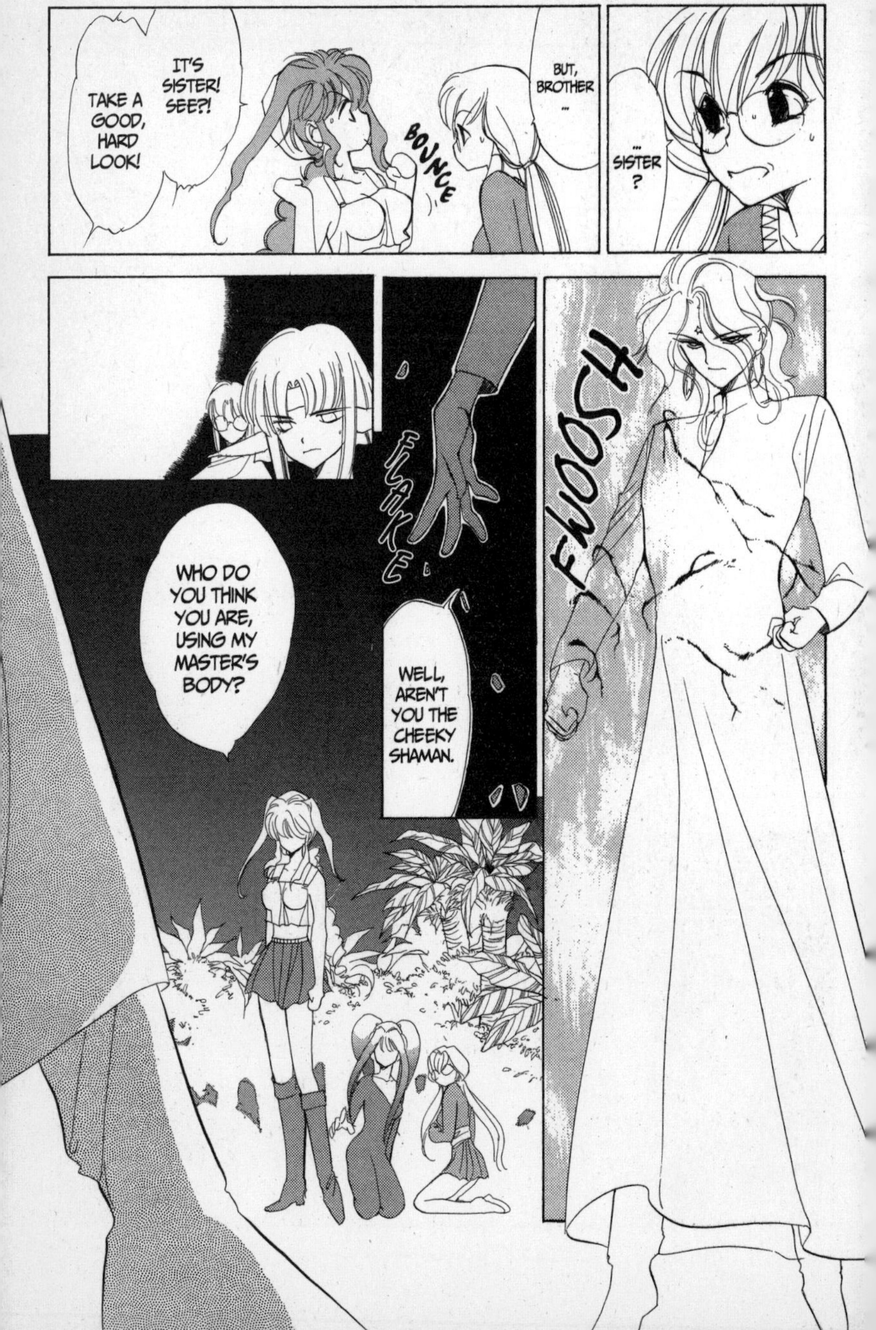

... SISTER?
BUT, BROTHER ...
BOUNCE
IT'S SISTER! SEE?!
TAKE A GOOD, HARD LOOK!
FWOOSH
FLAKE
WELL, AREN'T YOU THE CHEEKY SHAMAN.
WHO DO YOU THINK YOU ARE, USING MY MASTER'S BODY?

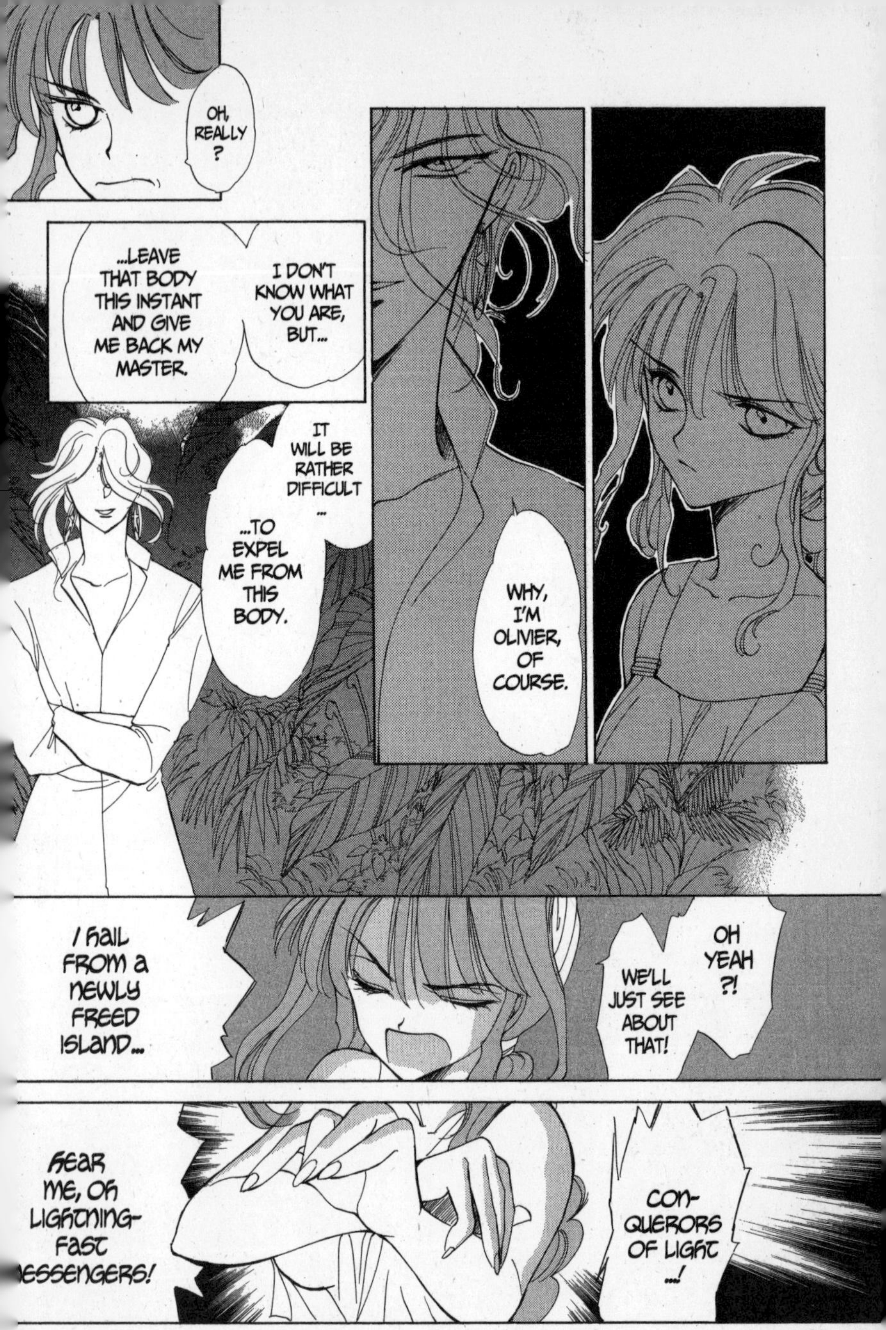
WHY, I'M OLIVIER, OF COURSE.
OH, REALLY?
I DON'T KNOW WHAT YOU ARE, BUT...
...LEAVE THAT BODY THIS INSTANT AND GIVE ME BACK MY MASTER.
IT WILL BE RATHER DIFFICULT...
...TO EXPEL ME FROM THIS BODY.
OH YEAH?!
WE'LL JUST SEE ABOUT THAT!
I hail from a newly freed island...
CON-QUERORS OF LIGHT...!
Hear me, oh lightning-fast messengers!

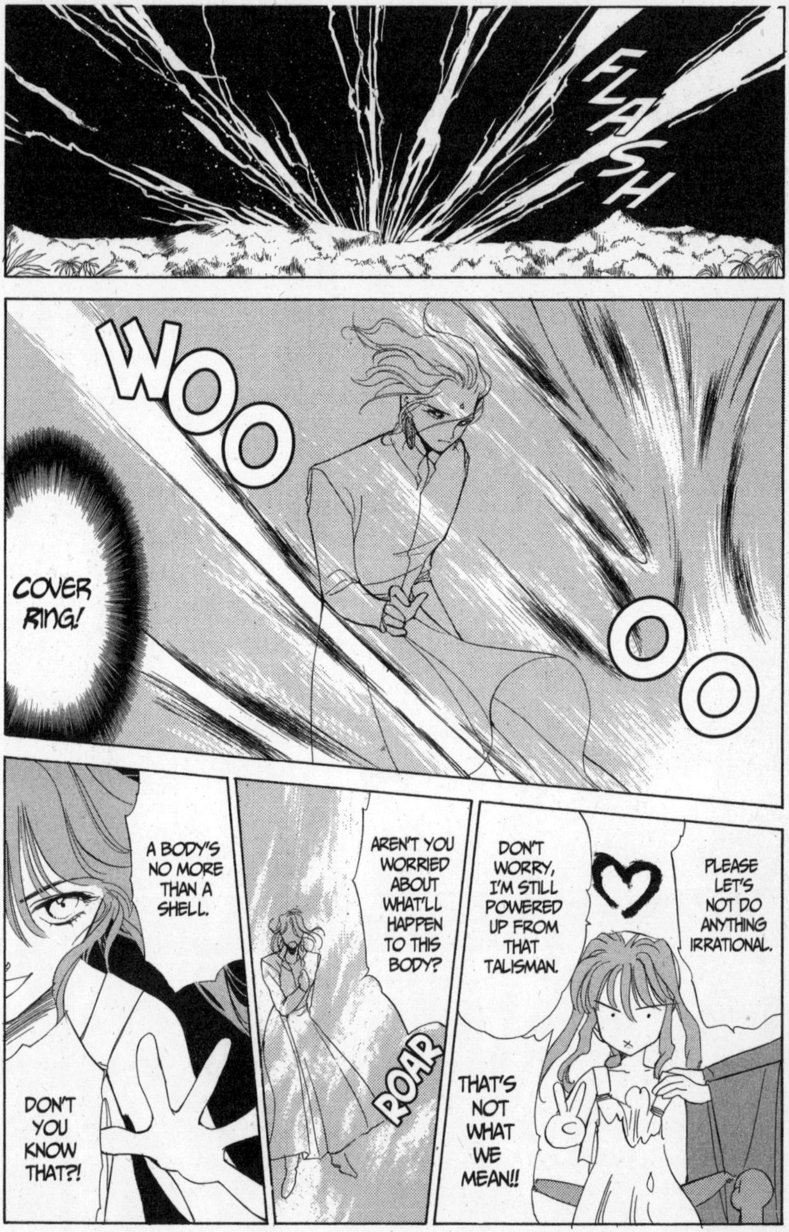
FLASH
WOO
OO
COVER RING!
PLEASE LET'S NOT DO ANYTHING IRRATIONAL.
DON'T WORRY, I'M STILL POWERED UP FROM THAT TALISMAN.
THAT'S NOT WHAT WE MEAN!!
AREN'T YOU WORRIED ABOUT WHAT'LL HAPPEN TO THIS BODY?
ROAR
A BODY'S NO MORE THAN A SHELL.
DON'T YOU KNOW THAT?!

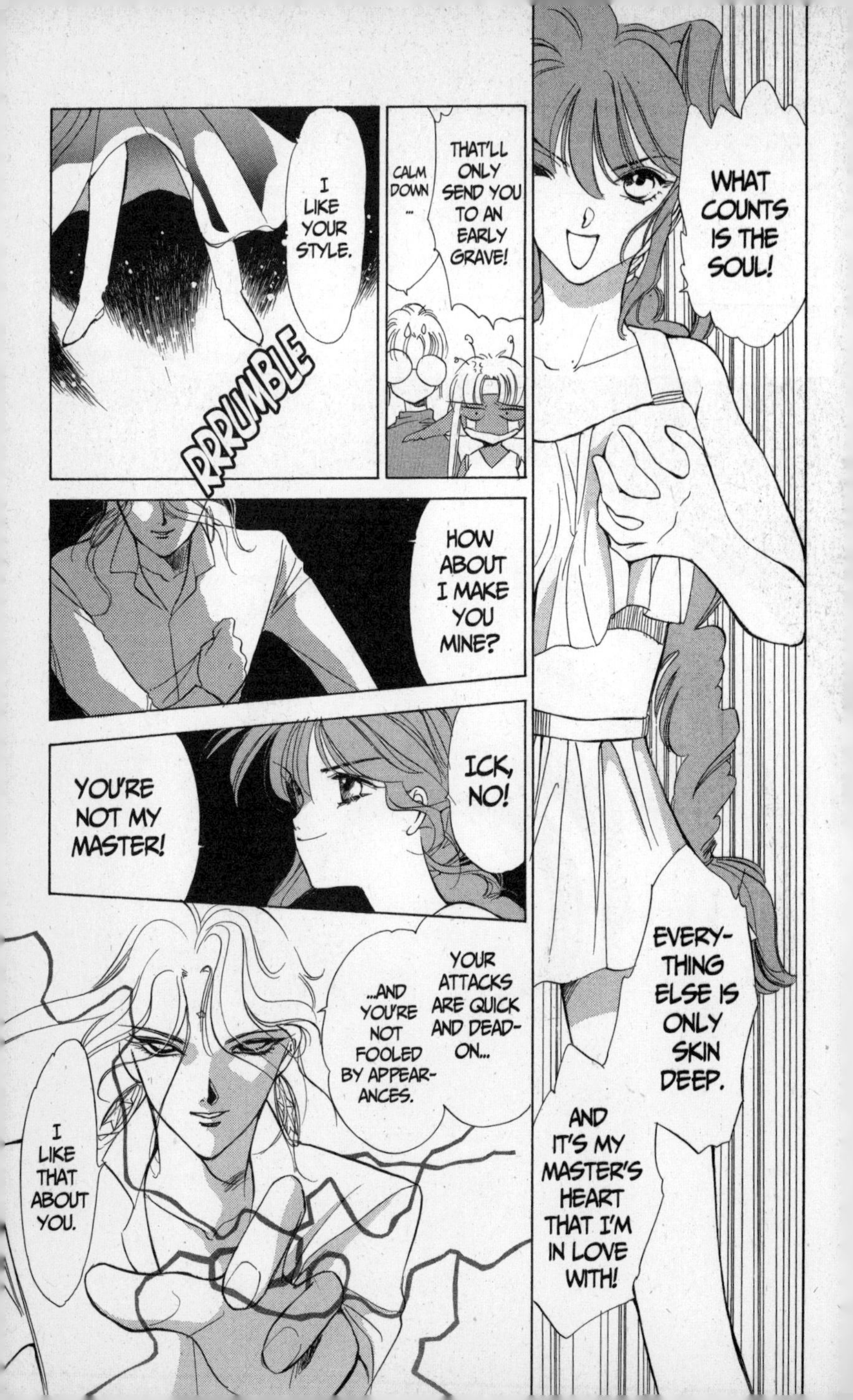
WHAT COUNTS IS THE SOUL!
EVERYTHING ELSE IS ONLY SKIN DEEP.
AND IT'S MY MASTER'S HEART THAT I'M IN LOVE WITH!
THAT'LL ONLY SEND YOU TO AN EARLY GRAVE!
CALM DOWN...
I LIKE YOUR STYLE.
RRRUMBLE
HOW ABOUT I MAKE YOU MINE?
ICK, NO!
YOU'RE NOT MY MASTER!
YOUR ATTACKS ARE QUICK AND DEAD-ON...
...AND YOU'RE NOT FOOLED BY APPEARANCES.
I LIKE THAT ABOUT YOU.

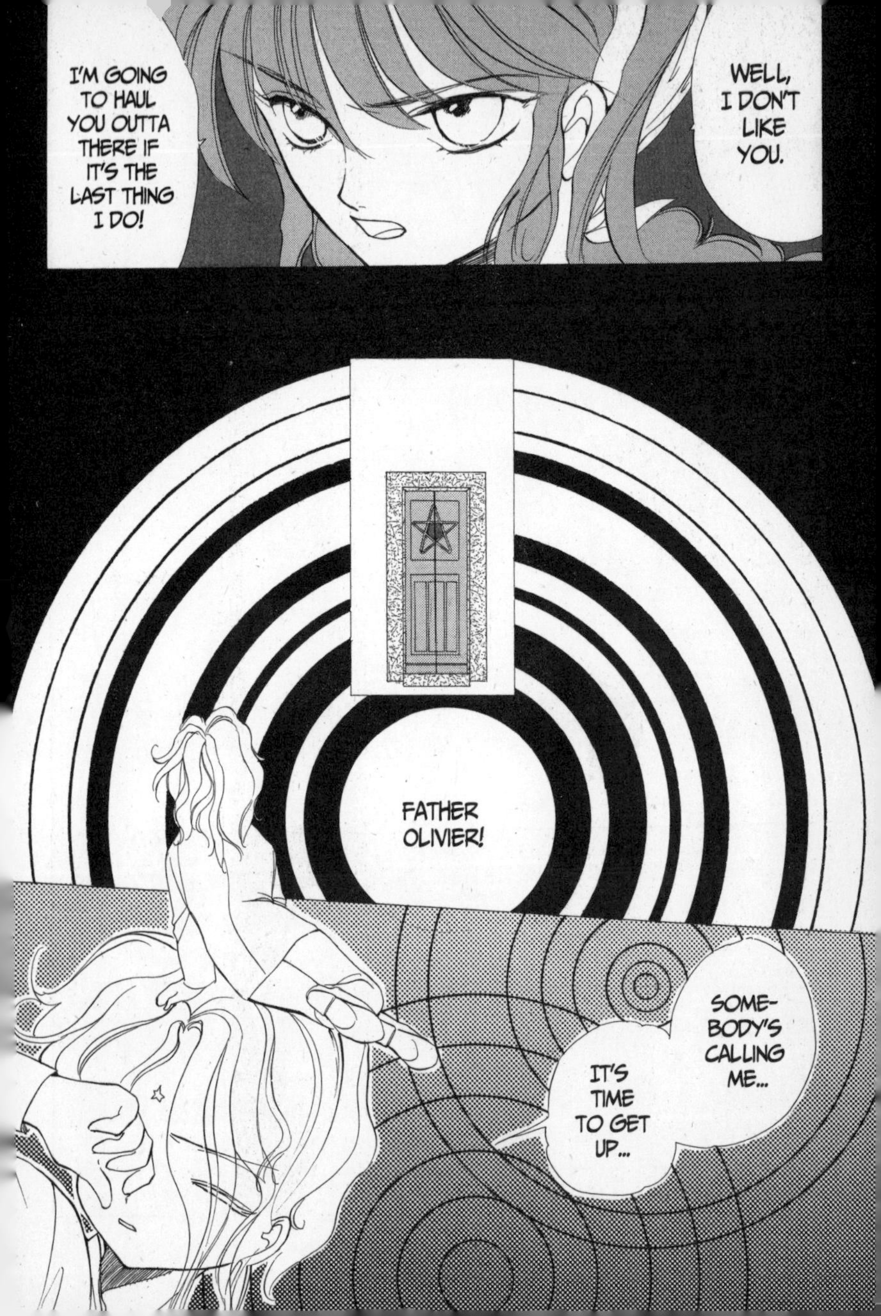
WELL, I DON'T LIKE YOU.
I'M GOING TO HAUL YOU OUTTA THERE IF IT'S THE LAST THING I DO!
FATHER OLIVIER!
SOME-BODY'S CALLING ME...
IT'S TIME TO GET UP...

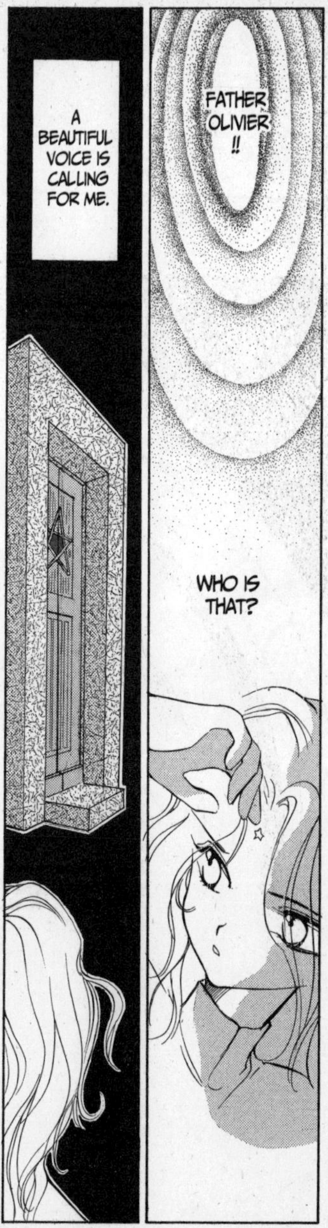
FATHER OLIVIER !!
WHO IS THAT?
A BEAUTIFUL VOICE IS CALLING FOR ME.

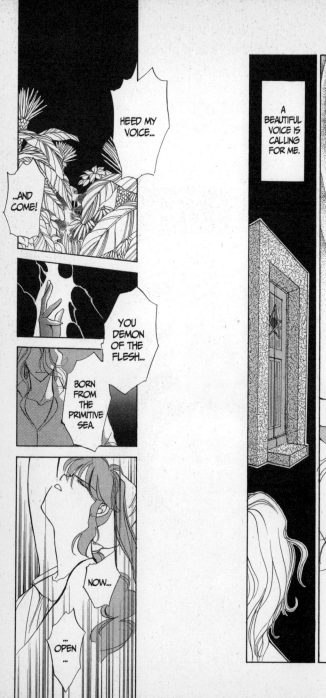

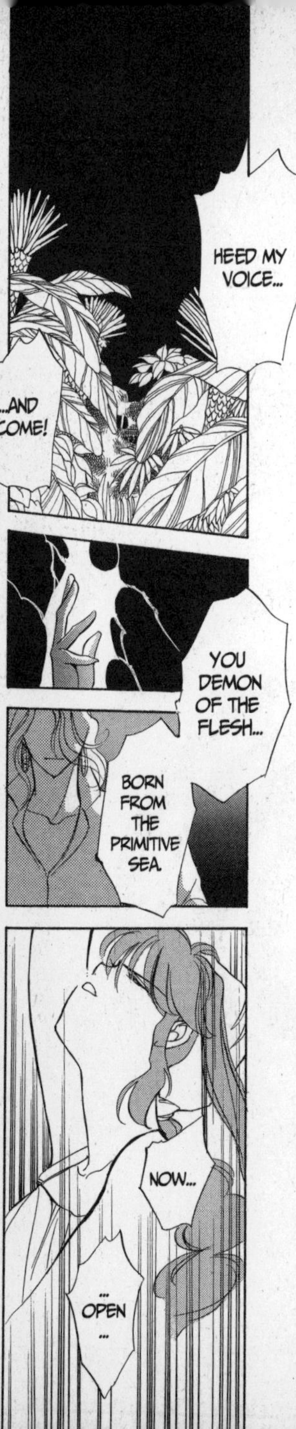
HEED MY VOICE...
...AND COME!
YOU DEMON OF THE FLESH...
BORN FROM THE PRIMITIVE SEA.
NOW...
... OPEN ...

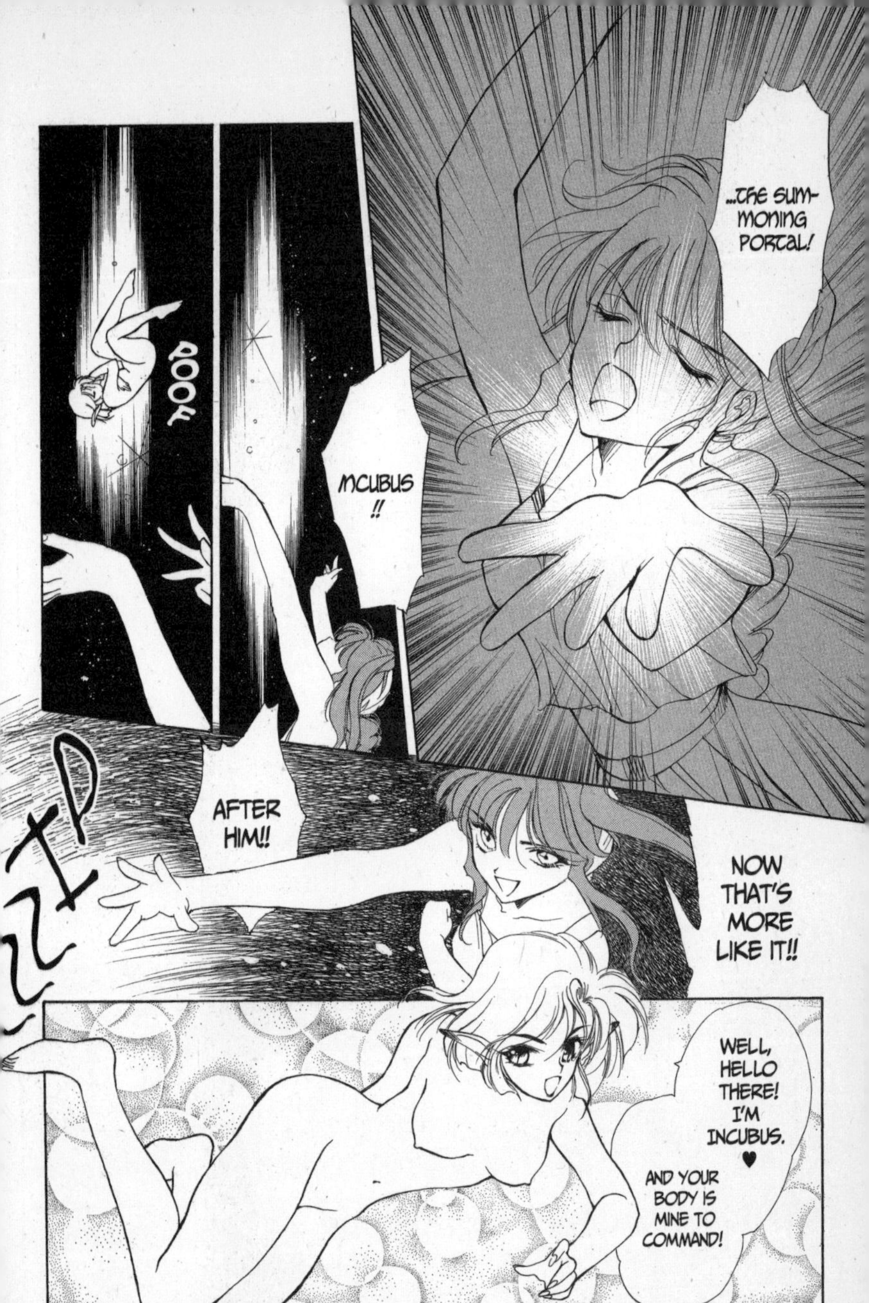
...THE SUMMONING PORTAL!
INCUBUS !!
POOF
AFTER HIM!!
NOW THAT'S MORE LIKE IT!!
WELL, HELLO THERE! I'M INCUBUS. ♥
AND YOUR BODY IS MINE TO COMMAND!

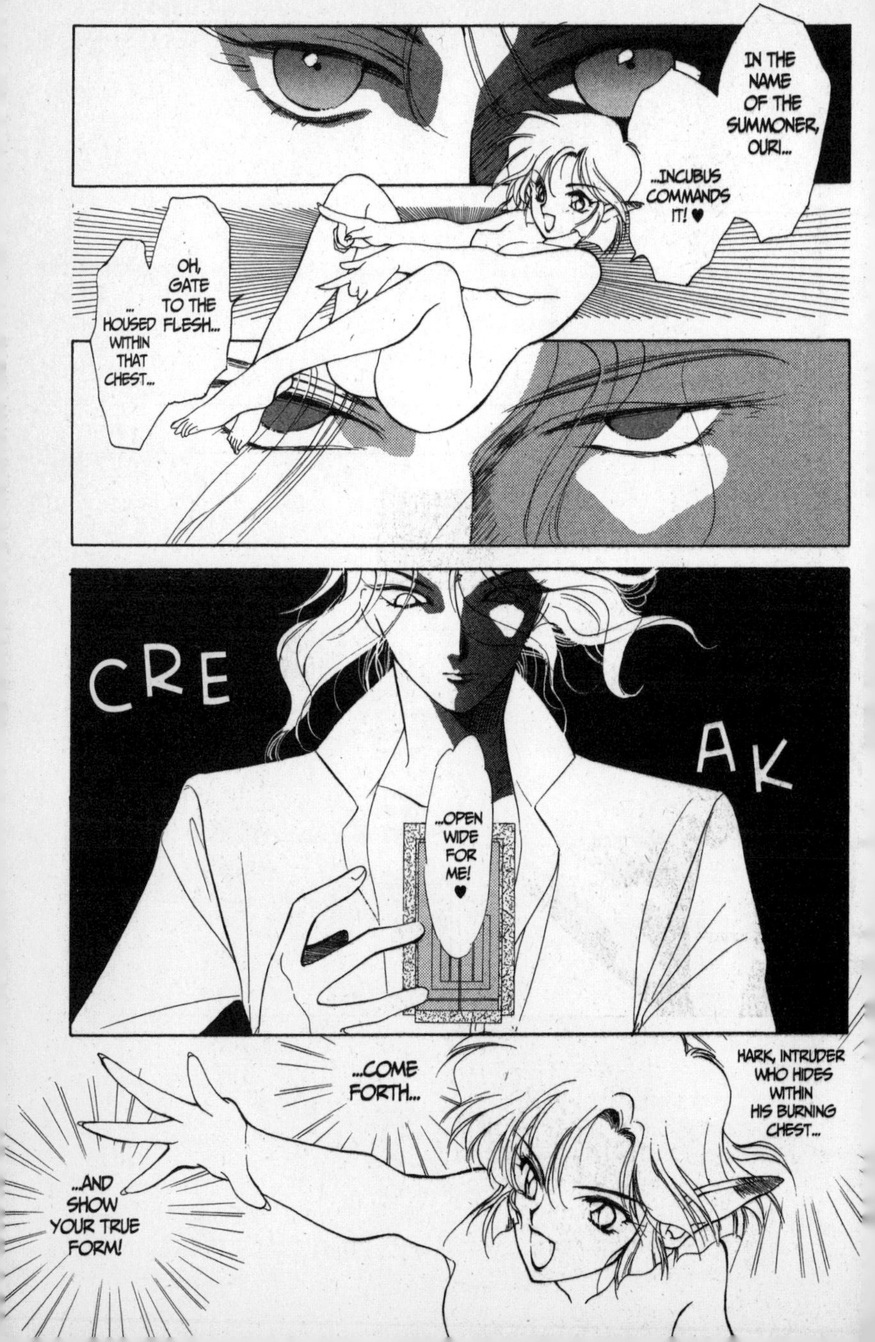
IN THE NAME OF THE SUMMONER, OURI...
...INCUBUS COMMANDS IT! ♥
OH, GATE TO THE FLESH...
...HOUSED WITHIN THAT CHEST...
CRE
AK
...OPEN WIDE FOR ME! ♥
HARK, INTRUDER WHO HIDES WITHIN HIS BURNING CHEST...
...COME FORTH...
...AND SHOW YOUR TRUE FORM!

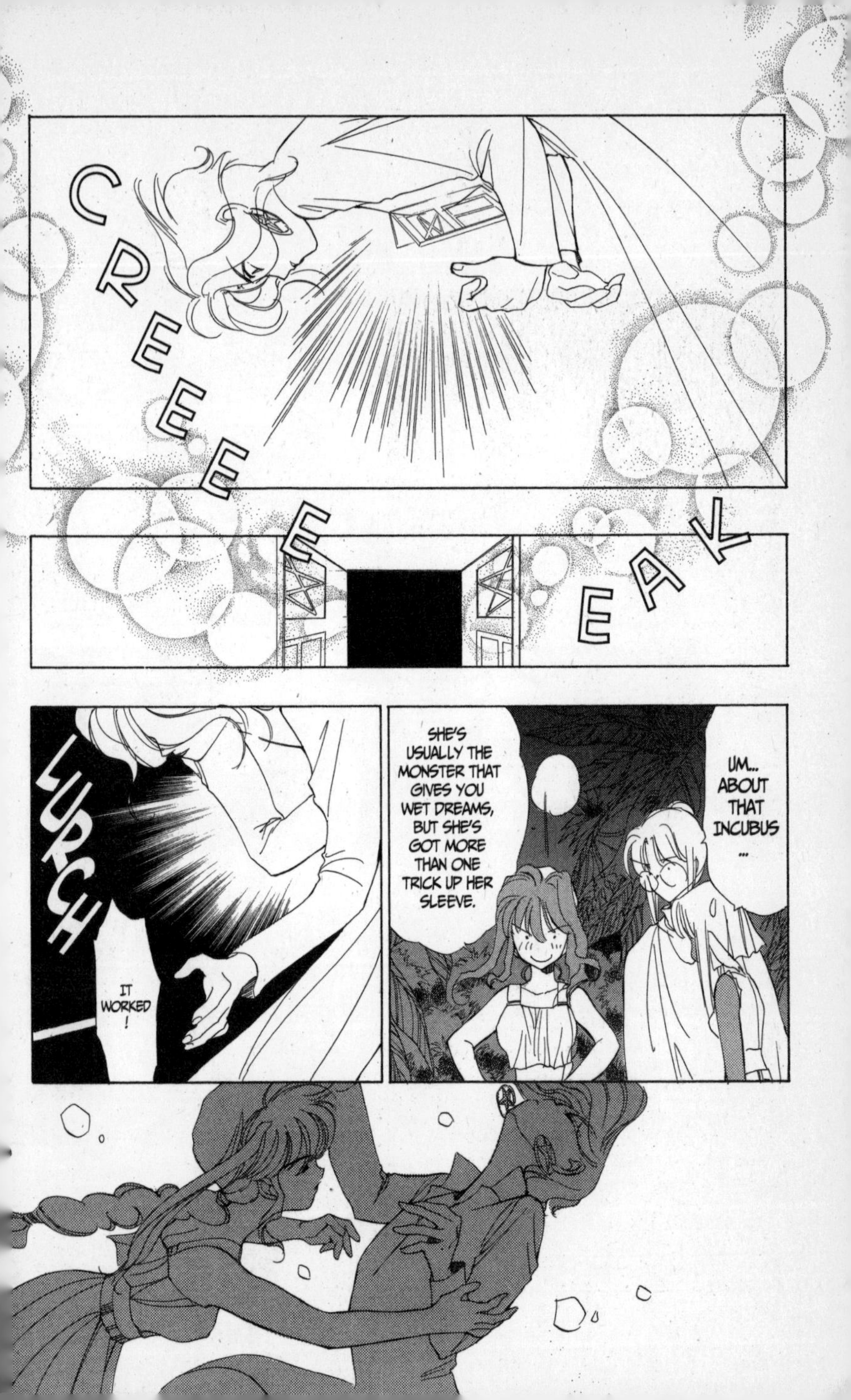
CREEEEEAK
UM... ABOUT THAT INCUBUS...
SHE'S USUALLY THE MONSTER THAT GIVES YOU WET DREAMS, BUT SHE'S GOT MORE THAN ONE TRICK UP HER SLEEVE.
LURCH
IT WORKED!

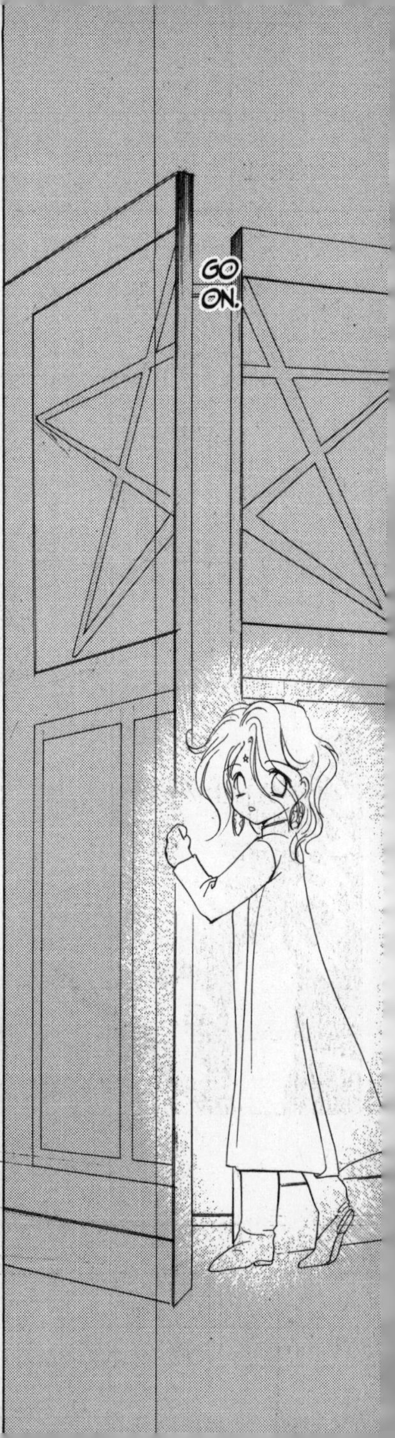
GO ON.

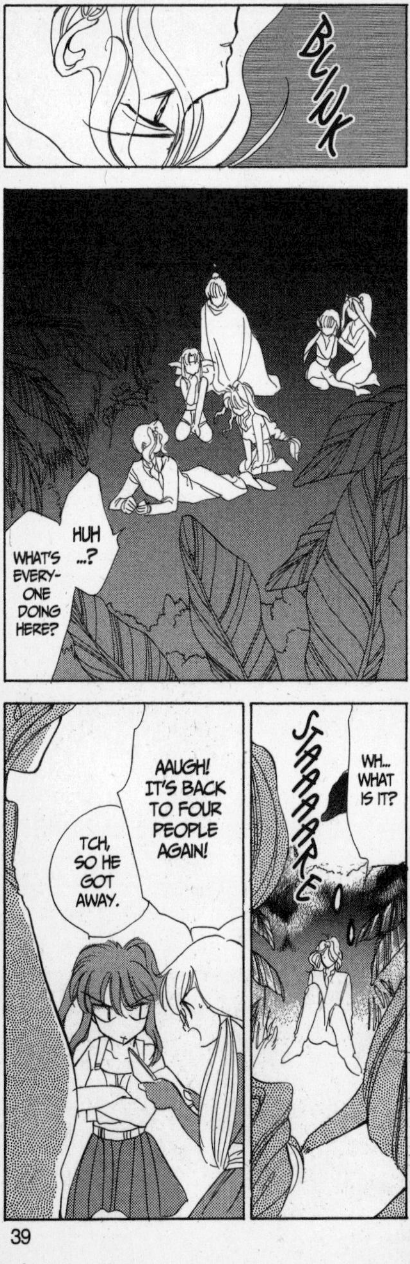
BLINK
HUH ...?
WHAT'S EVERYONE DOING HERE?
WH... WHAT IS IT?
STAAAAARE
AAUGH! IT'S BACK TO FOUR PEOPLE AGAIN!
TCH, SO HE GOT AWAY.

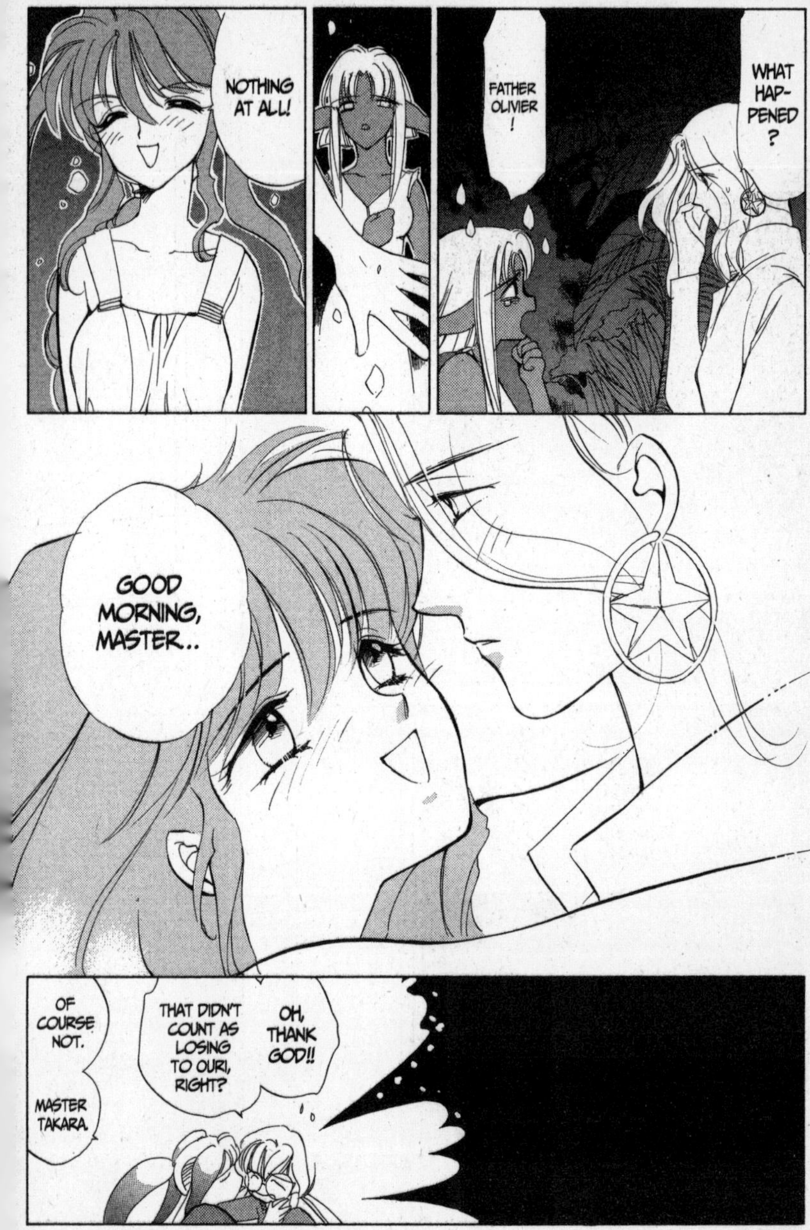
WHAT HAP-PENED?
FATHER OLIVIER!
NOTHING AT ALL!
GOOD MORNING, MASTER...
OH, THANK GOD!!
THAT DIDN'T COUNT AS LOSING TO OURI, RIGHT?
OF COURSE NOT.
MASTER TAKARA.

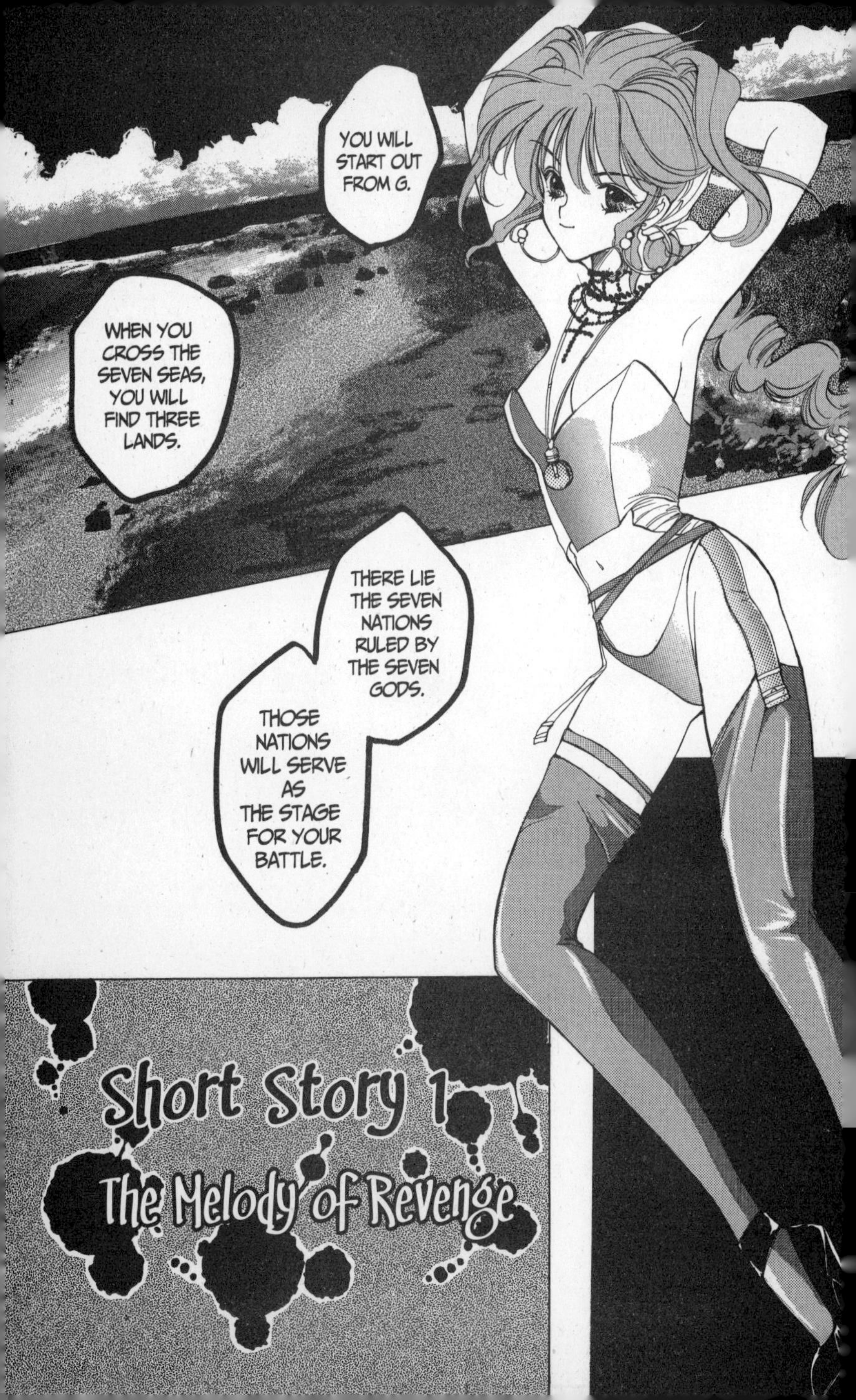
YOU WILL START OUT FROM G.
WHEN YOU CROSS THE SEVEN SEAS, YOU WILL FIND THREE LANDS.
THERE LIE THE SEVEN NATIONS RULED BY THE SEVEN GODS.
THOSE NATIONS WILL SERVE AS THE STAGE FOR YOUR BATTLE.
Short Story 1
The Melody of Revenge

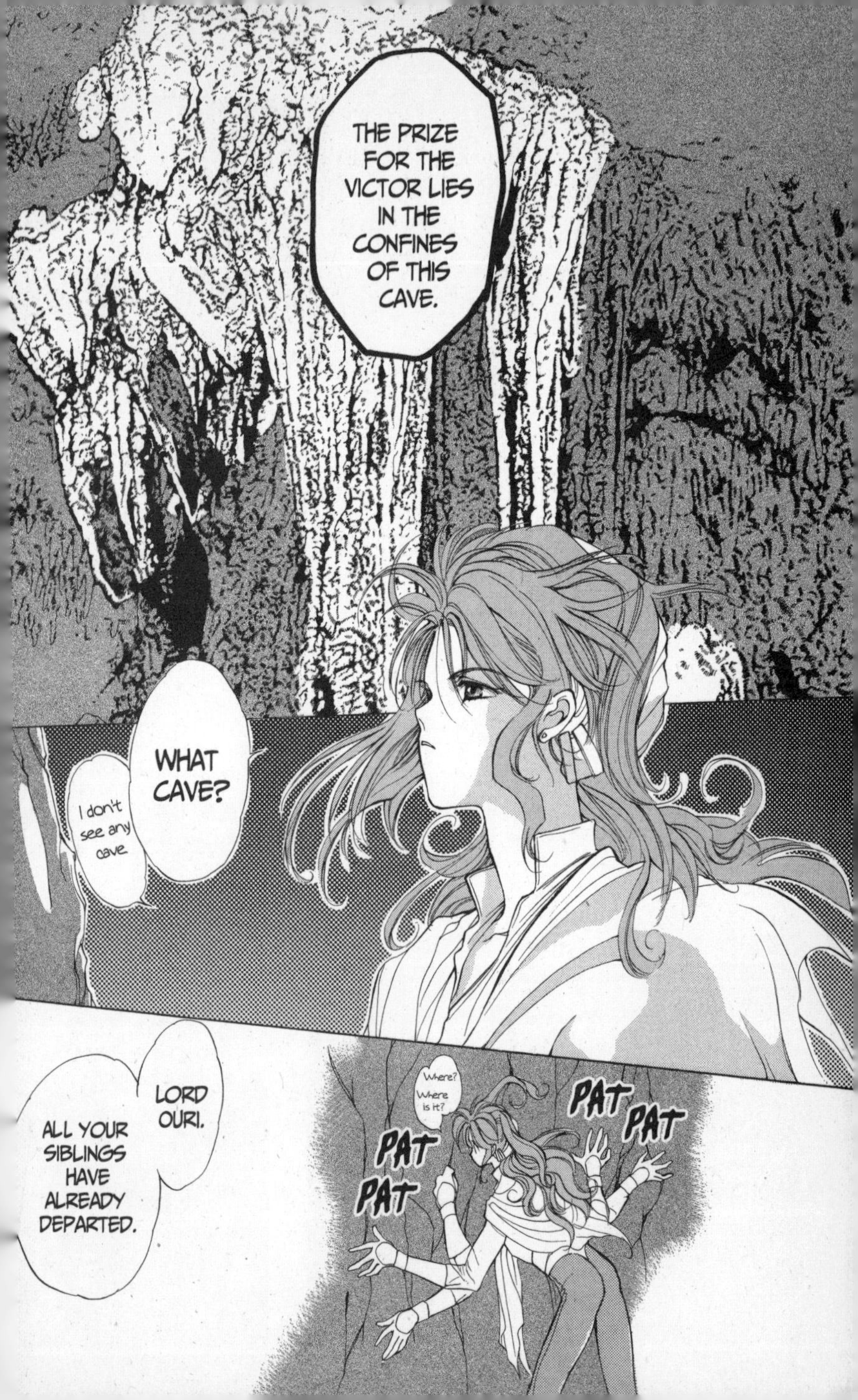
THE PRIZE FOR THE VICTOR LIES IN THE CONFINES OF THIS CAVE.
WHAT CAVE?
I don't see any cave
PAT PAT
Where? Where is it?
PAT PAT
LORD OURI.
ALL YOUR SIBLINGS HAVE ALREADY DEPARTED.

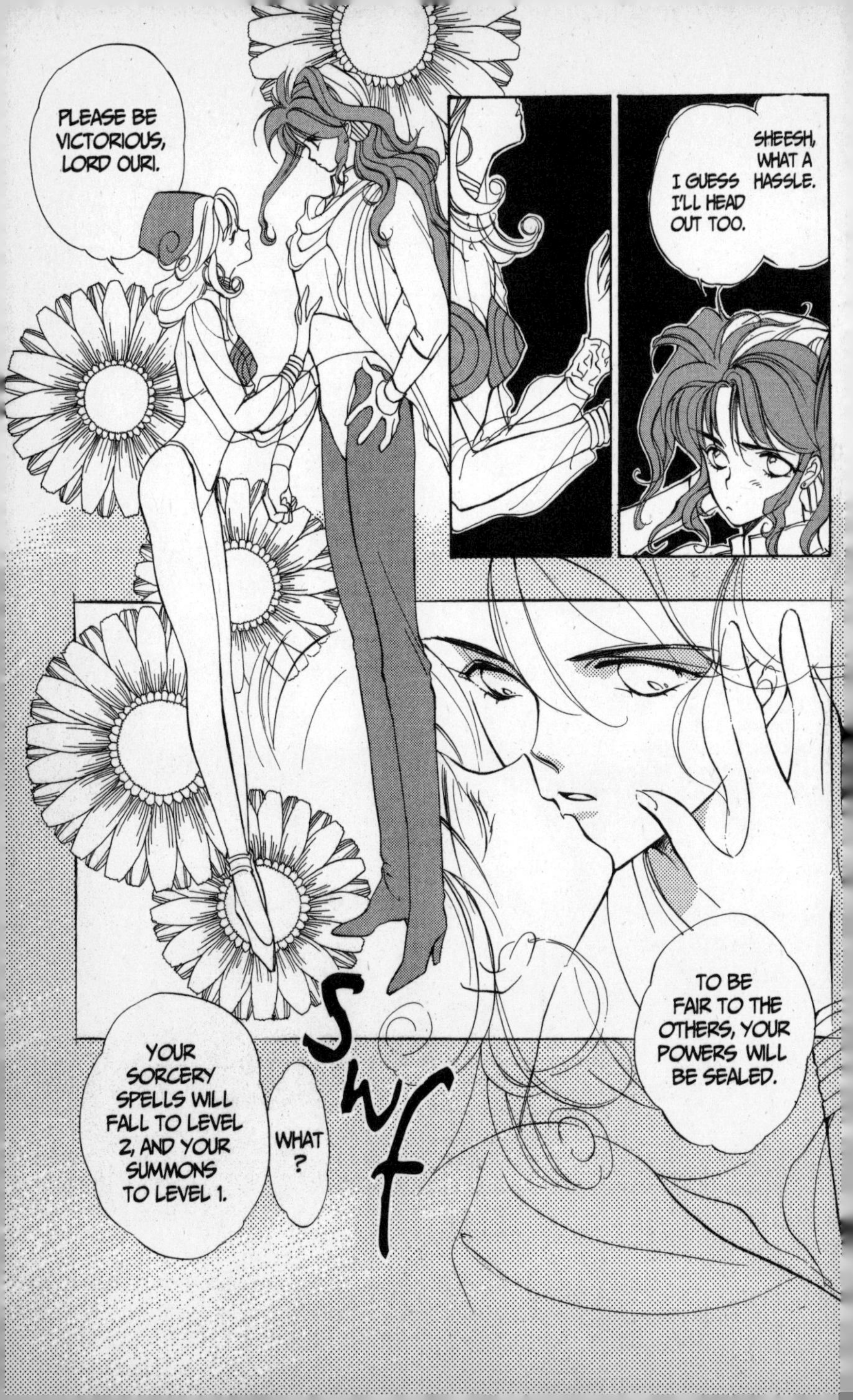
SHEESH, WHAT A HASSLE.
I GUESS I'LL HEAD OUT TOO.
PLEASE BE VICTORIOUS, LORD OURI.
TO BE FAIR TO THE OTHERS, YOUR POWERS WILL BE SEALED.
SWF
WHAT?
YOUR SORCERY SPELLS WILL FALL TO LEVEL 2, AND YOUR SUMMONS TO LEVEL 1.

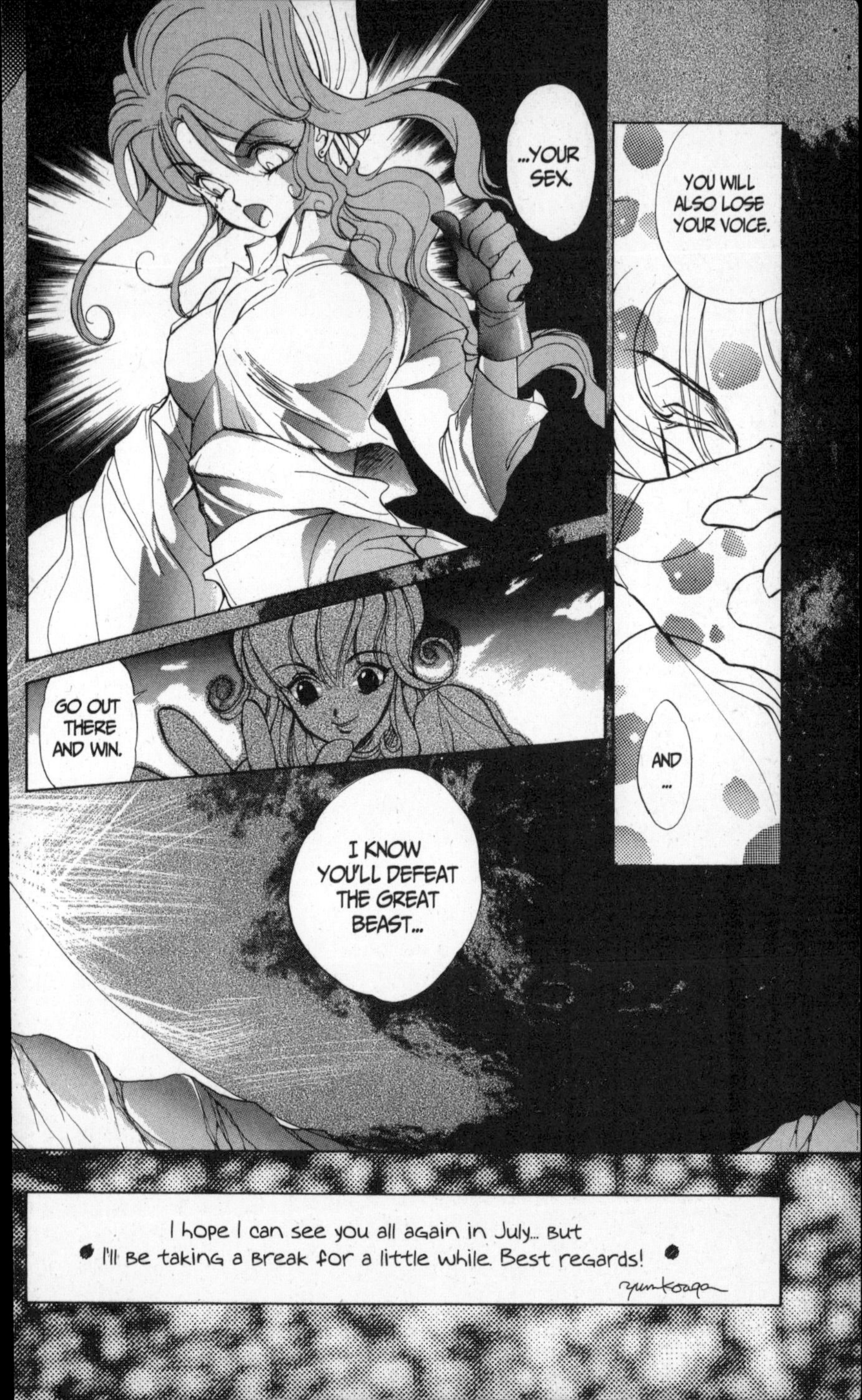
YOU WILL ALSO LOSE YOUR VOICE.
AND ...
...YOUR SEX.
GO OUT THERE AND WIN.
I KNOW YOU'LL DEFEAT THE GREAT BEAST...

I hope I can see you all again in July... But I'll be taking a break for a little while. Best regards!

Yun Kouga

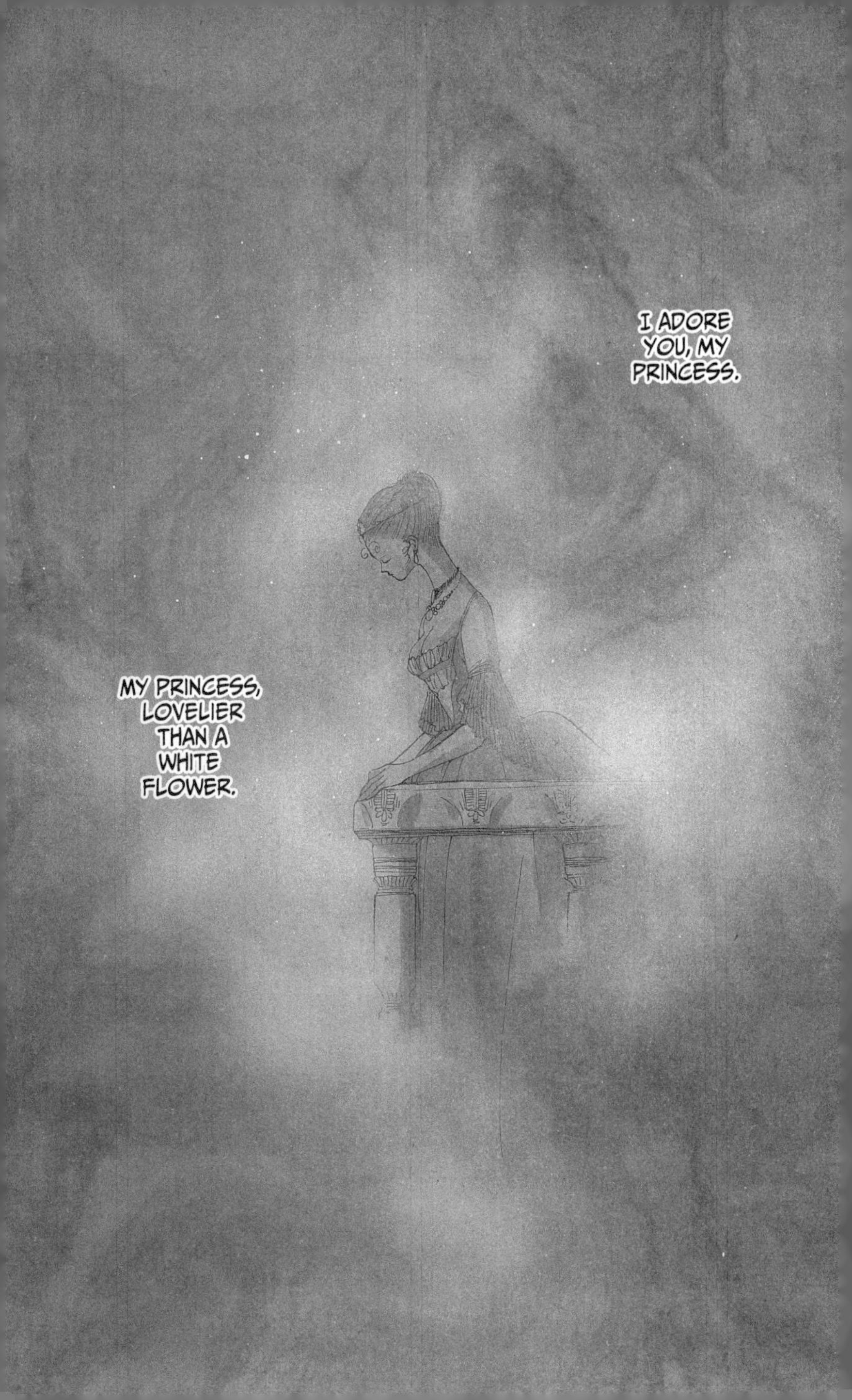
I ADORE YOU, MY PRINCESS.
MY PRINCESS, LOVELIER THAN A WHITE FLOWER.

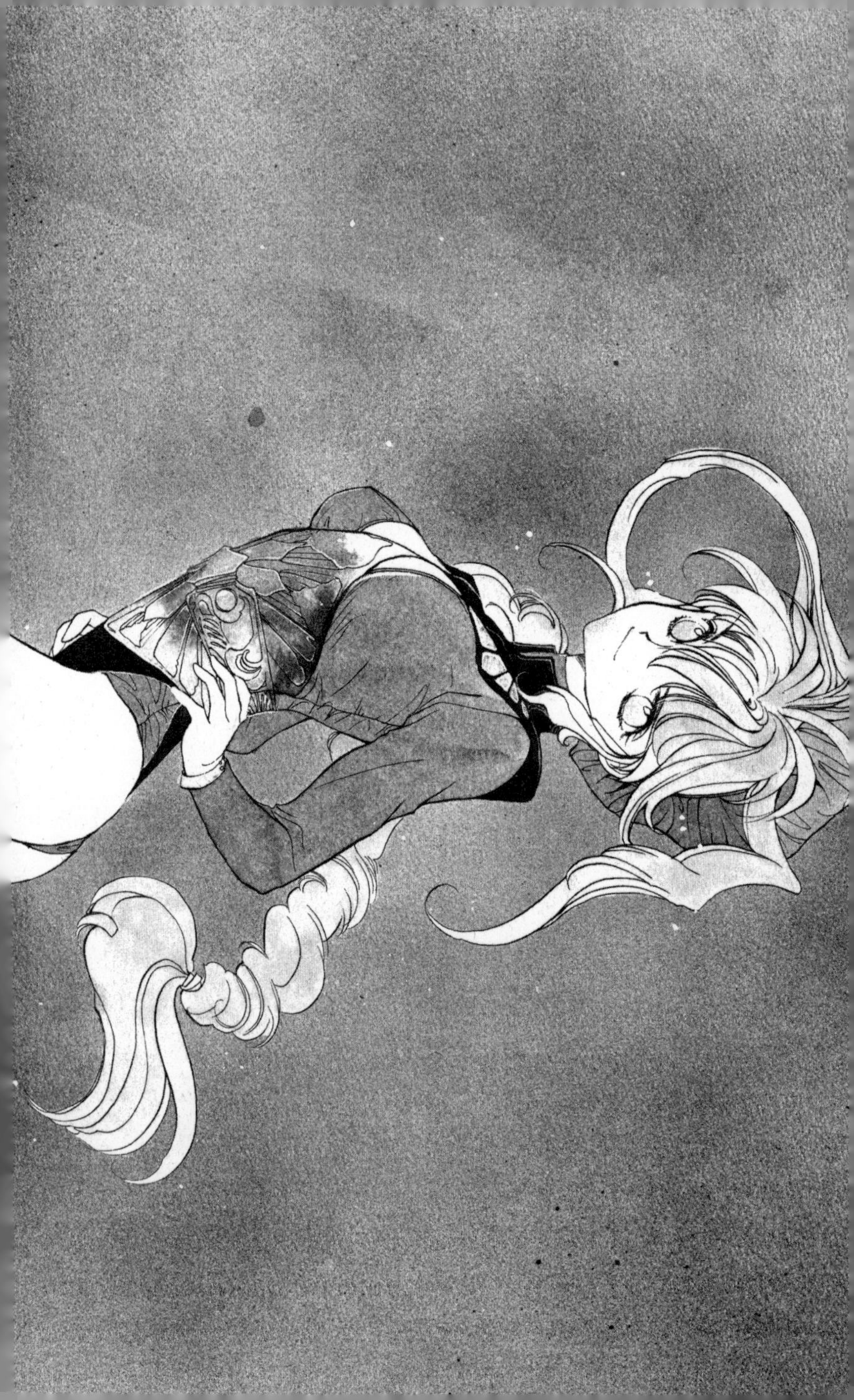

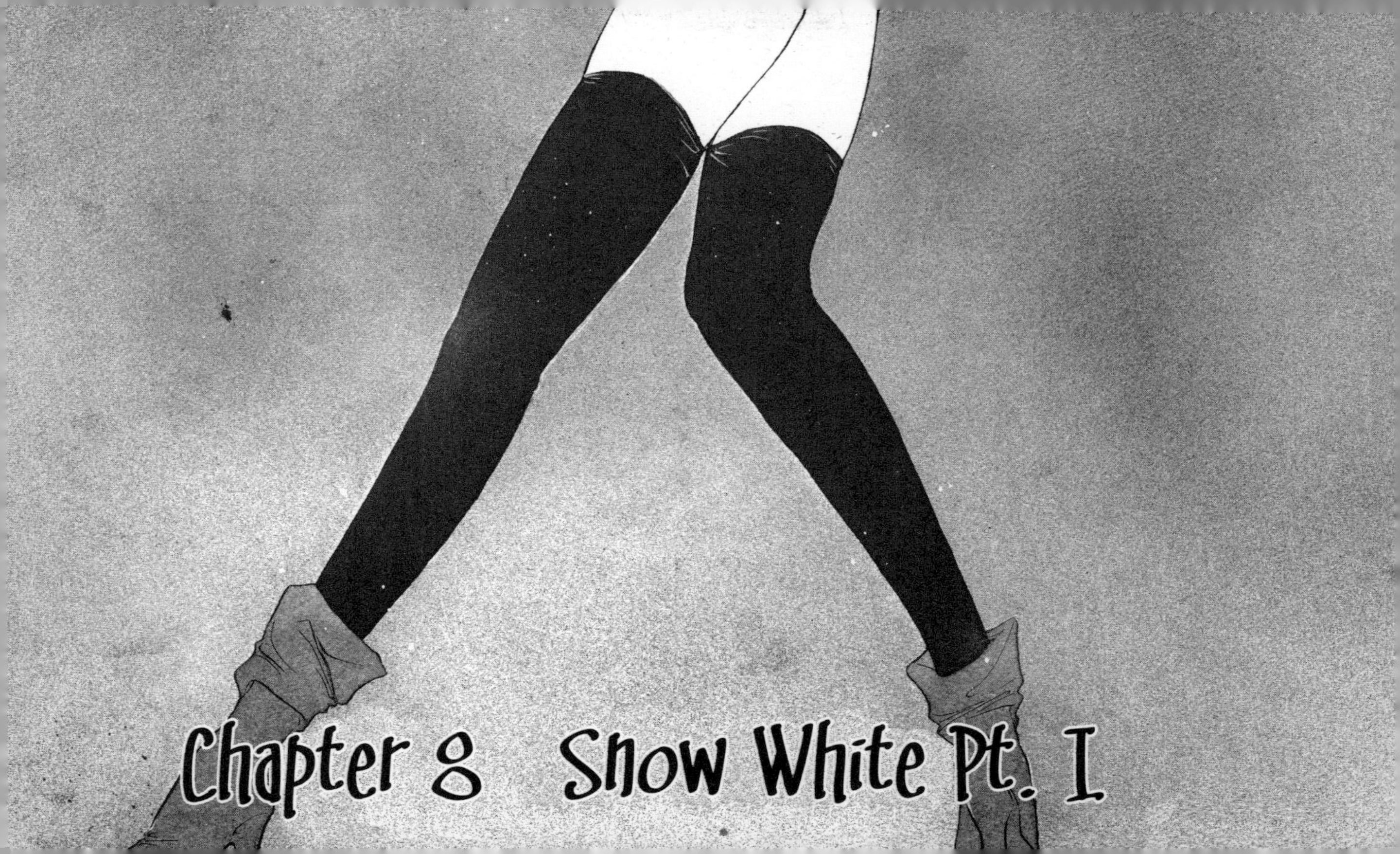
Chapter 8 Snow White Pt. 1

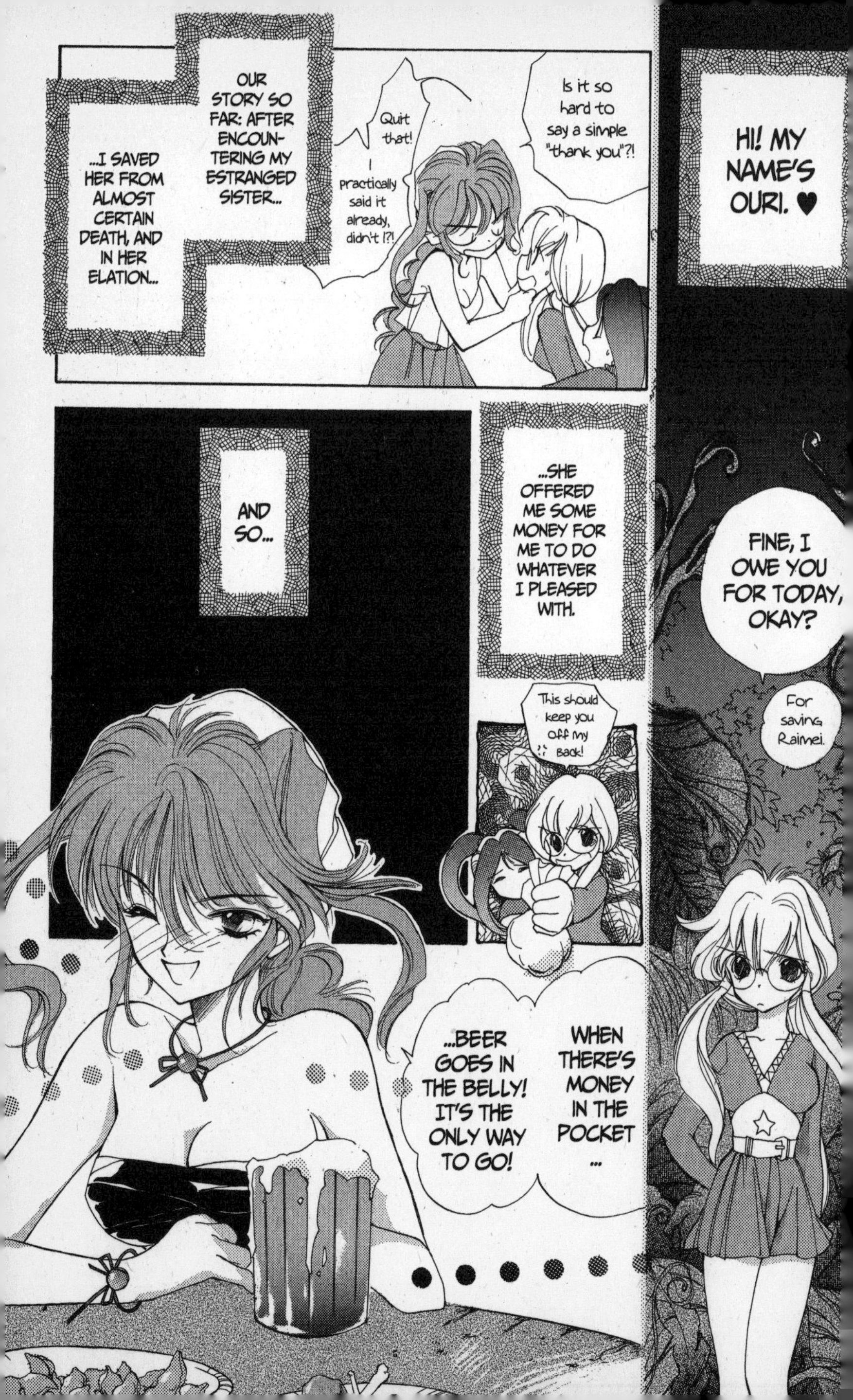
HI! MY NAME'S OURI. ♥
FINE, I OWE YOU FOR TODAY, OKAY?
For saving Raimei.
Is it so hard to say a simple "thank you"?!
Quit that!
I practically said it already, didn't I?!
OUR STORY SO FAR: AFTER ENCOUNTERING MY ESTRANGED SISTER...
...I SAVED HER FROM ALMOST CERTAIN DEATH, AND IN HER ELATION...
...SHE OFFERED ME SOME MONEY FOR ME TO DO WHATEVER I PLEASED WITH.
This should keep you off my back!
AND SO...
WHEN THERE'S MONEY IN THE POCKET...
...BEER GOES IN THE BELLY! IT'S THE ONLY WAY TO GO!

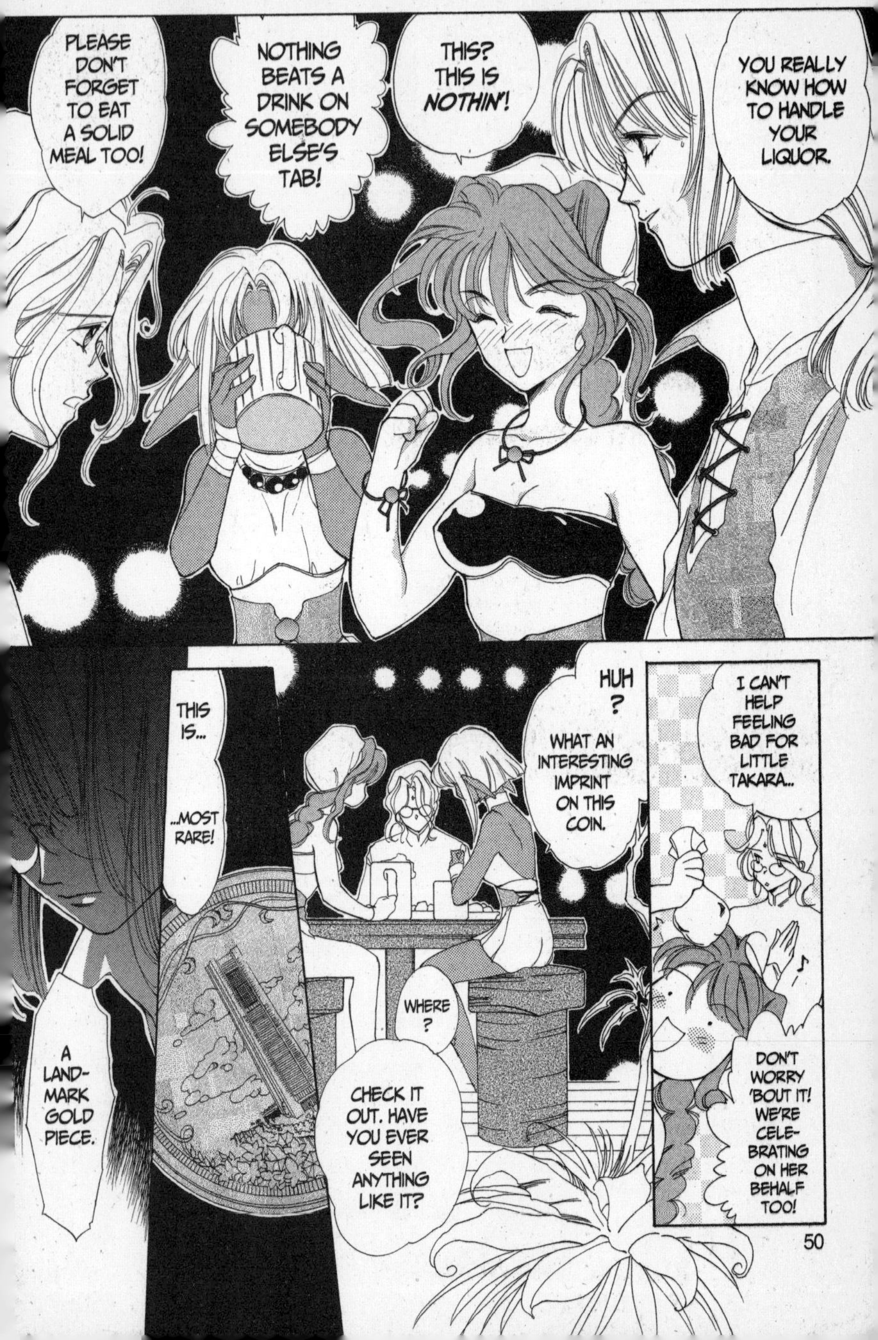
YOU REALLY KNOW HOW TO HANDLE YOUR LIQUOR.
THIS? THIS IS *NOTHIN'*!
NOTHING BEATS A DRINK ON SOMEBODY ELSE'S TAB!
PLEASE DON'T FORGET TO EAT A SOLID MEAL TOO!
I CAN'T HELP FEELING BAD FOR LITTLE TAKARA...
DON'T WORRY 'BOUT IT! WE'RE CELE-BRATING ON HER BEHALF TOO!
HUH?
WHAT AN INTERESTING IMPRINT ON THIS COIN.
WHERE?
CHECK IT OUT. HAVE YOU EVER SEEN ANYTHING LIKE IT?
THIS IS...
...MOST RARE!
A LAND-MARK GOLD PIECE.

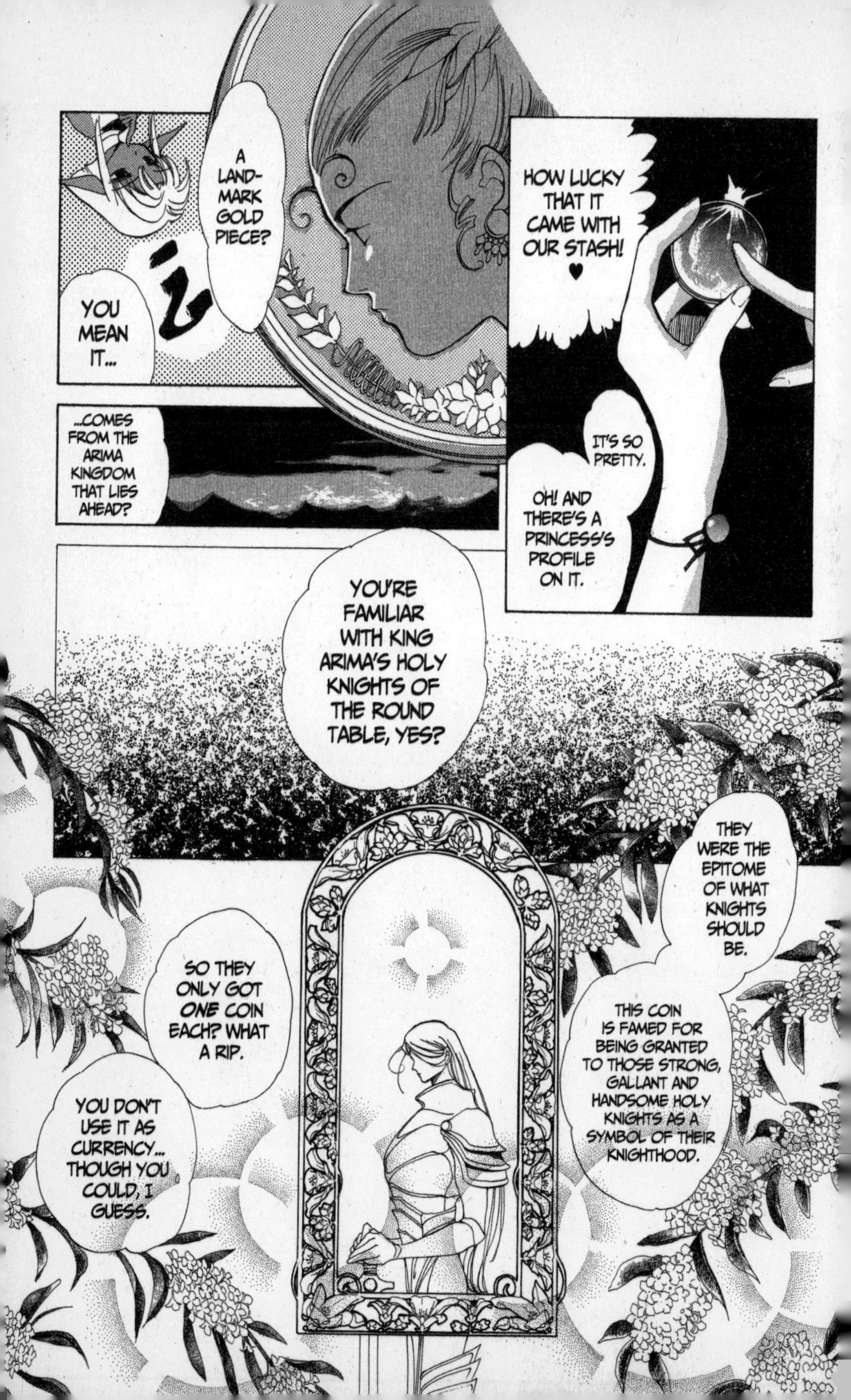
HOW LUCKY THAT IT CAME WITH OUR STASH! ♥
IT'S SO PRETTY.
OH! AND THERE'S A PRINCESS'S PROFILE ON IT.
A LAND-MARK GOLD PIECE?
YOU MEAN IT...
...COMES FROM THE ARIMA KINGDOM THAT LIES AHEAD?
YOU'RE FAMILIAR WITH KING ARIMA'S HOLY KNIGHTS OF THE ROUND TABLE, YES?
THEY WERE THE EPITOME OF WHAT KNIGHTS SHOULD BE.
THIS COIN IS FAMED FOR BEING GRANTED TO THOSE STRONG, GALLANT AND HANDSOME HOLY KNIGHTS AS A SYMBOL OF THEIR KNIGHTHOOD.
SO THEY ONLY GOT *ONE* COIN EACH? WHAT A RIP.
YOU DON'T USE IT AS CURRENCY... THOUGH YOU COULD, I GUESS.

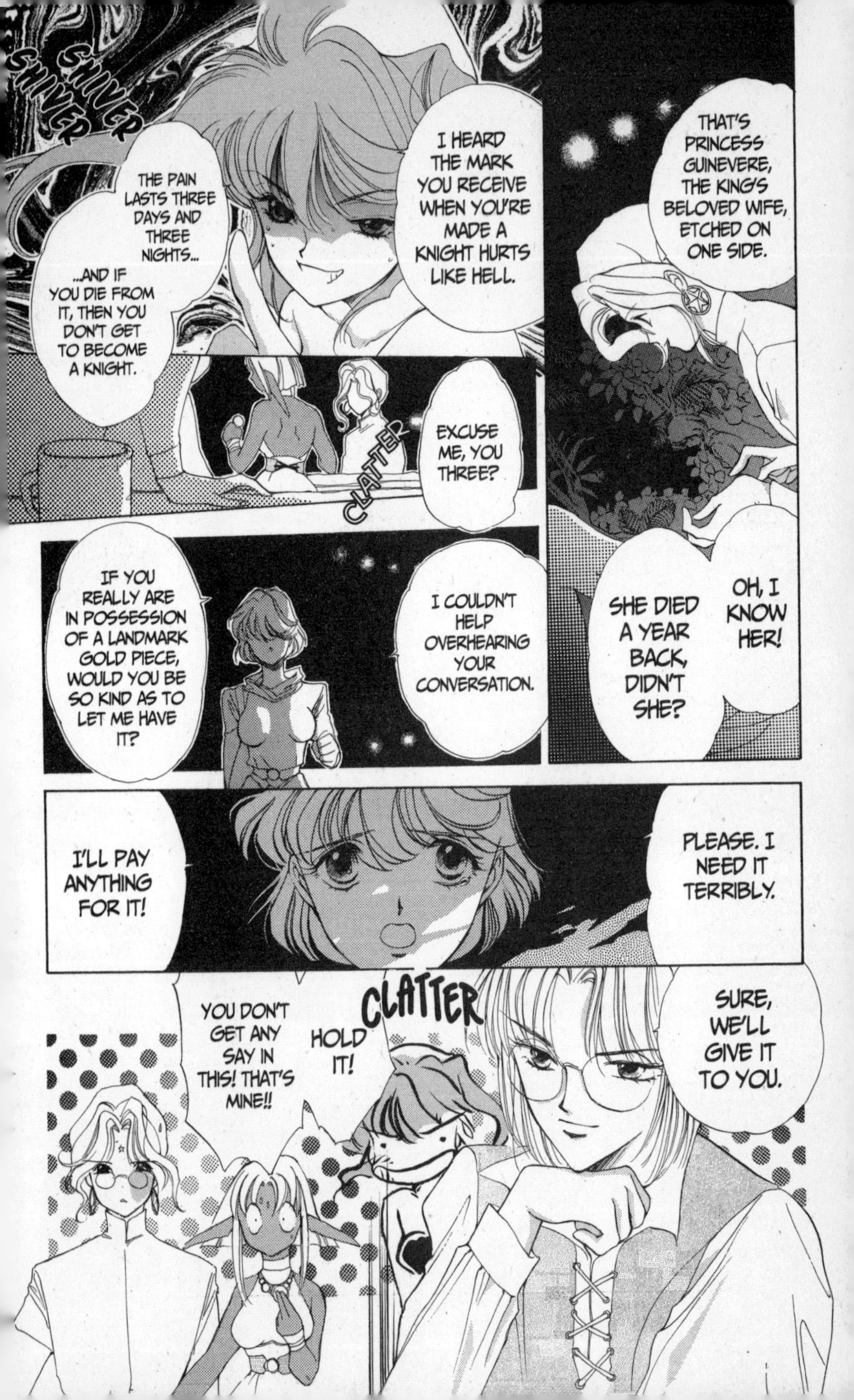
THAT'S PRINCESS GUINEVERE, THE KING'S BELOVED WIFE, ETCHED ON ONE SIDE.
OH, I KNOW HER!
SHE DIED A YEAR BACK, DIDN'T SHE?
I HEARD THE MARK YOU RECEIVE WHEN YOU'RE MADE A KNIGHT HURTS LIKE HELL.
THE PAIN LASTS THREE DAYS AND THREE NIGHTS...
...AND IF YOU DIE FROM IT, THEN YOU DON'T GET TO BECOME A KNIGHT.
SHIVER SHIVER
EXCUSE ME, YOU THREE?
CLATTER
I COULDN'T HELP OVERHEARING YOUR CONVERSATION.
IF YOU REALLY ARE IN POSSESSION OF A LANDMARK GOLD PIECE, WOULD YOU BE SO KIND AS TO LET ME HAVE IT?
PLEASE. I NEED IT TERRIBLY.
I'LL PAY ANYTHING FOR IT!
SURE, WE'LL GIVE IT TO YOU.
CLATTER
HOLD IT!
YOU DON'T GET ANY SAY IN THIS! THAT'S MINE!!

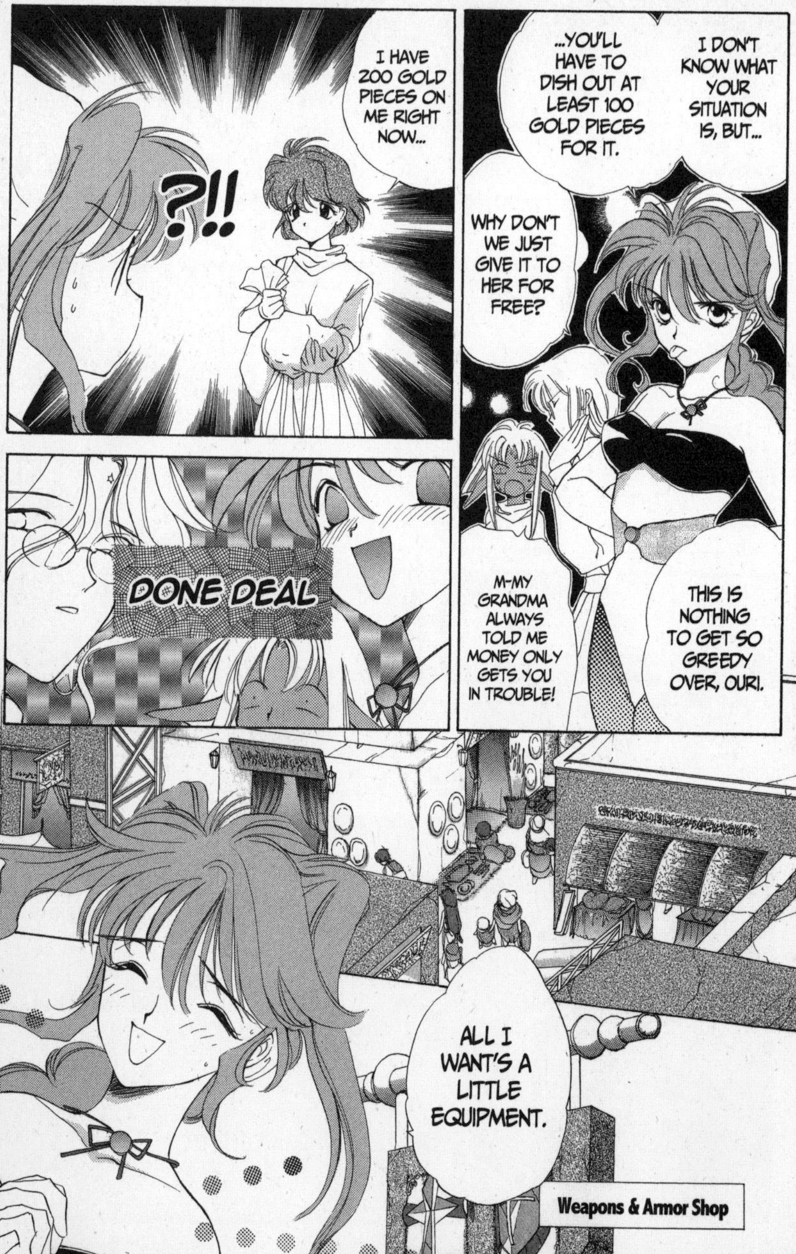
I DON'T KNOW WHAT YOUR SITUATION IS, BUT...
...YOU'LL HAVE TO DISH OUT AT LEAST 100 GOLD PIECES FOR IT.
WHY DON'T WE JUST GIVE IT TO HER FOR FREE?
THIS IS NOTHING TO GET SO GREEDY OVER, OURI.
M-MY GRANDMA ALWAYS TOLD ME MONEY ONLY GETS YOU IN TROUBLE!
I HAVE 200 GOLD PIECES ON ME RIGHT NOW...
?!!
DONE DEAL
ALL I WANT'S A LITTLE EQUIPMENT.
Weapons & Armor Shop

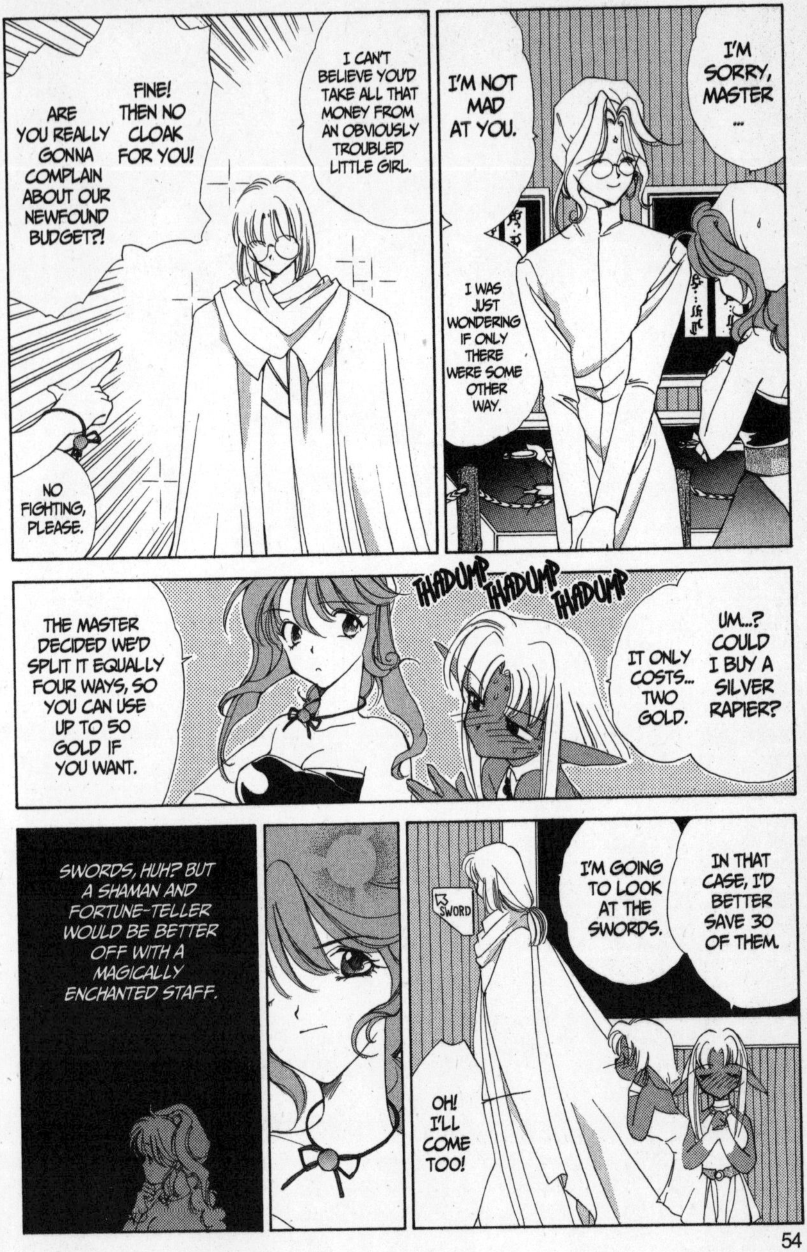
I'M SORRY, MASTER ...
I'M NOT MAD AT YOU.
I WAS JUST WONDERING IF ONLY THERE WERE SOME OTHER WAY.
I CAN'T BELIEVE YOU'D TAKE ALL THAT MONEY FROM AN OBVIOUSLY TROUBLED LITTLE GIRL.
FINE! THEN NO CLOAK FOR YOU!
ARE YOU REALLY GONNA COMPLAIN ABOUT OUR NEWFOUND BUDGET?!
NO FIGHTING, PLEASE.
UM...? COULD I BUY A SILVER RAPIER?
IT ONLY COSTS... TWO GOLD.
THADUMP THADUMP THADUMP
THE MASTER DECIDED WE'D SPLIT IT EQUALLY FOUR WAYS, SO YOU CAN USE UP TO 50 GOLD IF YOU WANT.
IN THAT CASE, I'D BETTER SAVE 30 OF THEM.
I'M GOING TO LOOK AT THE SWORDS.
SWORD
OH! I'LL COME TOO!
SWORDS, HUH? BUT A SHAMAN AND FORTUNE-TELLER WOULD BE BETTER OFF WITH A MAGICALLY ENCHANTED STAFF.

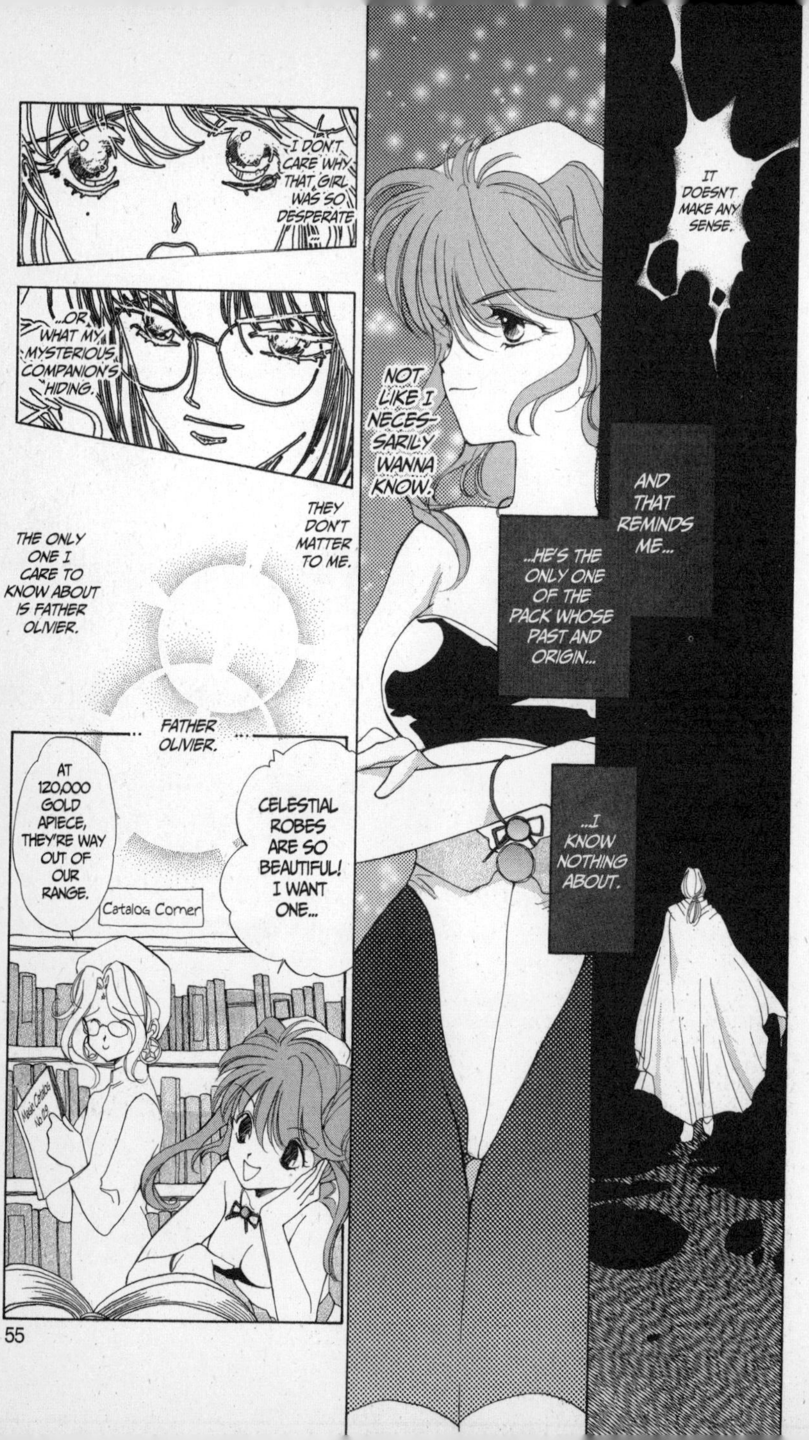
IT DOESN'T MAKE ANY SENSE.
AND THAT REMINDS ME...
...HE'S THE ONLY ONE OF THE PACK WHOSE PAST AND ORIGIN...
...I KNOW NOTHING ABOUT.
I DON'T CARE WHY THAT GIRL WAS SO DESPERATE...
...OR WHAT MY MYSTERIOUS COMPANION'S HIDING.
NOT LIKE I NECES-SARILY WANNA KNOW.
THEY DON'T MATTER TO ME.
THE ONLY ONE I CARE TO KNOW ABOUT IS FATHER OLIVIER.
...FATHER OLIVIER.
CELESTIAL ROBES ARE SO BEAUTIFUL! I WANT ONE...
AT 120,000 GOLD APIECE, THEY'RE WAY OUT OF OUR RANGE.
Catalog Corner

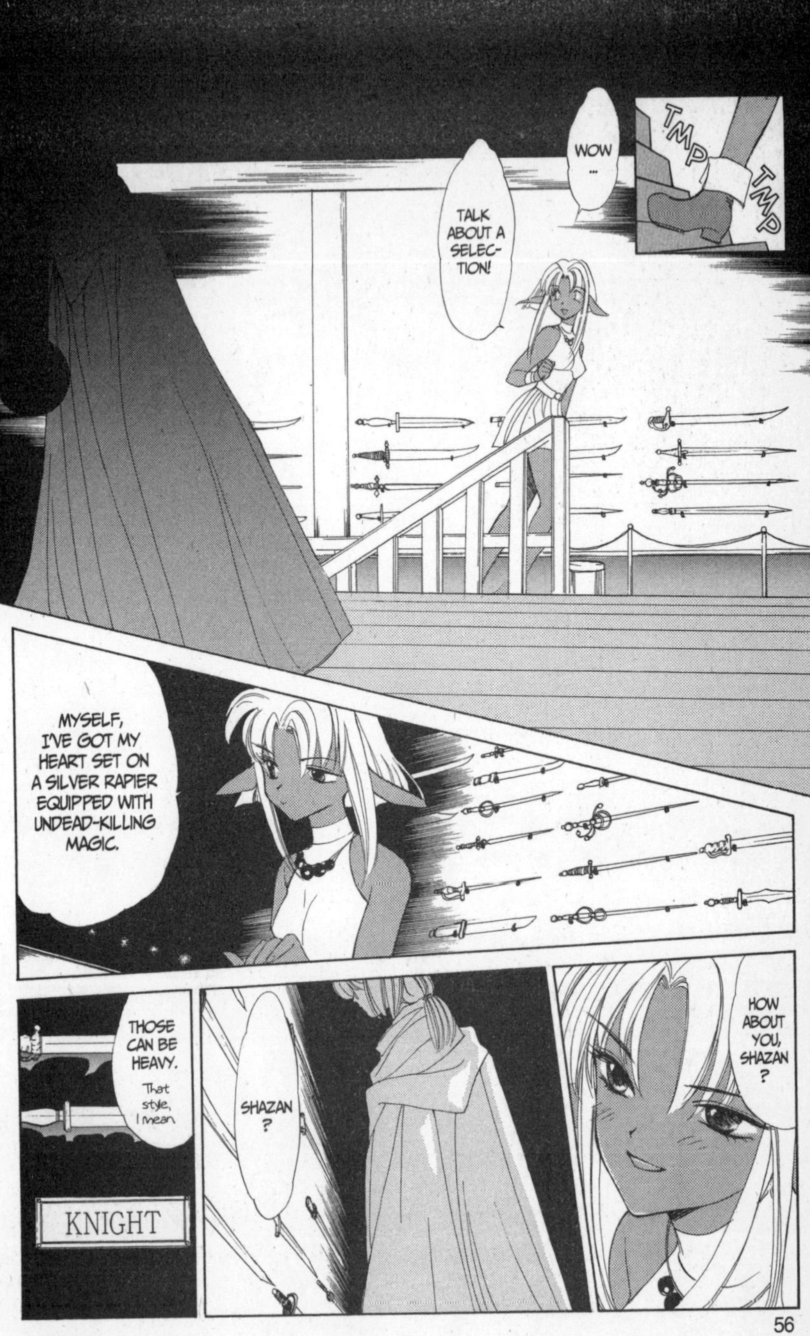
TMP TMP
WOW ...
TALK ABOUT A SELECTION!
MYSELF, I'VE GOT MY HEART SET ON A SILVER RAPIER EQUIPPED WITH UNDEAD-KILLING MAGIC.
HOW ABOUT YOU, SHAZAN?
SHAZAN?
THOSE CAN BE HEAVY.
That style, I mean.
KNIGHT

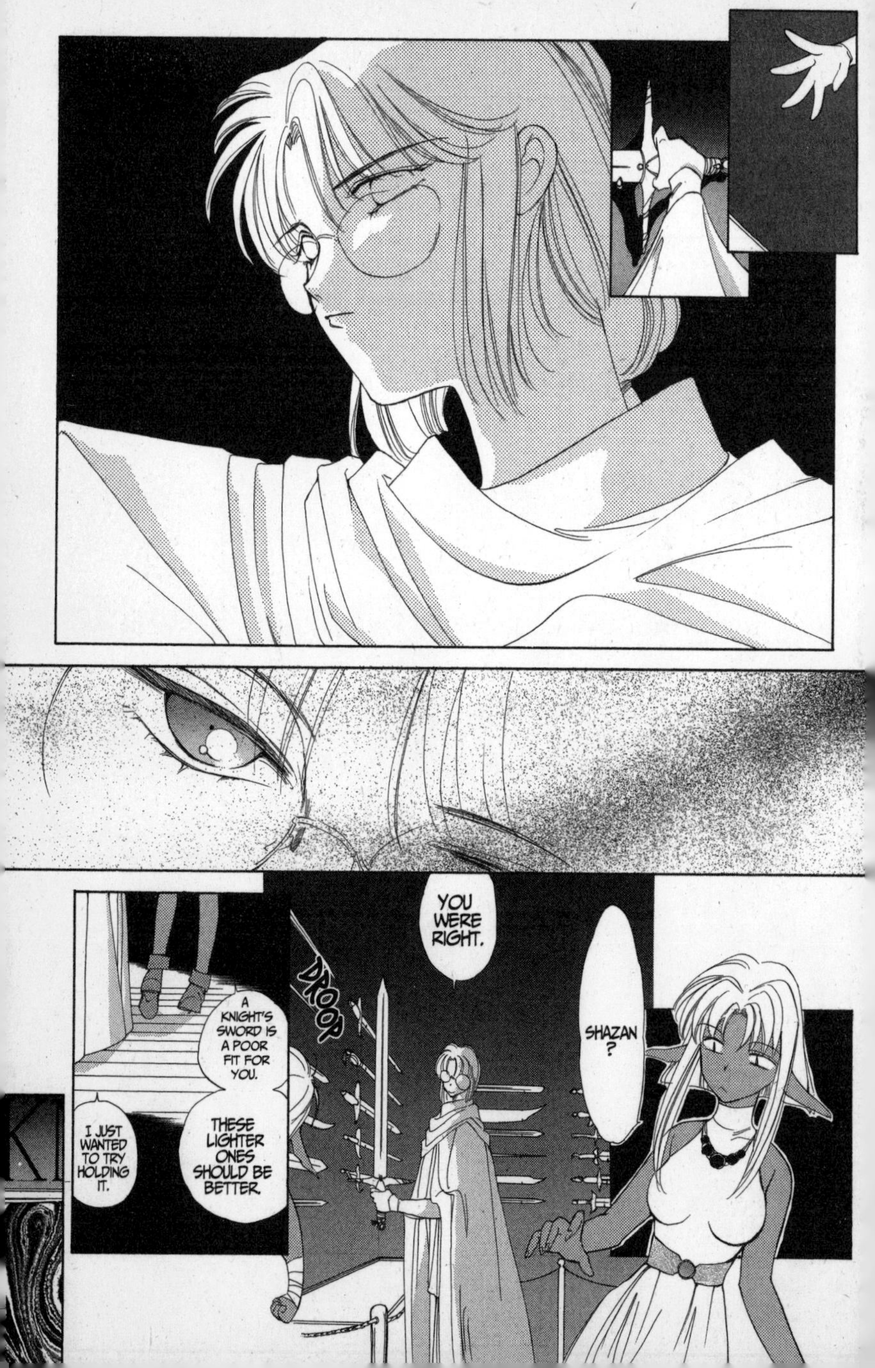
SHAZAN?
YOU WERE RIGHT.
DROOP
A KNIGHT'S SWORD IS A POOR FIT FOR YOU.
THESE LIGHTER ONES SHOULD BE BETTER.
I JUST WANTED TO TRY HOLDING IT.

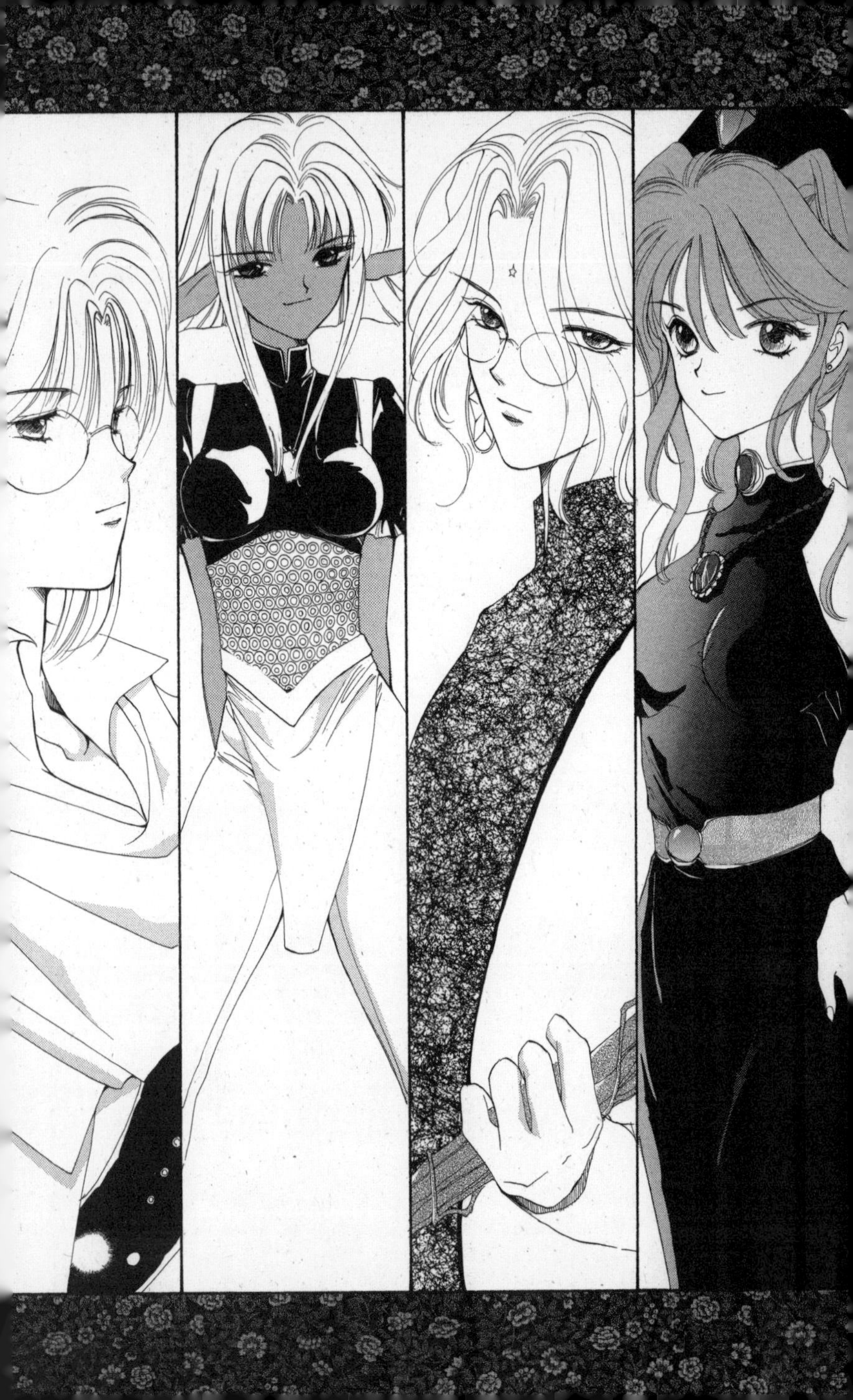

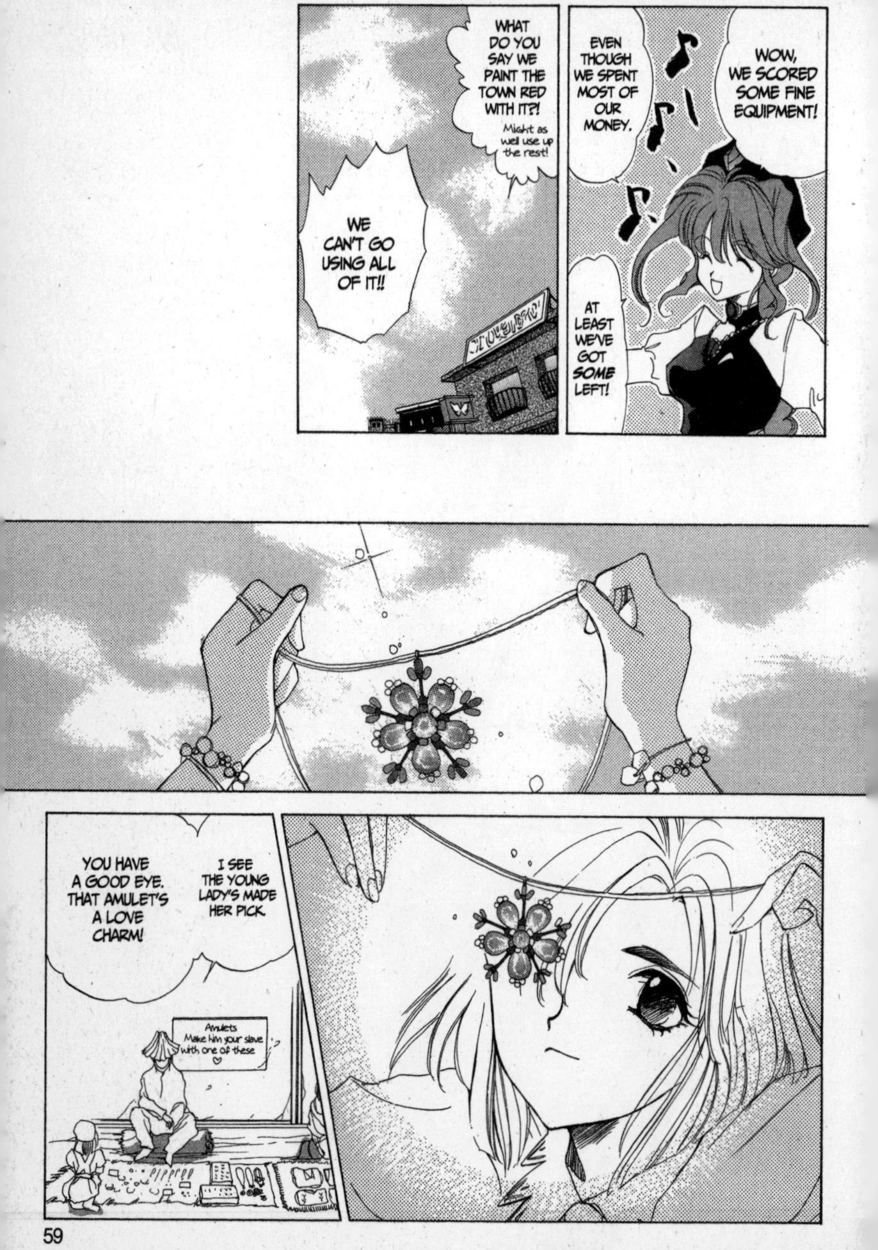
WOW, WE SCORED SOME FINE EQUIPMENT!
EVEN THOUGH WE SPENT MOST OF OUR MONEY.
AT LEAST WE'VE GOT SOME LEFT!
WHAT DO YOU SAY WE PAINT THE TOWN RED WITH IT?!
Might as well use up the rest!
WE CAN'T GO USING ALL OF IT!!
I SEE THE YOUNG LADY'S MADE HER PICK.
YOU HAVE A GOOD EYE. THAT AMULET'S A LOVE CHARM!
Amulets
Make him your slave with one of these ♡

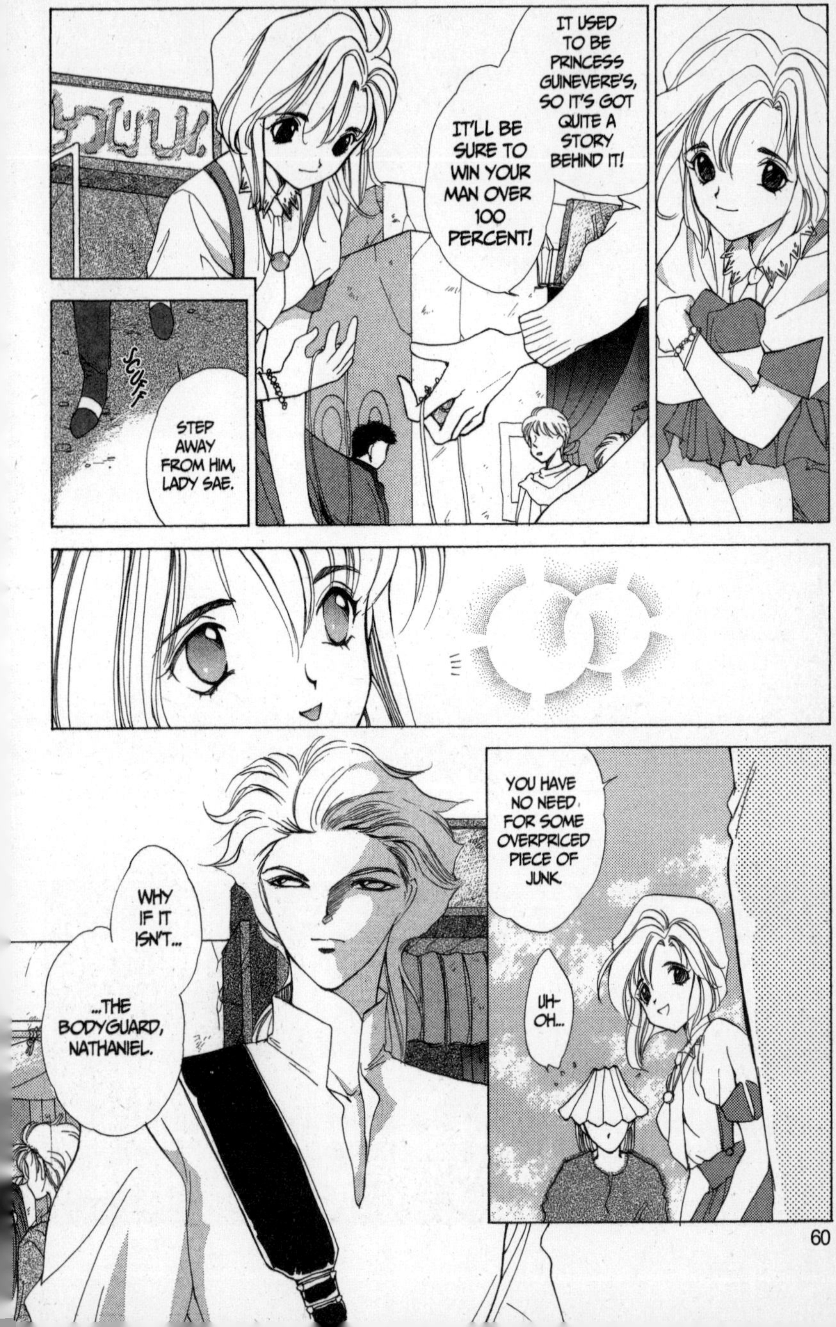
IT USED TO BE PRINCESS GUINEVERE'S, SO IT'S GOT QUITE A STORY BEHIND IT!
IT'LL BE SURE TO WIN YOUR MAN OVER 100 PERCENT!
SCUFF
STEP AWAY FROM HIM, LADY SAE.
YOU HAVE NO NEED FOR SOME OVERPRICED PIECE OF JUNK.
UH-OH...
WHY IF IT ISN'T...
...THE BODYGUARD, NATHANIEL.

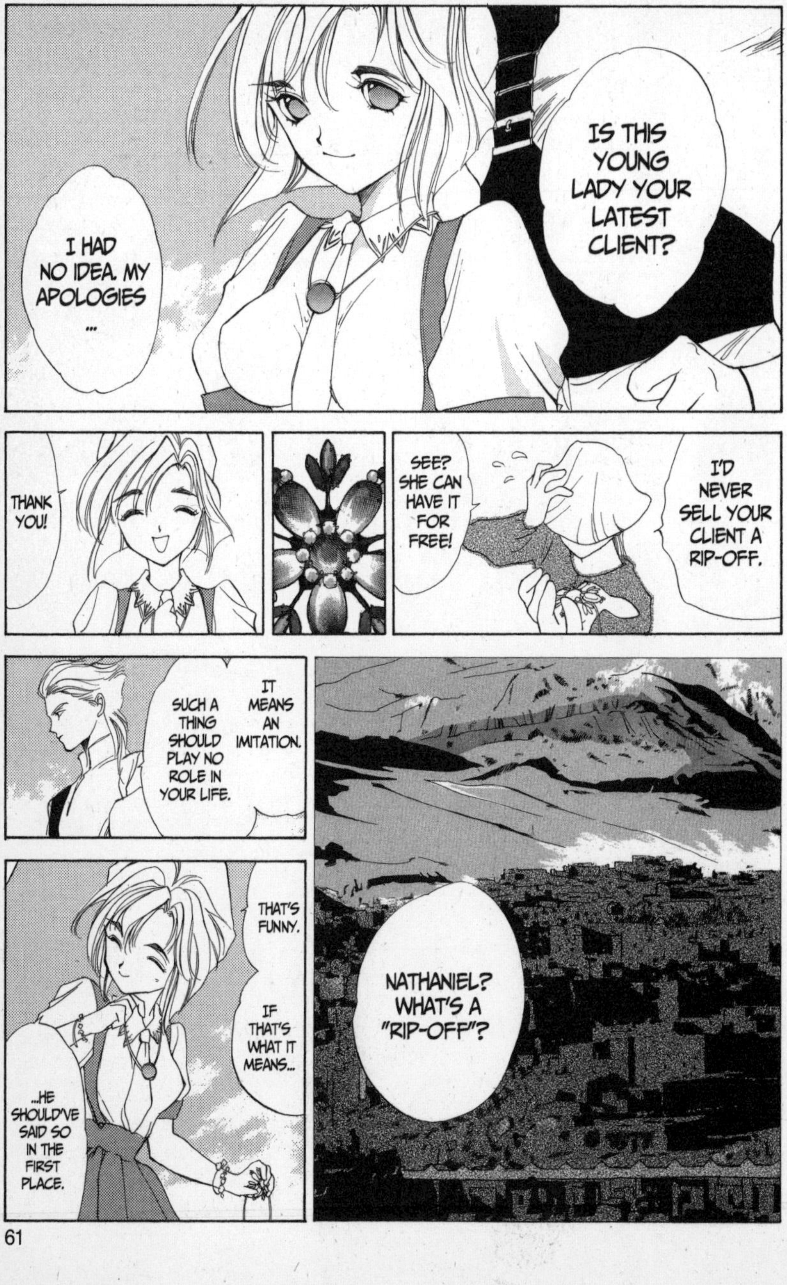
IS THIS YOUNG LADY YOUR LATEST CLIENT?
I HAD NO IDEA. MY APOLOGIES ...
I'D NEVER SELL YOUR CLIENT A RIP-OFF.
SEE? SHE CAN HAVE IT FOR FREE!
THANK YOU!
NATHANIEL? WHAT'S A "RIP-OFF"?
IT MEANS AN IMITATION.
SUCH A THING SHOULD PLAY NO ROLE IN YOUR LIFE.
THAT'S FUNNY.
IF THAT'S WHAT IT MEANS...
...HE SHOULD'VE SAID SO IN THE FIRST PLACE.

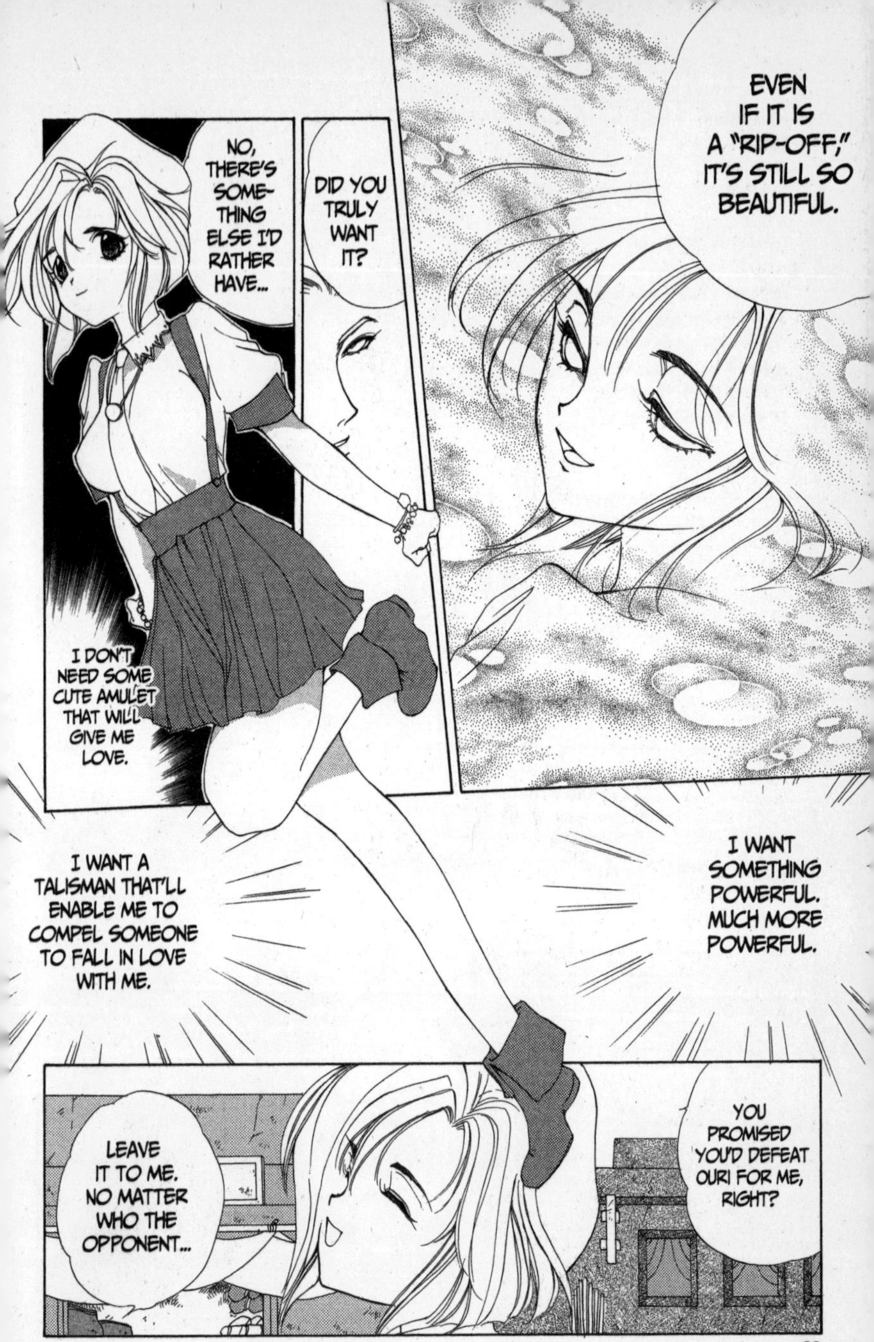
EVEN IF IT IS A "RIP-OFF," IT'S STILL SO BEAUTIFUL.
DID YOU TRULY WANT IT?
NO, THERE'S SOME-THING ELSE I'D RATHER HAVE...
I DON'T NEED SOME CUTE AMULET THAT WILL GIVE ME LOVE.
I WANT SOMETHING POWERFUL. MUCH MORE POWERFUL.
I WANT A TALISMAN THAT'LL ENABLE ME TO COMPEL SOMEONE TO FALL IN LOVE WITH ME.
YOU PROMISED YOU'D DEFEAT OURI FOR ME, RIGHT?
LEAVE IT TO ME. NO MATTER WHO THE OPPONENT...

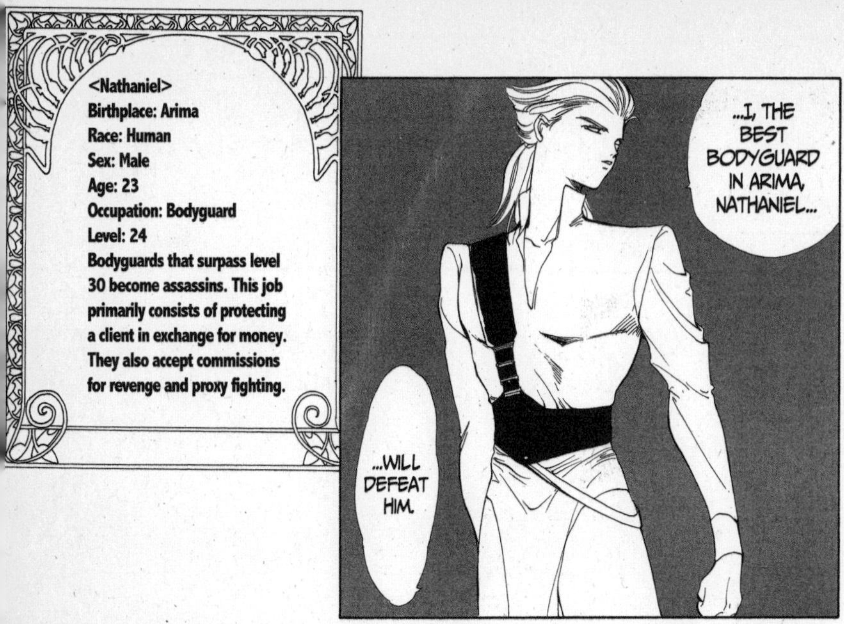
...I, THE BEST BODYGUARD IN ARIMA, NATHANIEL...
...WILL DEFEAT HIM.

<Nathaniel>
Birthplace: Arima
Race: Human
Sex: Male
Age: 23
Occupation: Bodyguard
Level: 24
Bodyguards that surpass level 30 become assassins. This job primarily consists of protecting a client in exchange for money. They also accept commissions for revenge and proxy fighting.

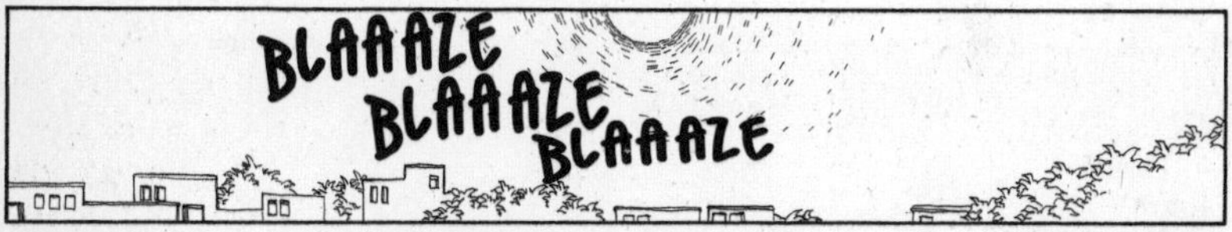
BLAAAZE
BLAAAZE
BLAAAZE

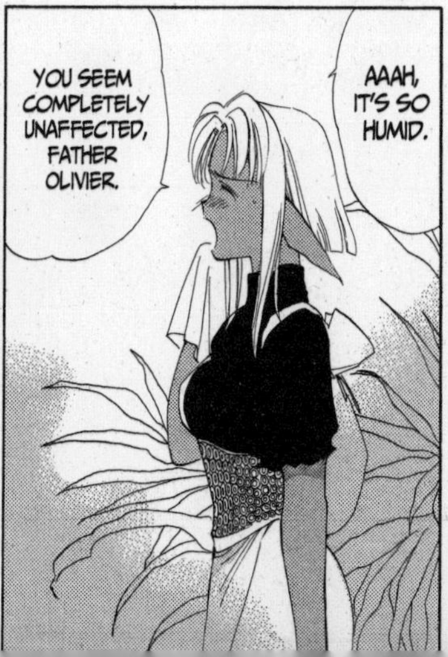
AAAH, IT'S SO HUMID.
YOU SEEM COMPLETELY UNAFFECTED, FATHER OLIVIER.

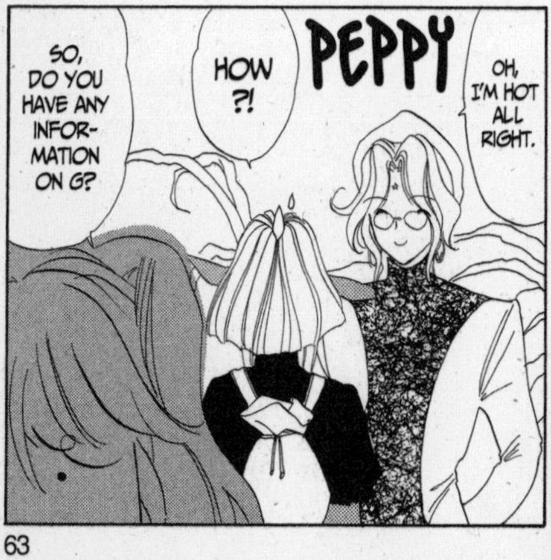
OH, I'M HOT ALL RIGHT.
PEPPY
HOW ?!
SO, DO YOU HAVE ANY INFOR-MATION ON G?

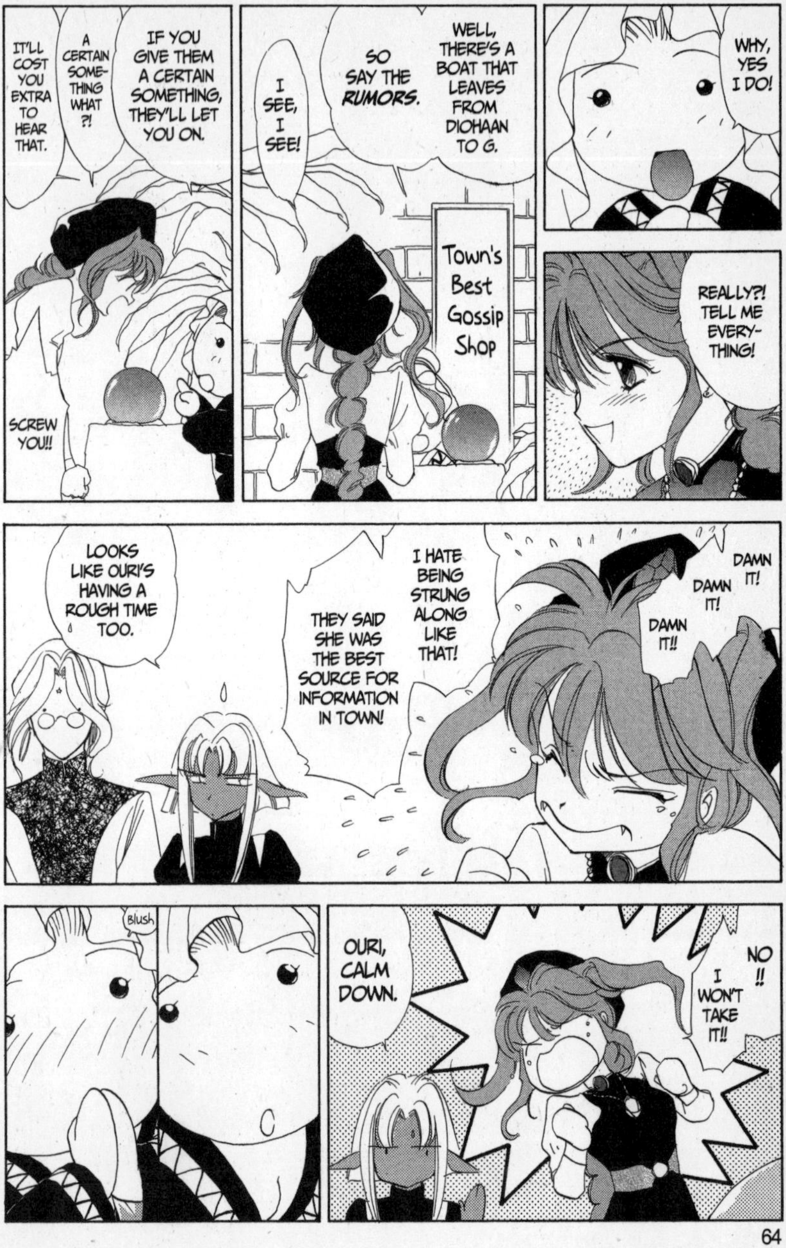
WHY, YES I DO!
REALLY?! TELL ME EVERYTHING!
WELL, THERE'S A BOAT THAT LEAVES FROM DIOHAAN TO G.
SO SAY THE *RUMORS.*
I SEE, I SEE!
Town's Best Gossip Shop
IF YOU GIVE THEM A CERTAIN SOMETHING, THEY'LL LET YOU ON.
A CERTAIN SOMETHING WHAT?!
IT'LL COST YOU EXTRA TO HEAR THAT.
SCREW YOU!!
DAMN IT!
DAMN IT!
DAMN IT!!
I HATE BEING STRUNG ALONG LIKE THAT!
THEY SAID SHE WAS THE BEST SOURCE FOR INFORMATION IN TOWN!
LOOKS LIKE OURI'S HAVING A ROUGH TIME TOO.
NO!!
I WON'T TAKE IT!!
OURI, CALM DOWN.
Blush

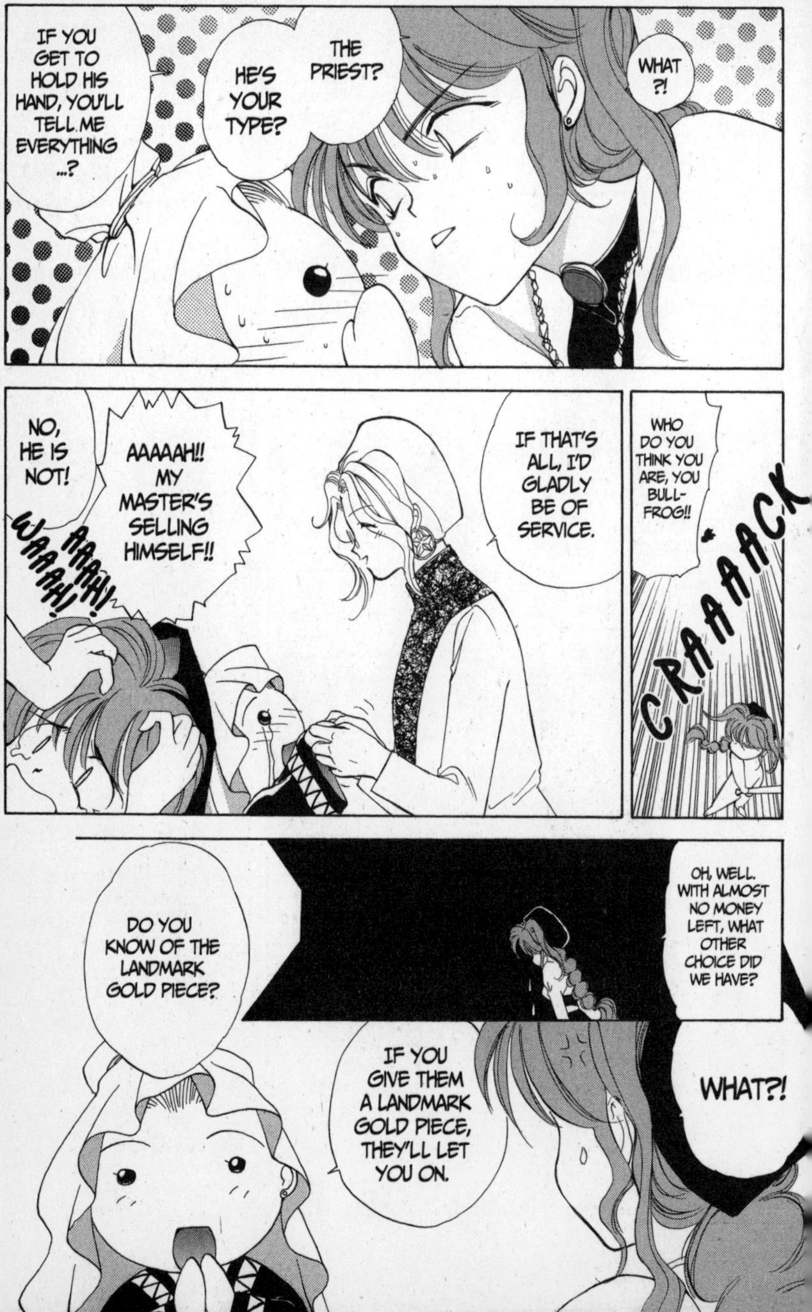
WHAT ?!
THE PRIEST?
HE'S YOUR TYPE?
IF YOU GET TO HOLD HIS HAND, YOU'LL TELL ME EVERYTHING ...?
WHO DO YOU THINK YOU ARE, YOU BULL-FROG!!
CRAAAACK
IF THAT'S ALL, I'D GLADLY BE OF SERVICE.
AAAAAH!! MY MASTER'S SELLING HIMSELF!!
NO, HE IS NOT!
AAARH! WAAAAH!
OH, WELL. WITH ALMOST NO MONEY LEFT, WHAT OTHER CHOICE DID WE HAVE?
DO YOU KNOW OF THE LANDMARK GOLD PIECE?
IF YOU GIVE THEM A LANDMARK GOLD PIECE, THEY'LL LET YOU ON.
WHAT?!

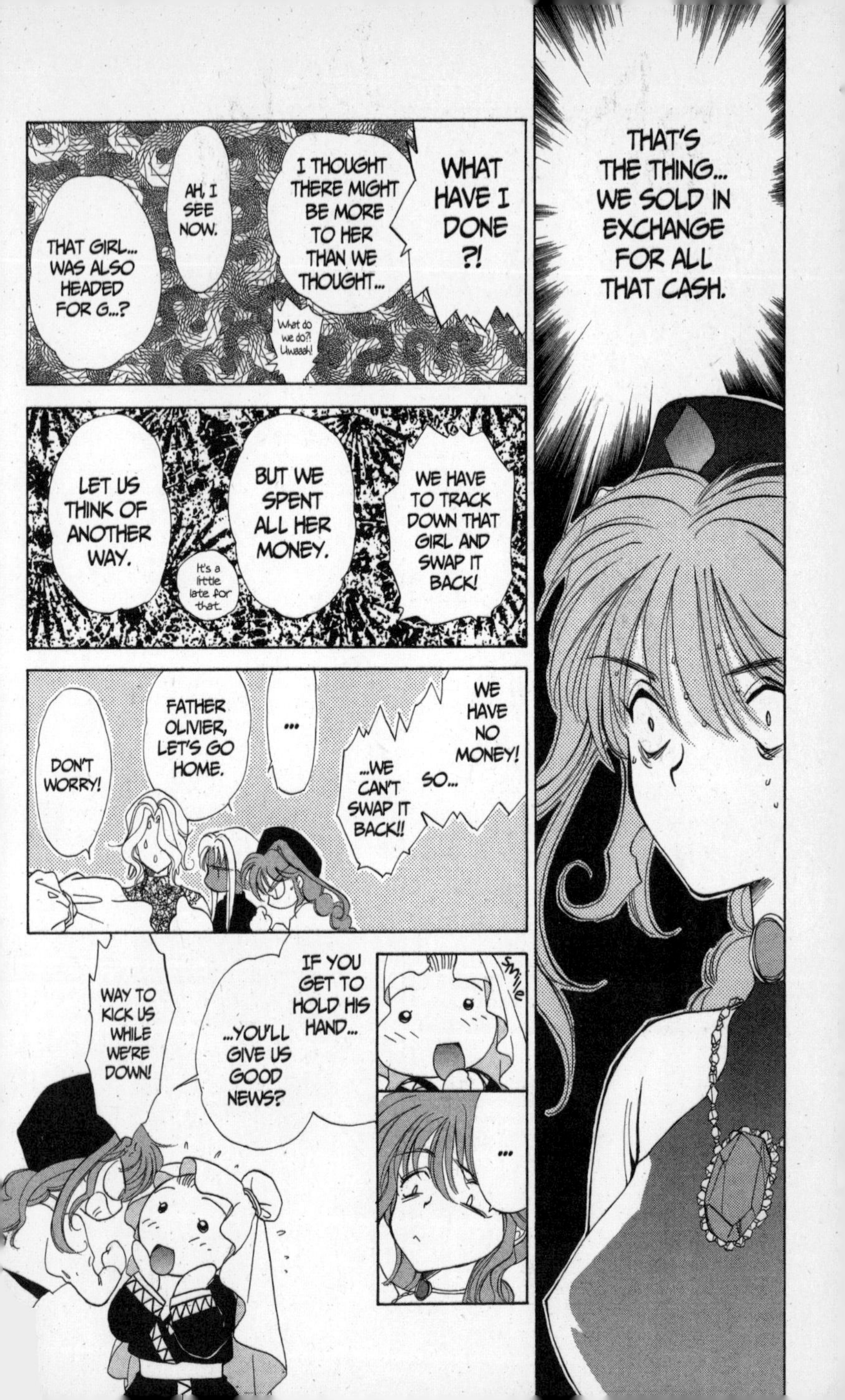
THAT'S THE THING... WE SOLD IN EXCHANGE FOR ALL THAT CASH.
WHAT HAVE I DONE ?!
I THOUGHT THERE MIGHT BE MORE TO HER THAN WE THOUGHT...
What do we do?! Uwaaah!
AH, I SEE NOW.
THAT GIRL... WAS ALSO HEADED FOR G...?
WE HAVE TO TRACK DOWN THAT GIRL AND SWAP IT BACK!
BUT WE SPENT ALL HER MONEY.
It's a little late for that.
LET US THINK OF ANOTHER WAY.
WE HAVE NO MONEY!
SO...
...WE CAN'T SWAP IT BACK!!
...
FATHER OLIVIER, LET'S GO HOME.
DON'T WORRY!
Smile
IF YOU GET TO HOLD HIS HAND...
...YOU'LL GIVE US GOOD NEWS?
...
WAY TO KICK US WHILE WE'RE DOWN!

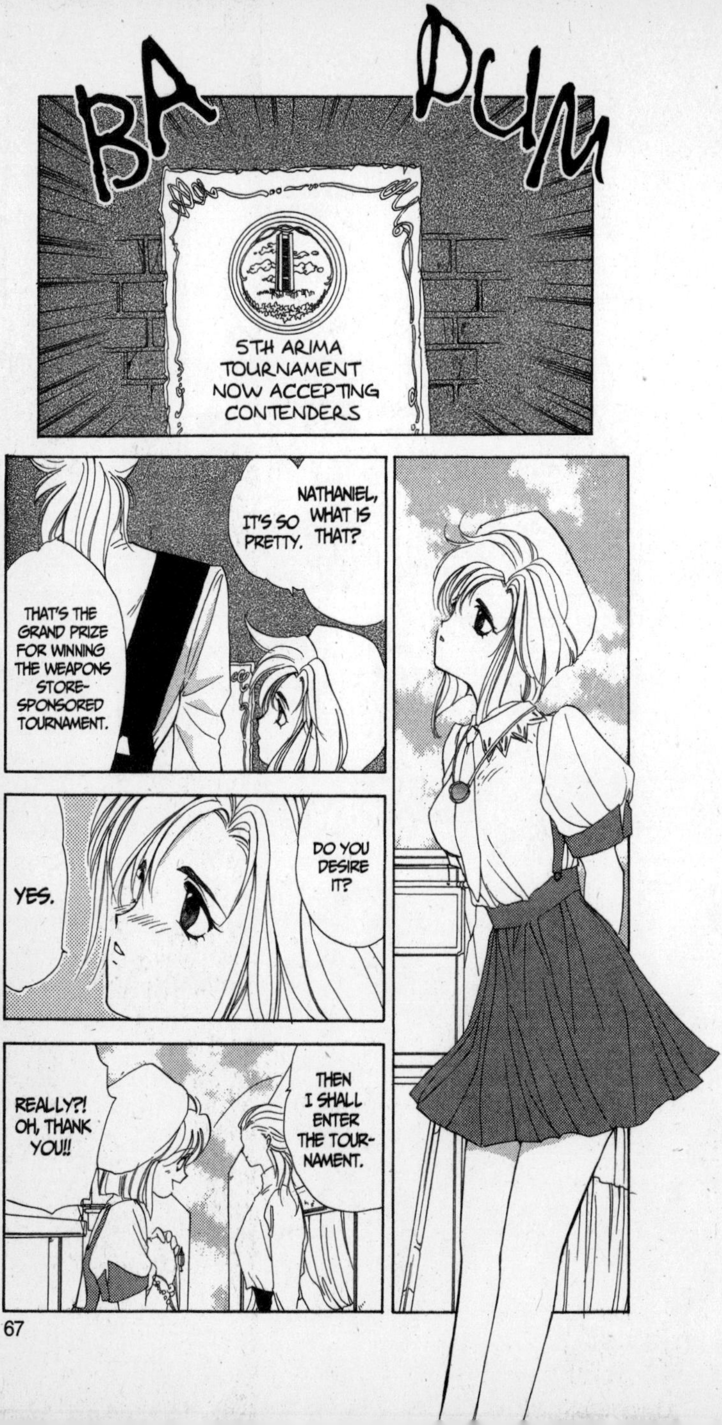
BA DUM
5TH ARIMA TOURNAMENT NOW ACCEPTING CONTENDERS
NATHANIEL, WHAT IS THAT?
IT'S SO PRETTY.
THAT'S THE GRAND PRIZE FOR WINNING THE WEAPONS STORE-SPONSORED TOURNAMENT.
DO YOU DESIRE IT?
YES.
THEN I SHALL ENTER THE TOUR-NAMENT.
REALLY?! OH, THANK YOU!!

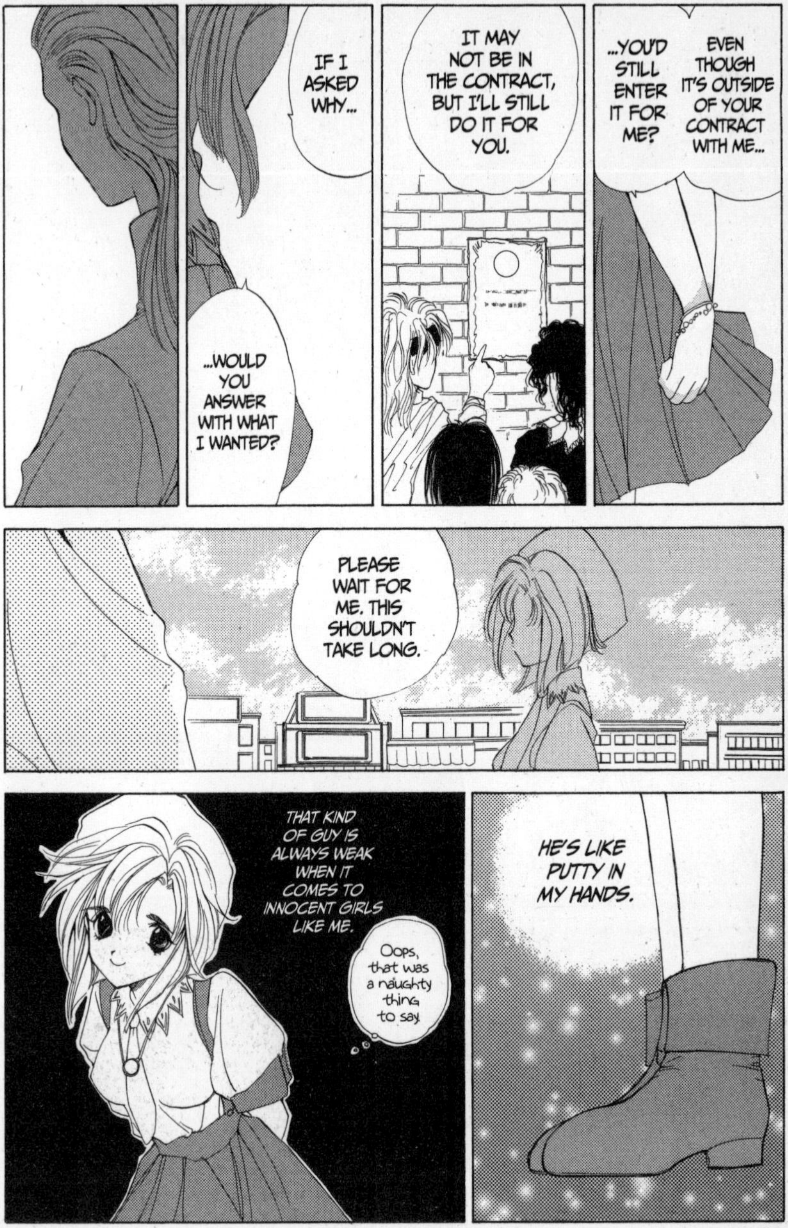
EVEN THOUGH IT'S OUTSIDE OF YOUR CONTRACT WITH ME...
...YOU'D STILL ENTER IT FOR ME?
IT MAY NOT BE IN THE CONTRACT, BUT I'LL STILL DO IT FOR YOU.
IF I ASKED WHY...
...WOULD YOU ANSWER WITH WHAT I WANTED?
PLEASE WAIT FOR ME. THIS SHOULDN'T TAKE LONG.
HE'S LIKE PUTTY IN MY HANDS.
THAT KIND OF GUY IS ALWAYS WEAK WHEN IT COMES TO INNOCENT GIRLS LIKE ME.
Oops, that was a naughty thing to say.

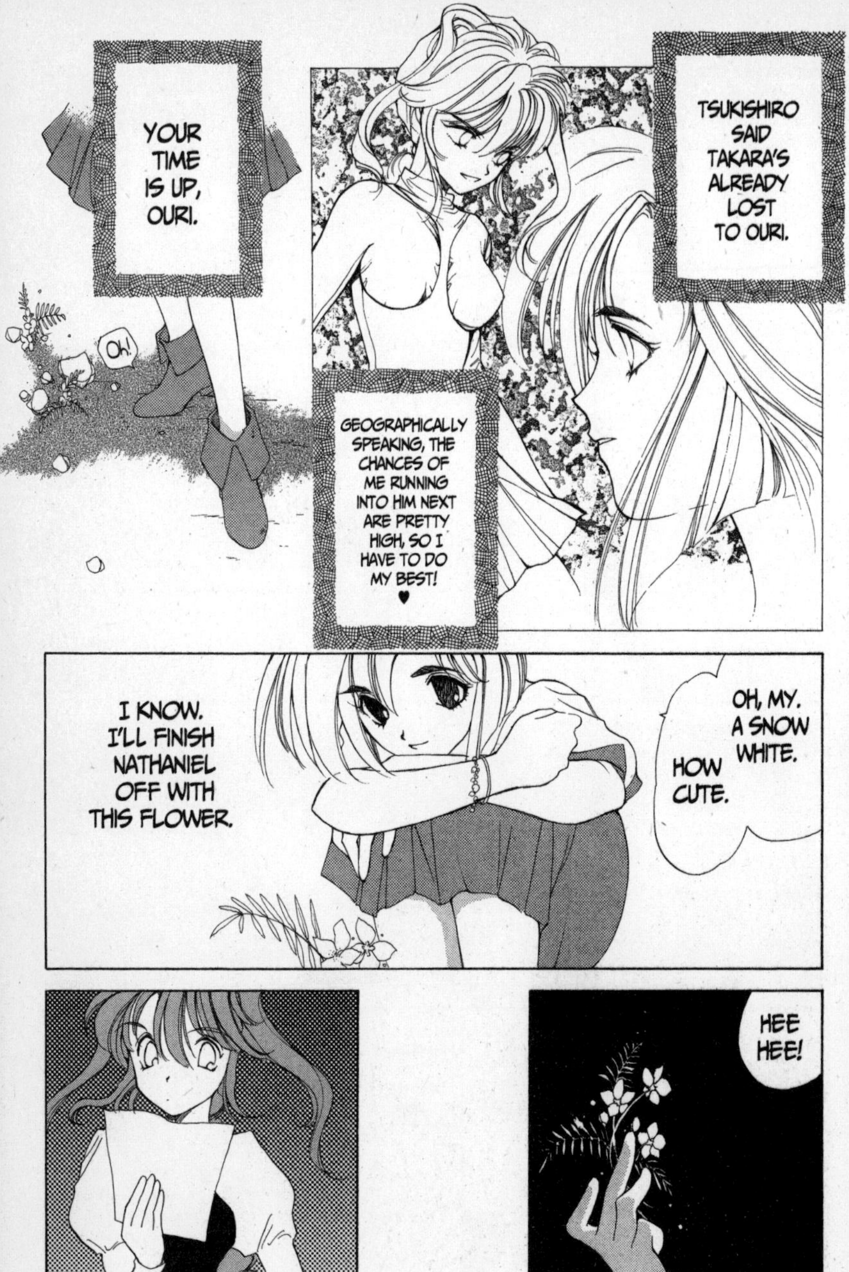
TSUKISHIRO SAID TAKARA'S ALREADY LOST TO OURI.
GEOGRAPHICALLY SPEAKING, THE CHANCES OF ME RUNNING INTO HIM NEXT ARE PRETTY HIGH, SO I HAVE TO DO MY BEST! ♥
YOUR TIME IS UP, OURI.
OH!
OH, MY. A SNOW WHITE.
HOW CUTE.
I KNOW. I'LL FINISH NATHANIEL OFF WITH THIS FLOWER.
HEE HEE!

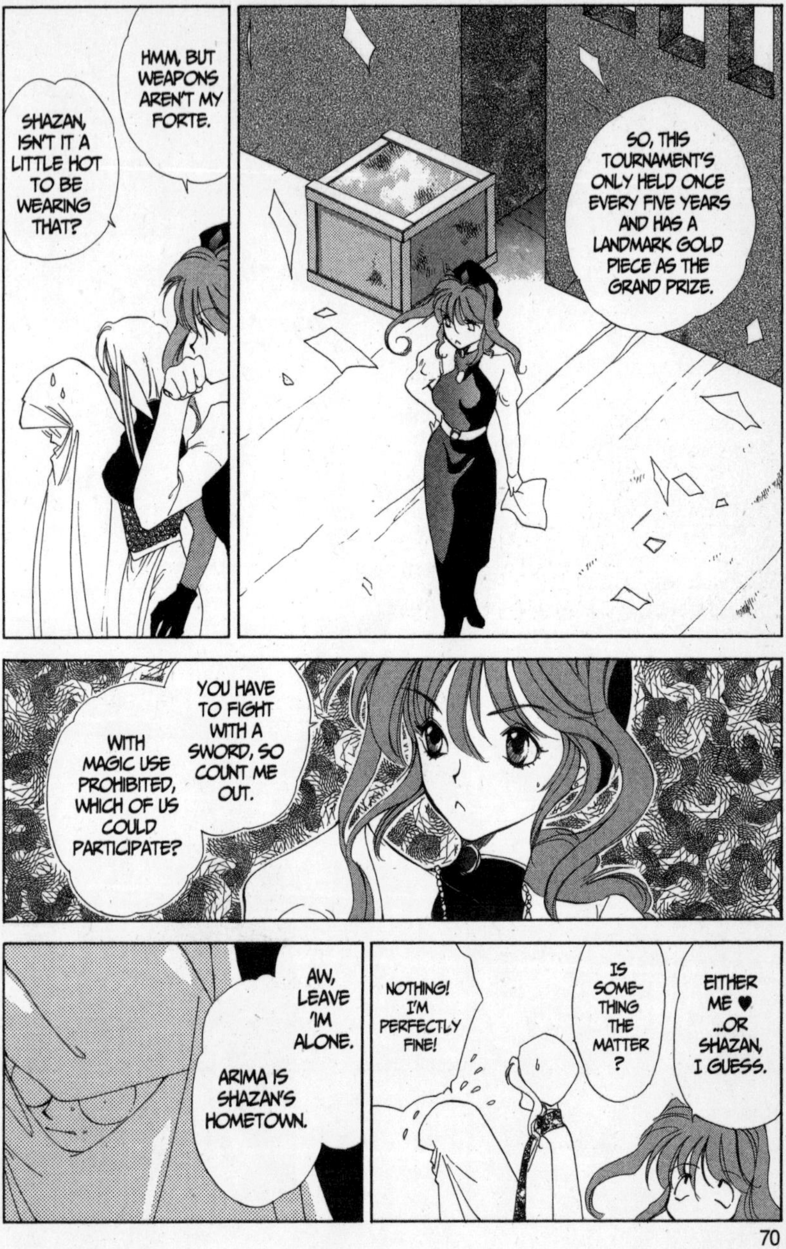
SO, THIS TOURNAMENT'S ONLY HELD ONCE EVERY FIVE YEARS AND HAS A LANDMARK GOLD PIECE AS THE GRAND PRIZE.
HMM, BUT WEAPONS AREN'T MY FORTE.
SHAZAN, ISN'T IT A LITTLE HOT TO BE WEARING THAT?
YOU HAVE TO FIGHT WITH A SWORD, SO COUNT ME OUT.
WITH MAGIC USE PROHIBITED, WHICH OF US COULD PARTICIPATE?
EITHER ME ♥ ...OR SHAZAN, I GUESS.
IS SOME-THING THE MATTER?
NOTHING! I'M PERFECTLY FINE!
AW, LEAVE 'IM ALONE.
ARIMA IS SHAZAN'S HOMETOWN.

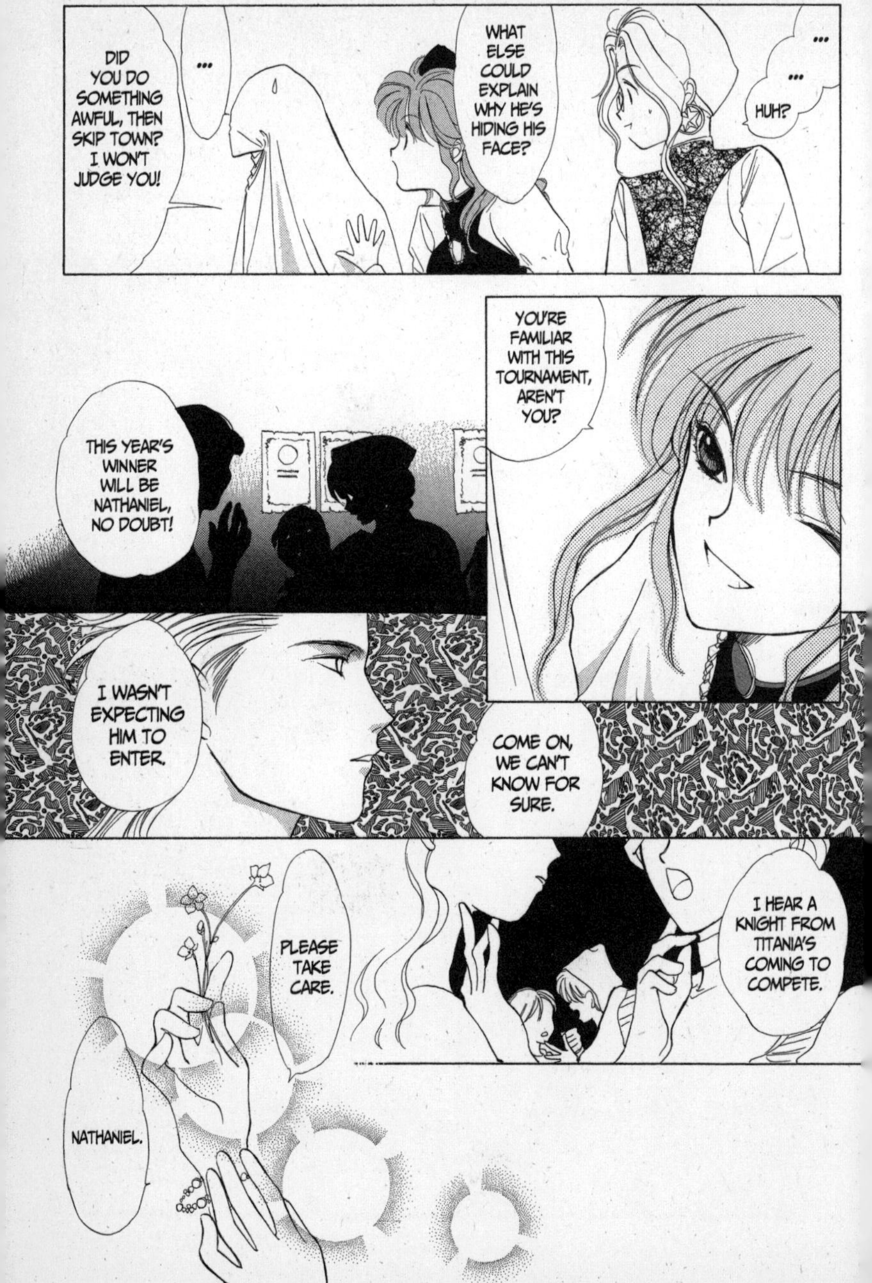
...
...
HUH?
WHAT ELSE COULD EXPLAIN WHY HE'S HIDING HIS FACE?
...
DID YOU DO SOMETHING AWFUL, THEN SKIP TOWN? I WON'T JUDGE YOU!
YOU'RE FAMILIAR WITH THIS TOURNAMENT, AREN'T YOU?
THIS YEAR'S WINNER WILL BE NATHANIEL, NO DOUBT!
COME ON, WE CAN'T KNOW FOR SURE.
I WASN'T EXPECTING HIM TO ENTER.
I HEAR A KNIGHT FROM TITANIA'S COMING TO COMPETE.
PLEASE TAKE CARE.
NATHANIEL.

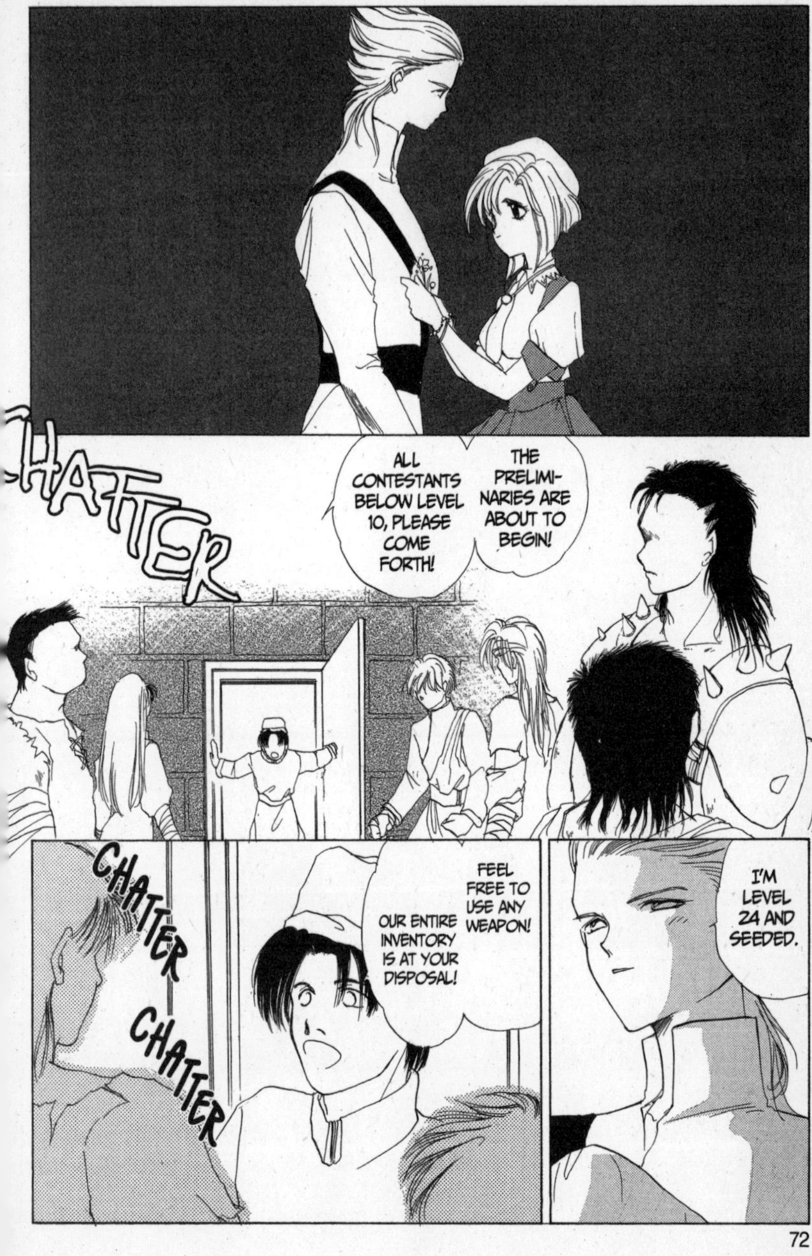
THE PRELIMINARIES ARE ABOUT TO BEGIN!
ALL CONTESTANTS BELOW LEVEL 10, PLEASE COME FORTH!
CHATTER
I'M LEVEL 24 AND SEEDED.
FEEL FREE TO USE ANY WEAPON!
OUR ENTIRE INVENTORY IS AT YOUR DISPOSAL!
CHATTER
CHATTER

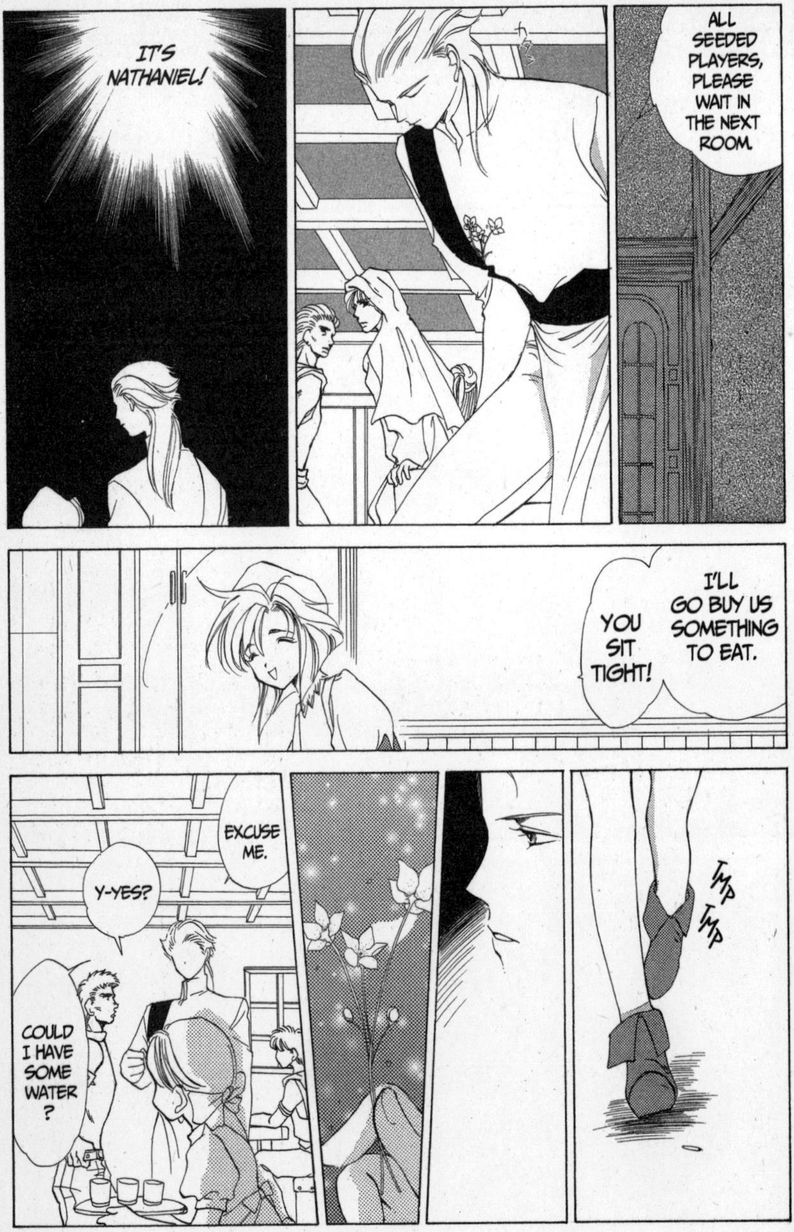
ALL SEEDED PLAYERS, PLEASE WAIT IN THE NEXT ROOM.
IT'S NATHANIEL!
I'LL GO BUY US SOMETHING TO EAT.
YOU SIT TIGHT!
TMP TMP
EXCUSE ME.
Y-YES?
COULD I HAVE SOME WATER?

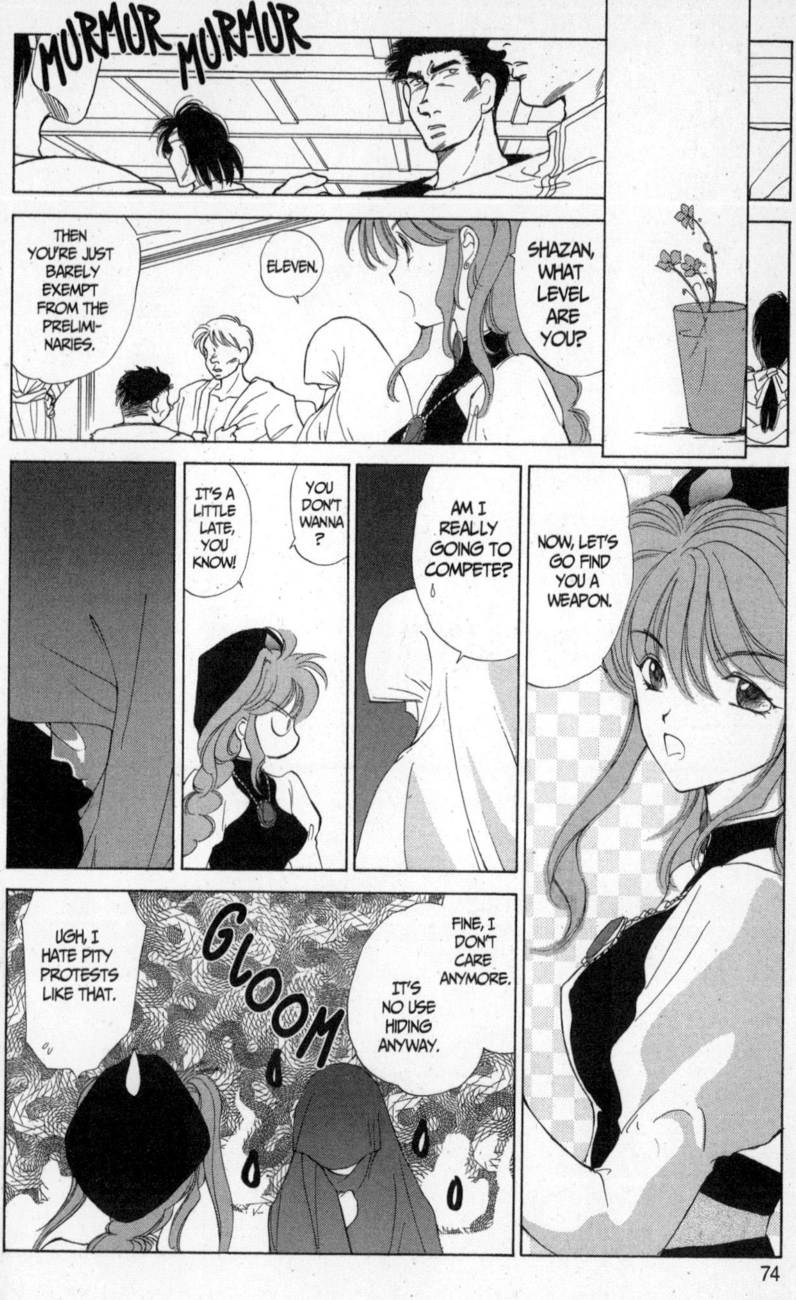
MURMUR MURMUR
SHAZAN, WHAT LEVEL ARE YOU?
ELEVEN.
THEN YOU'RE JUST BARELY EXEMPT FROM THE PRELIMI-NARIES.
NOW, LET'S GO FIND YOU A WEAPON.
AM I REALLY GOING TO COMPETE?
YOU DON'T WANNA?
IT'S A LITTLE LATE, YOU KNOW!
FINE, I DON'T CARE ANYMORE.
IT'S NO USE HIDING ANYWAY.
GLOOM
UGH, I HATE PITY PROTESTS LIKE THAT.

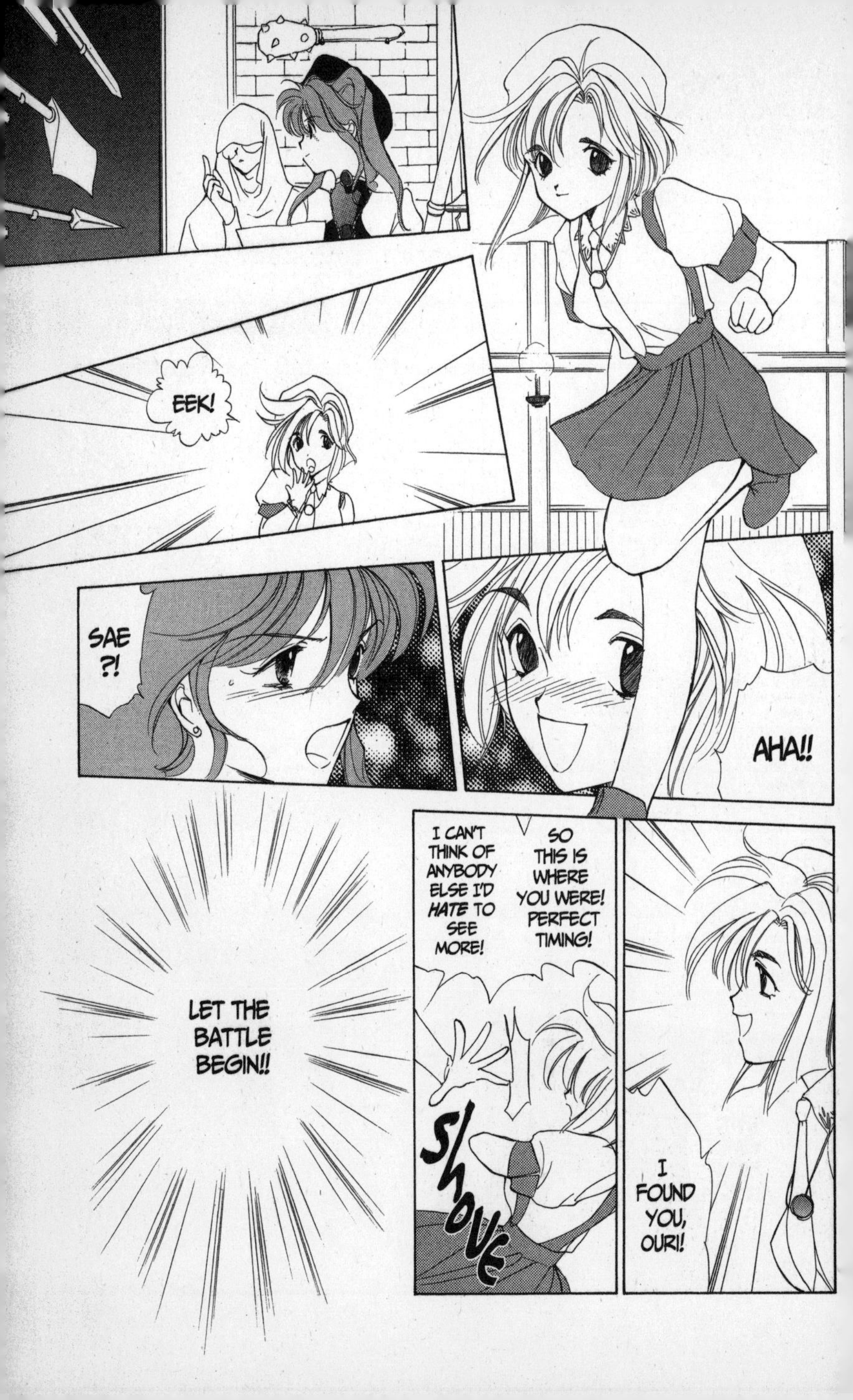
EEK!
AHA!!
SAE ?!
I FOUND YOU, OURI!
SO THIS IS WHERE YOU WERE! PERFECT TIMING!
I CAN'T THINK OF ANYBODY ELSE I'D *HATE* TO SEE MORE!
SHOVE
LET THE BATTLE BEGIN!!

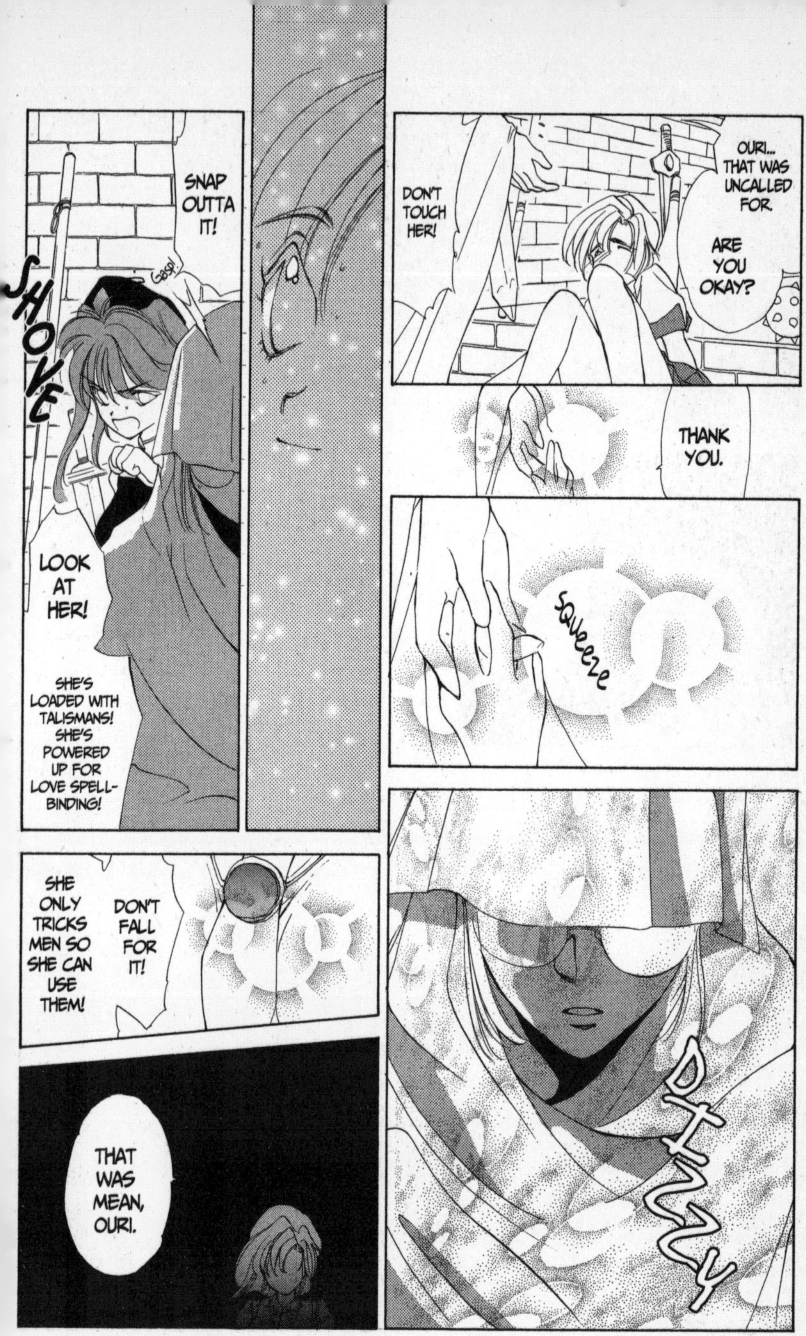
OURI... THAT WAS UNCALLED FOR.
ARE YOU OKAY?
DON'T TOUCH HER!
THANK YOU.
squeeze
SNAP OUTTA IT!
Gasp!
SHOVE
LOOK AT HER!
SHE'S LOADED WITH TALISMANS! SHE'S POWERED UP FOR LOVE SPELL-BINDING!
DIZZY
DON'T FALL FOR IT!
SHE ONLY TRICKS MEN SO SHE CAN USE THEM!
THAT WAS MEAN, OURI.

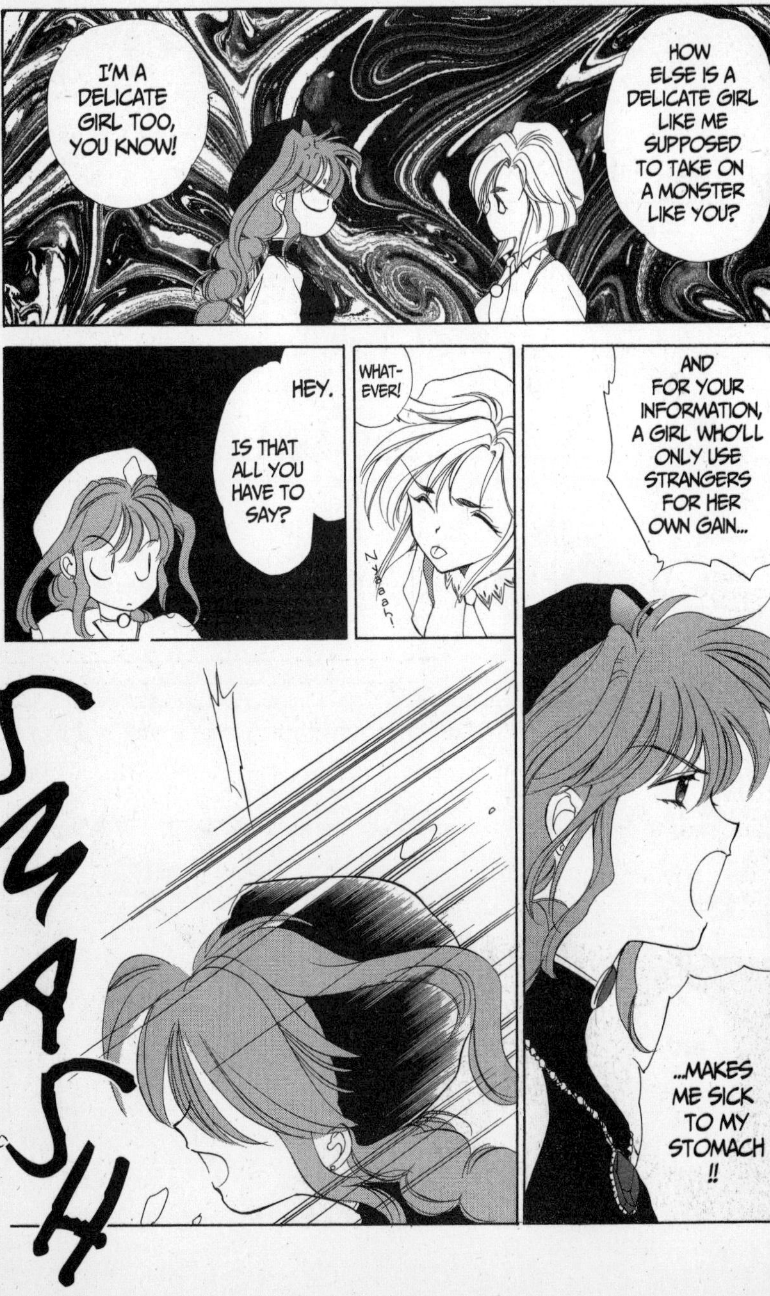
HOW ELSE IS A DELICATE GIRL LIKE ME SUPPOSED TO TAKE ON A MONSTER LIKE YOU?
I'M A DELICATE GIRL TOO, YOU KNOW!
AND FOR YOUR INFORMATION, A GIRL WHO'LL ONLY USE STRANGERS FOR HER OWN GAIN...
...MAKES ME SICK TO MY STOMACH!!
WHAT-EVER!
Nyaaah!
HEY.
IS THAT ALL YOU HAVE TO SAY?
SMASH

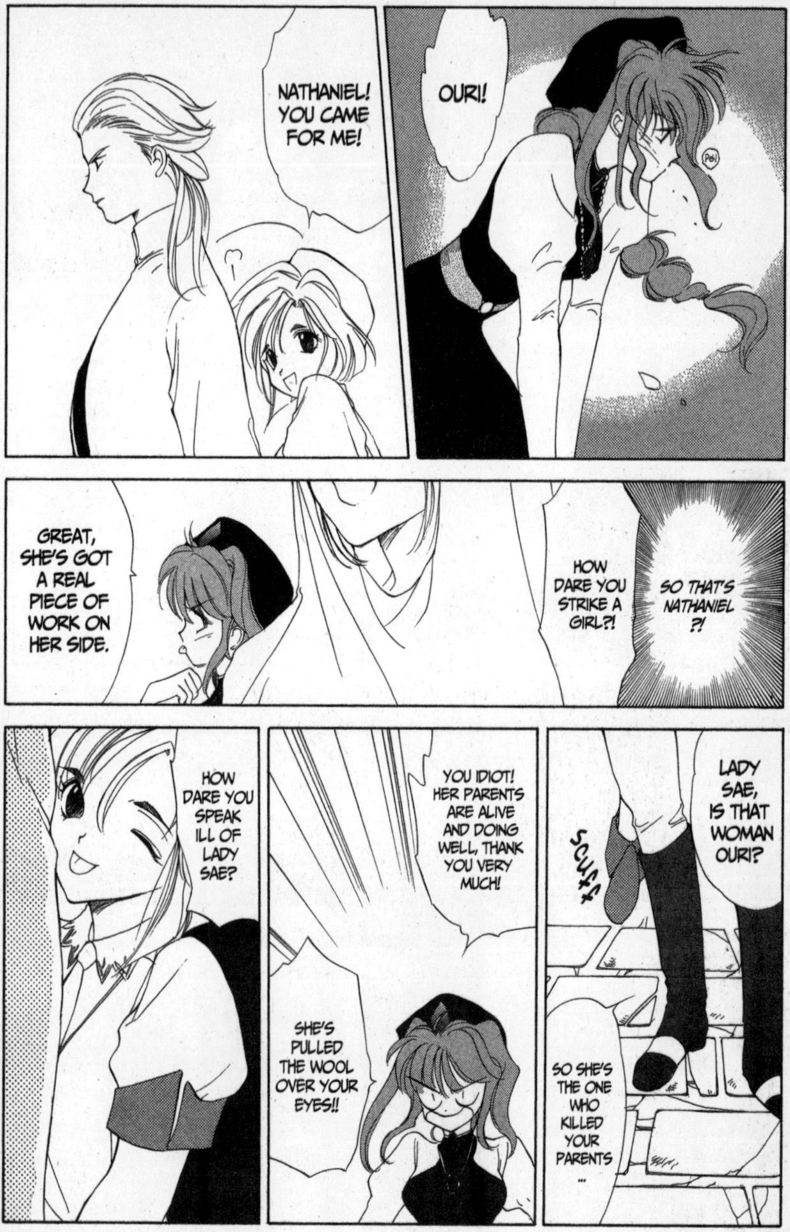
OURI!
NATHANIEL! YOU CAME FOR ME!
SO THAT'S NATHANIEL ?!
HOW DARE YOU STRIKE A GIRL?!
GREAT, SHE'S GOT A REAL PIECE OF WORK ON HER SIDE.
LADY SAE, IS THAT WOMAN OURI?
SCUFF
SO SHE'S THE ONE WHO KILLED YOUR PARENTS ...
YOU IDIOT! HER PARENTS ARE ALIVE AND DOING WELL, THANK YOU VERY MUCH!
SHE'S PULLED THE WOOL OVER YOUR EYES!!
HOW DARE YOU SPEAK ILL OF LADY SAE?

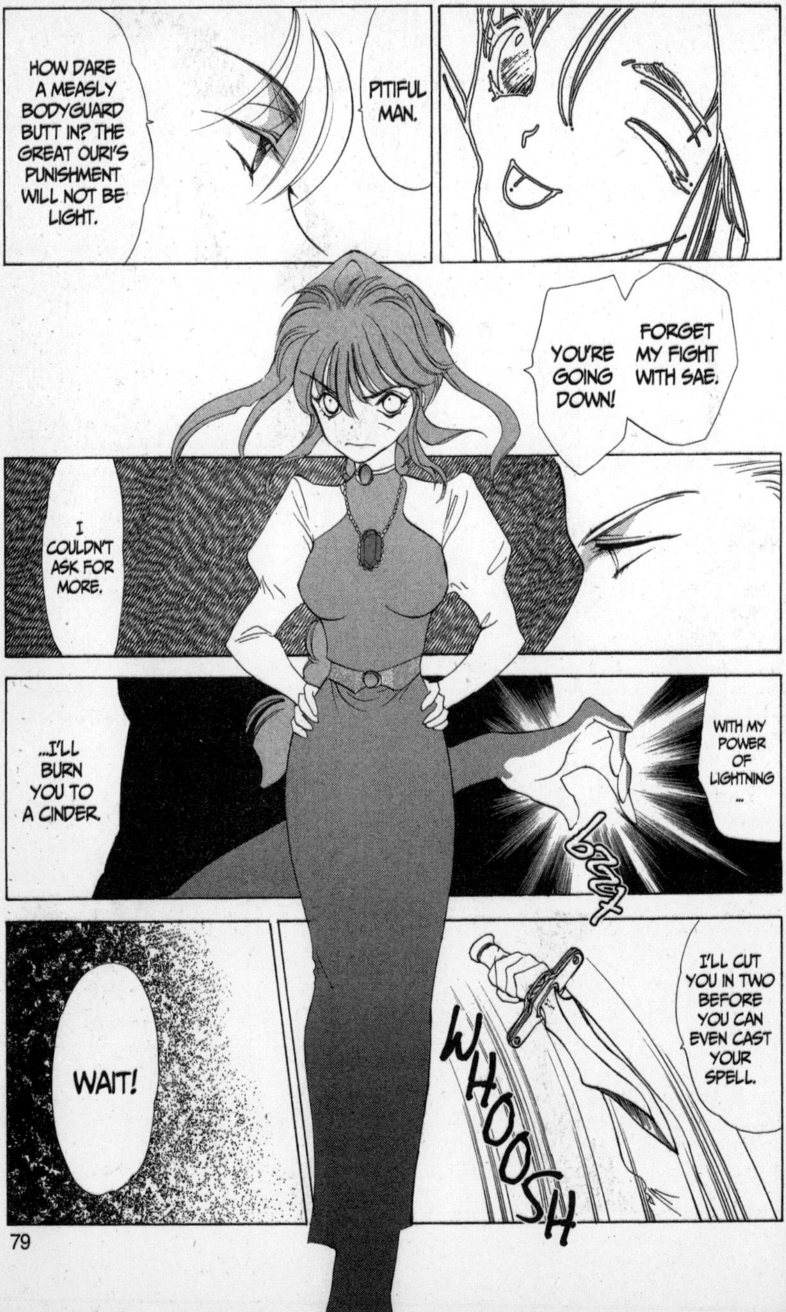
PITIFUL MAN.
HOW DARE A MEASLY BODYGUARD BUTT IN? THE GREAT OURI'S PUNISHMENT WILL NOT BE LIGHT.
FORGET MY FIGHT WITH SAE.
YOU'RE GOING DOWN!
I COULDN'T ASK FOR MORE.
WITH MY POWER OF LIGHTNING...
bzzt
...I'LL BURN YOU TO A CINDER.
I'LL CUT YOU IN TWO BEFORE YOU CAN EVEN CAST YOUR SPELL.
WHOOSH
WAIT!

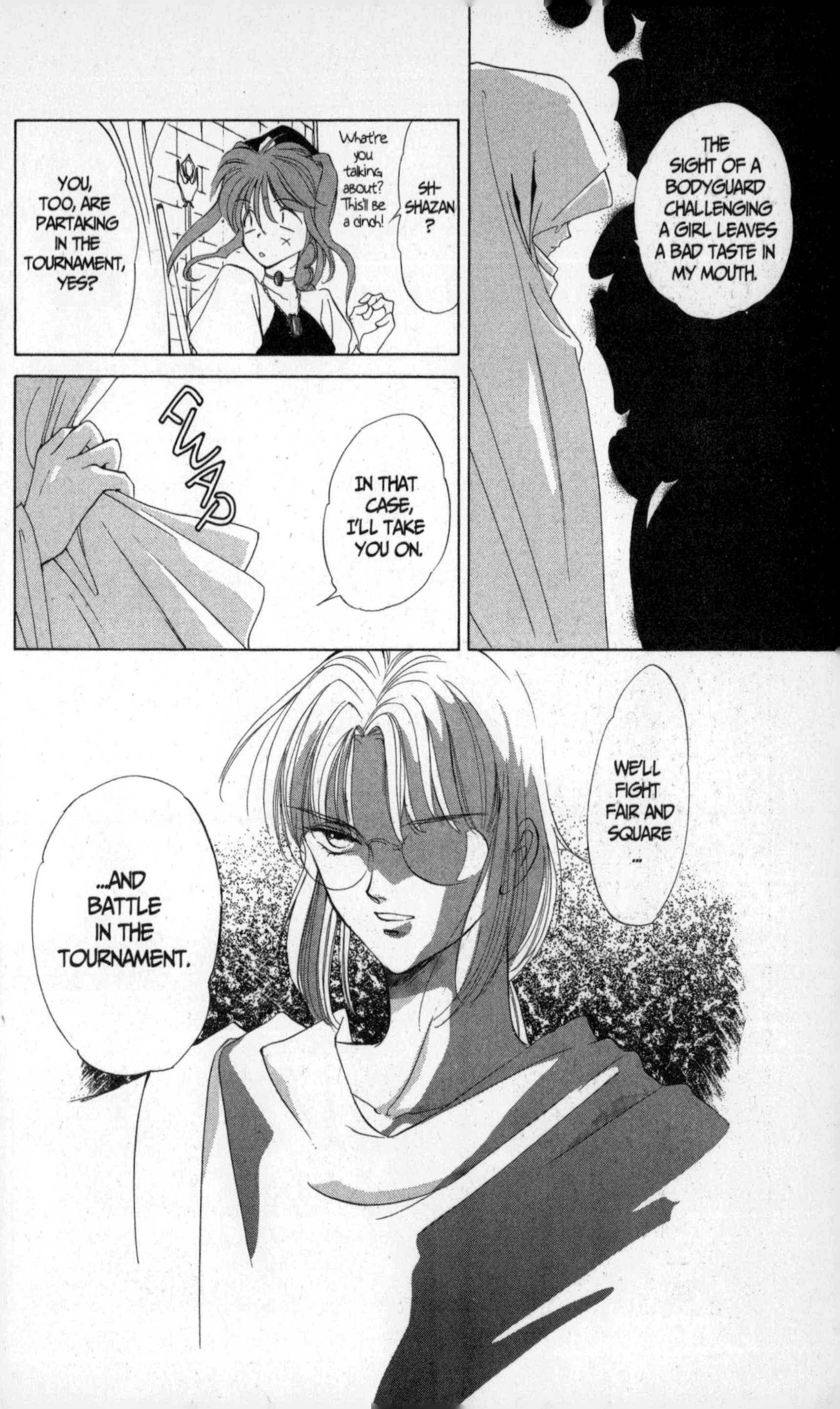
THE SIGHT OF A BODYGUARD CHALLENGING A GIRL LEAVES A BAD TASTE IN MY MOUTH.
SH-SHAZAN?
What're you talking about? This'll be a cinch!
YOU, TOO, ARE PARTAKING IN THE TOURNAMENT, YES?
IN THAT CASE, I'LL TAKE YOU ON.
FWAP
WE'LL FIGHT FAIR AND SQUARE...
...AND BATTLE IN THE TOURNAMENT.

Short Story 2

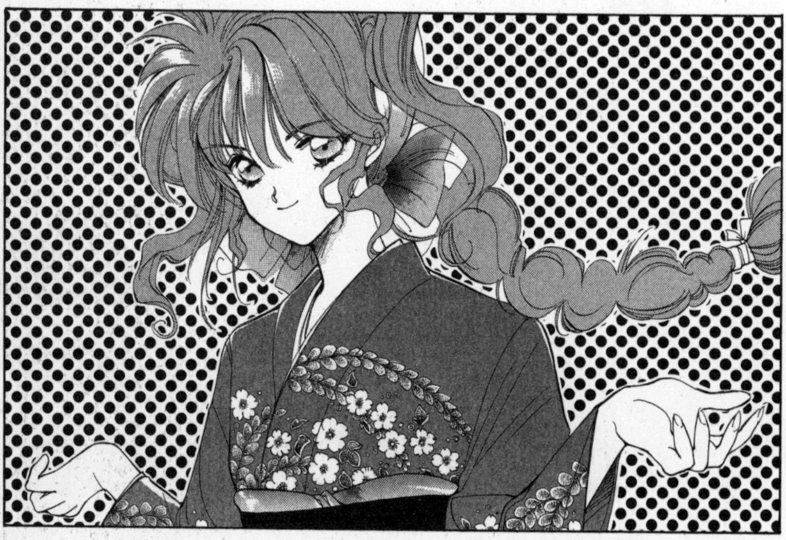

Riddles of the New Year

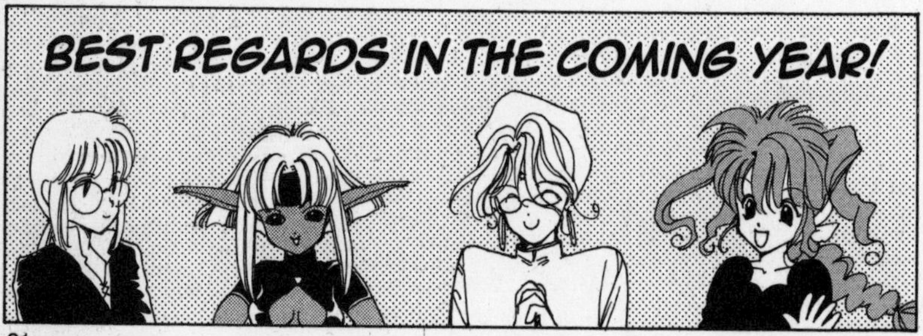
BEST REGARDS IN THE COMING YEAR!

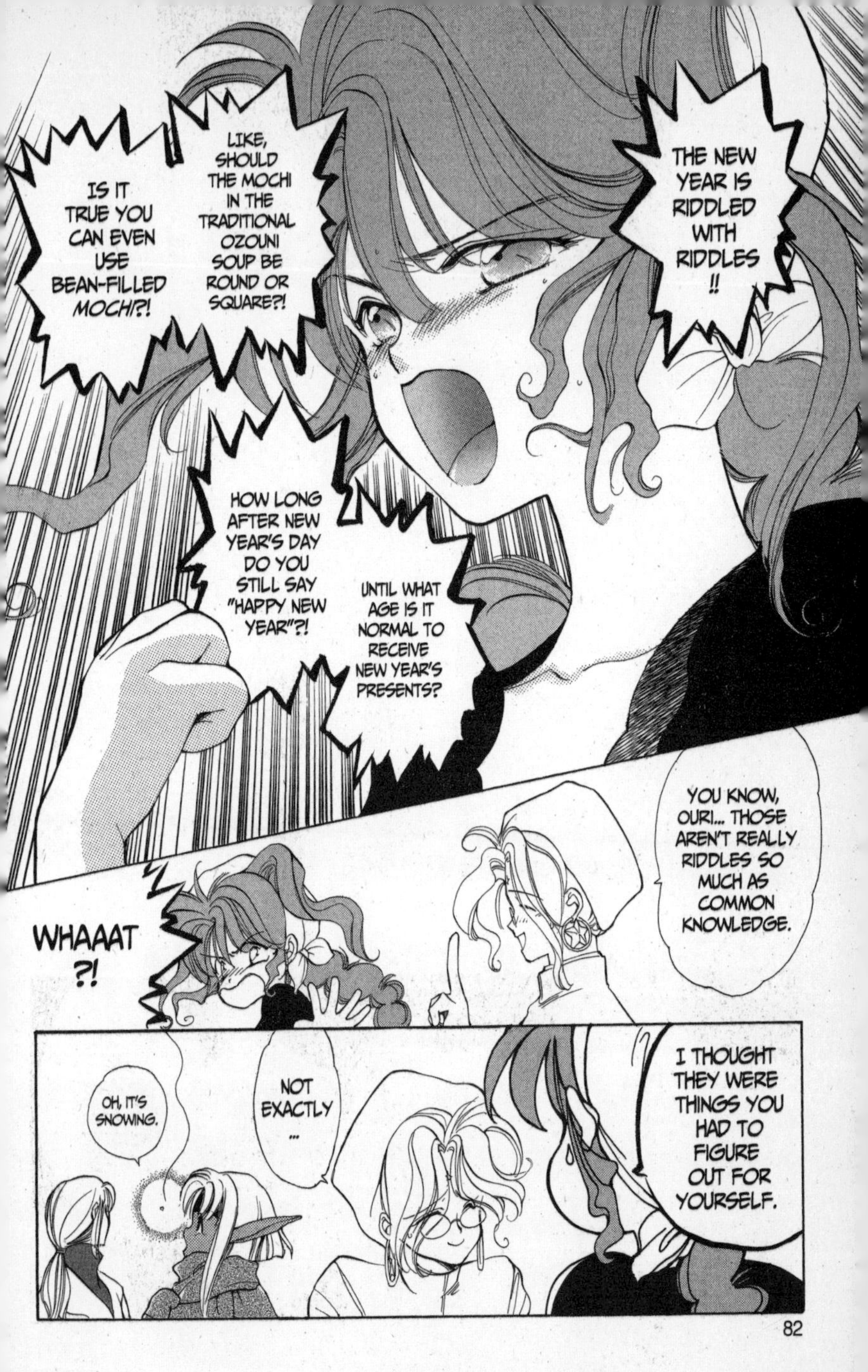
THE NEW YEAR IS RIDDLED WITH RIDDLES !!
LIKE, SHOULD THE MOCHI IN THE TRADITIONAL OZOUNI SOUP BE ROUND OR SQUARE?!
IS IT TRUE YOU CAN EVEN USE BEAN-FILLED *MOCHI*?!
HOW LONG AFTER NEW YEAR'S DAY DO YOU STILL SAY "HAPPY NEW YEAR"?!
UNTIL WHAT AGE IS IT NORMAL TO RECEIVE NEW YEAR'S PRESENTS?
YOU KNOW, OURI... THOSE AREN'T REALLY RIDDLES SO MUCH AS COMMON KNOWLEDGE.
WHAAAT ?!
I THOUGHT THEY WERE THINGS YOU HAD TO FIGURE OUT FOR YOURSELF.
NOT EXACTLY ...
OH, IT'S SNOWING.

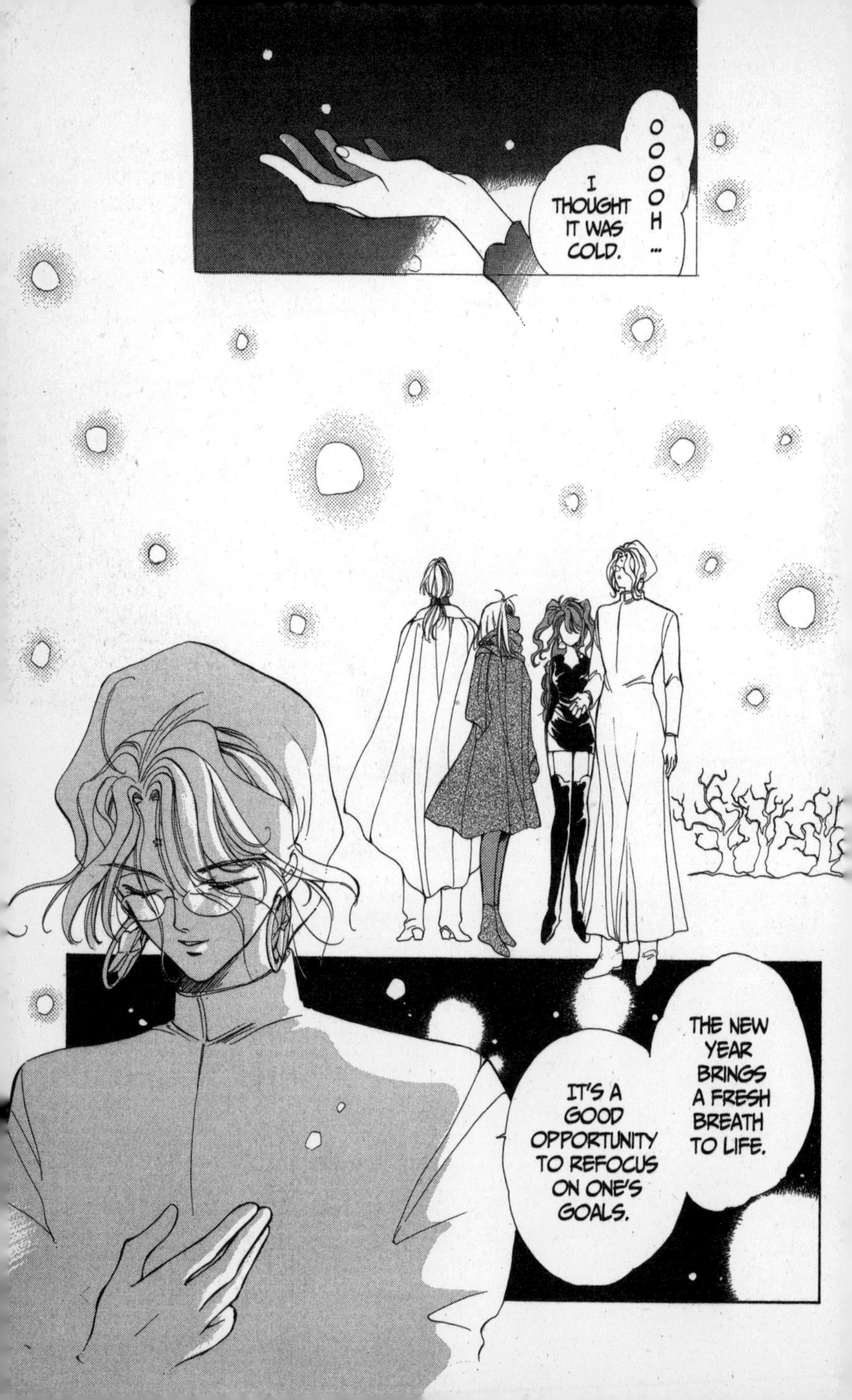

OOOOH...
I THOUGHT IT WAS COLD.
THE NEW YEAR BRINGS A FRESH BREATH TO LIFE.
IT'S A GOOD OPPORTUNITY TO REFOCUS ON ONE'S GOALS.

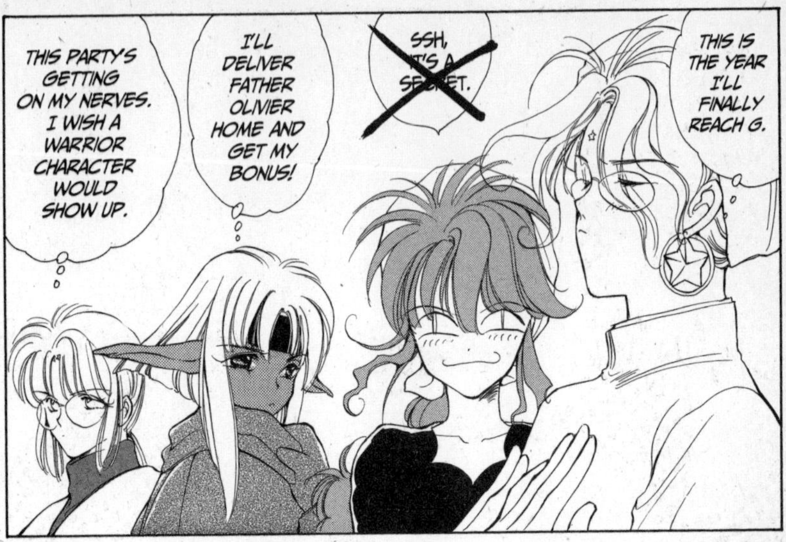
THIS IS THE YEAR I'LL FINALLY REACH G.
SSH, IT'S A SECRET.
I'LL DELIVER FATHER OLIVIER HOME AND GET MY BONUS!
THIS PARTY'S GETTING ON MY NERVES. I WISH A WARRIOR CHARACTER WOULD SHOW UP.

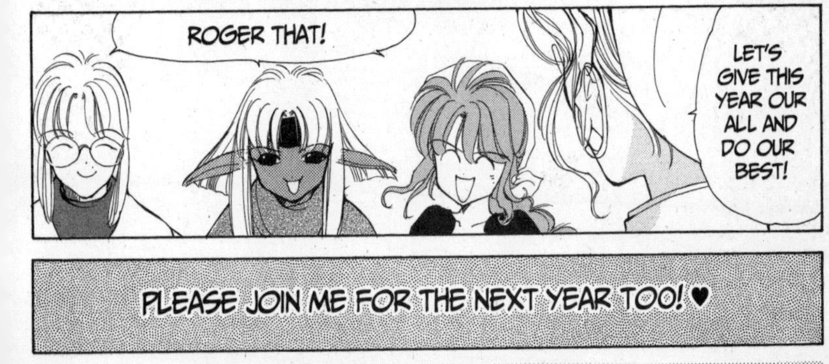
LET'S GIVE THIS YEAR OUR ALL AND DO OUR BEST!
ROGER THAT!

PLEASE JOIN ME FOR THE NEXT YEAR TOO! ♥

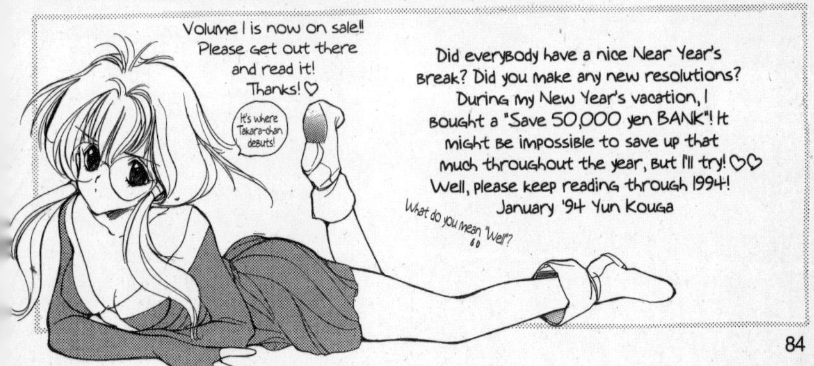
Did everybody have a nice Near Year's break? Did you make any new resolutions? During my New Year's vacation, I bought a "Save 50,000 yen BANK"! It might be impossible to save up that much throughout the year, but I'll try! ♡♡
Well, please keep reading through 1994!
January '94 Yun Kouga
What do you mean "Well"?
Volume 1 is now on sale!! Please get out there and read it! Thanks! ♡
It's where Takara-chan debuts!

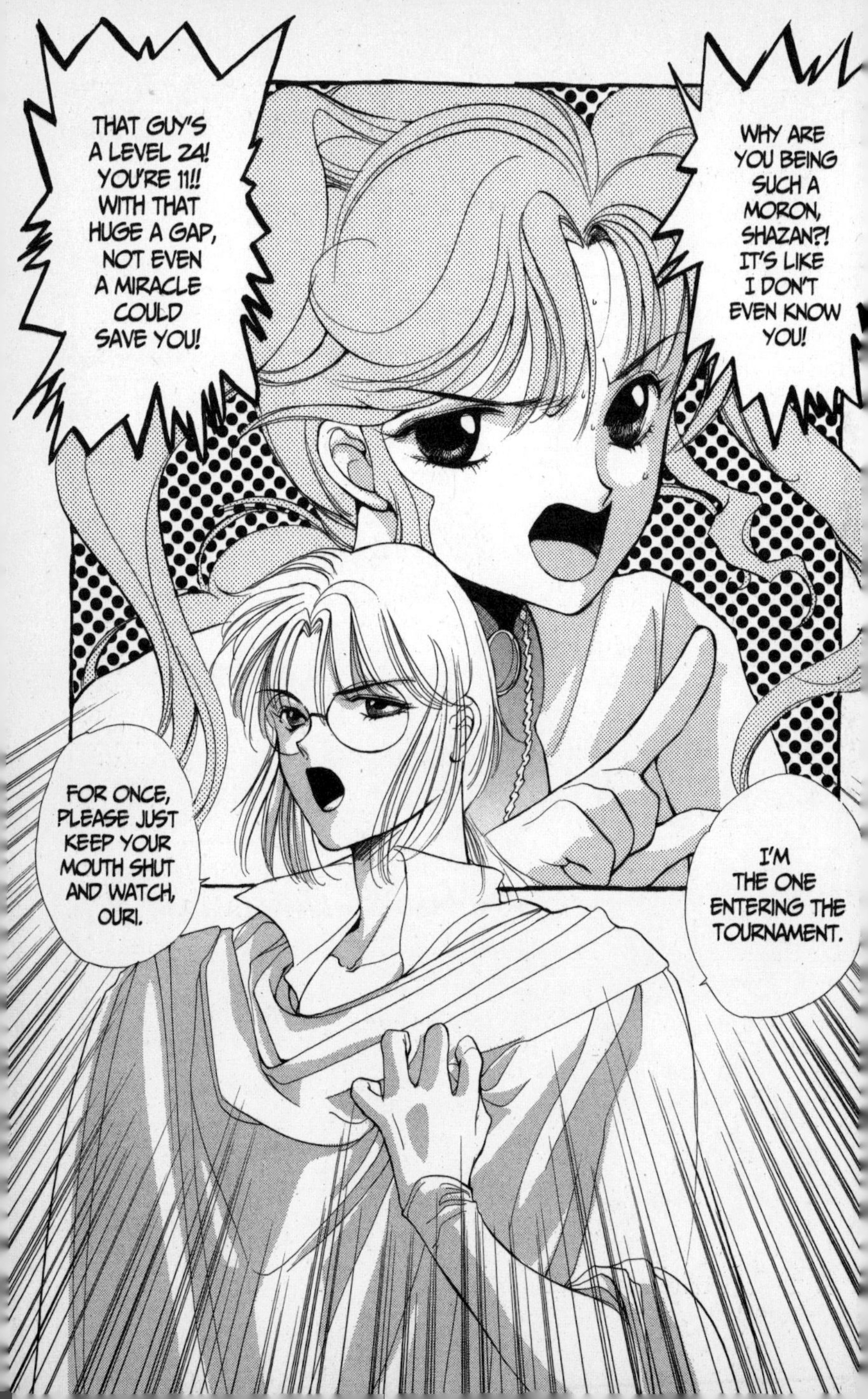
WHY ARE YOU BEING SUCH A MORON, SHAZAN?! IT'S LIKE I DON'T EVEN KNOW YOU!
THAT GUY'S A LEVEL 24! YOU'RE 11!! WITH THAT HUGE A GAP, NOT EVEN A MIRACLE COULD SAVE YOU!
I'M THE ONE ENTERING THE TOURNAMENT.
FOR ONCE, PLEASE JUST KEEP YOUR MOUTH SHUT AND WATCH, OURI.

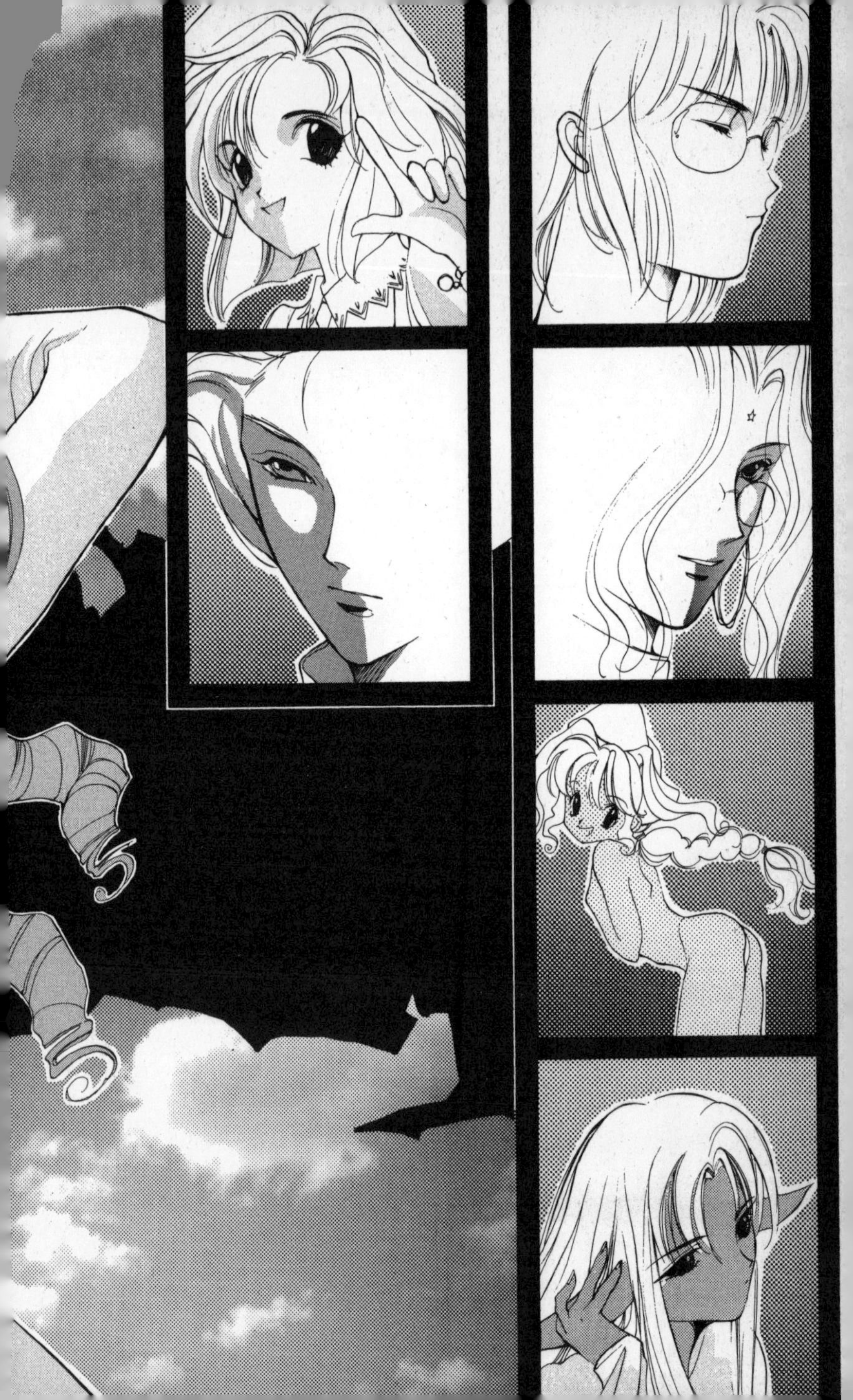

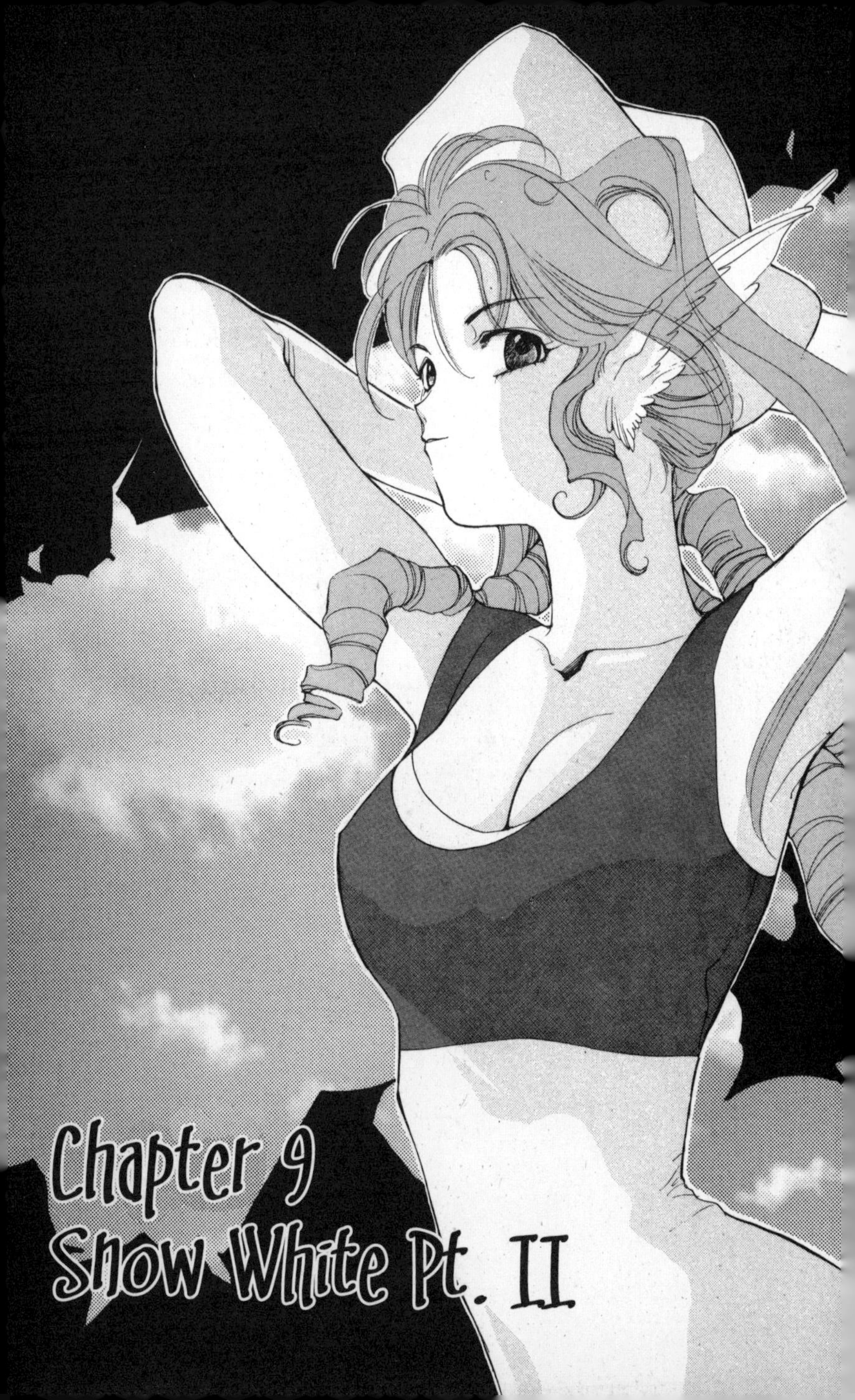
Chapter 9
Snow White Pt. II

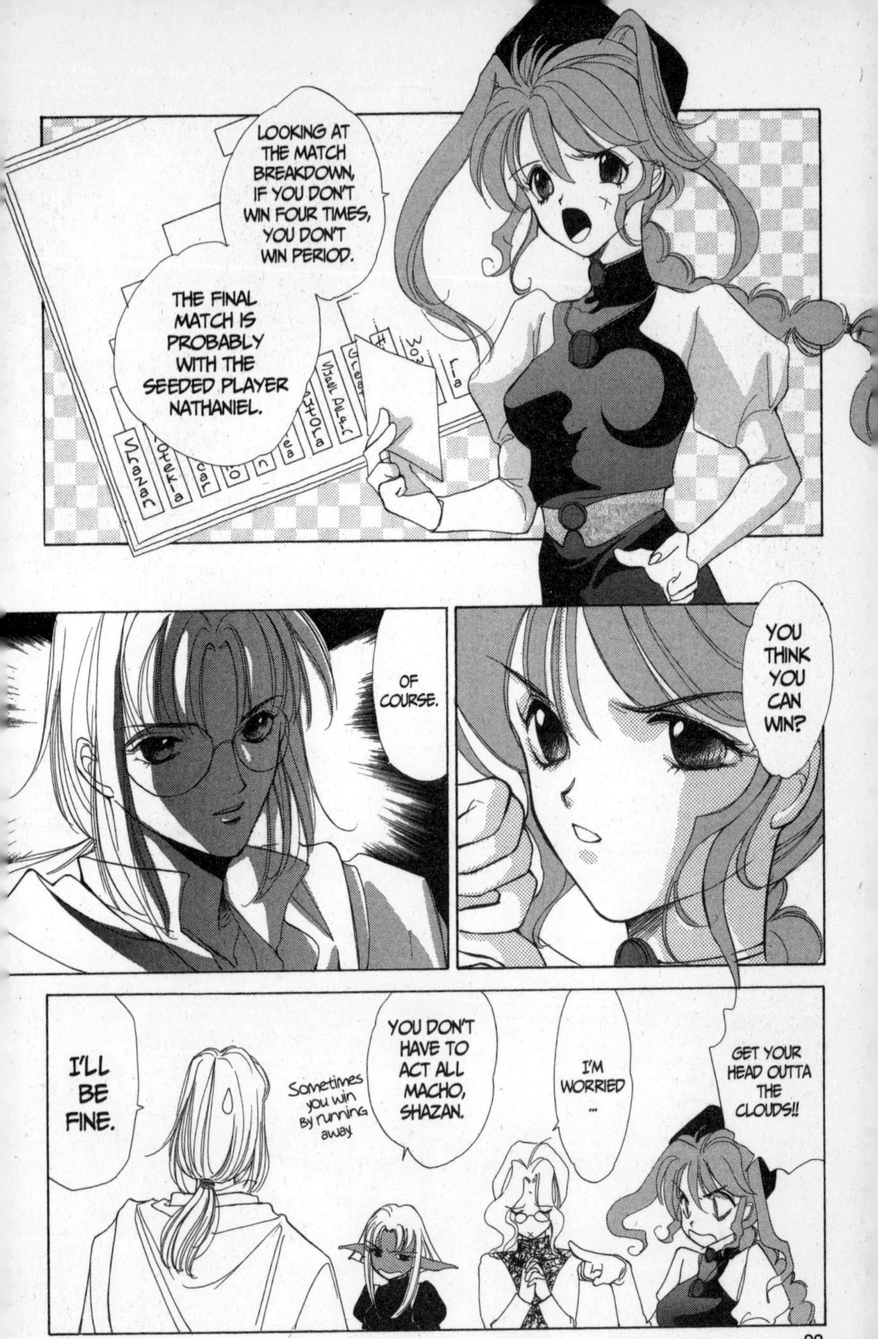
LOOKING AT THE MATCH BREAKDOWN, IF YOU DON'T WIN FOUR TIMES, YOU DON'T WIN PERIOD.
THE FINAL MATCH IS PROBABLY WITH THE SEEDED PLAYER NATHANIEL.
Shazan
YOU THINK YOU CAN WIN?
OF COURSE.
GET YOUR HEAD OUTTA THE CLOUDS!!
I'M WORRIED ...
YOU DON'T HAVE TO ACT ALL MACHO, SHAZAN.
Sometimes you win by running away.
I'LL BE FINE.

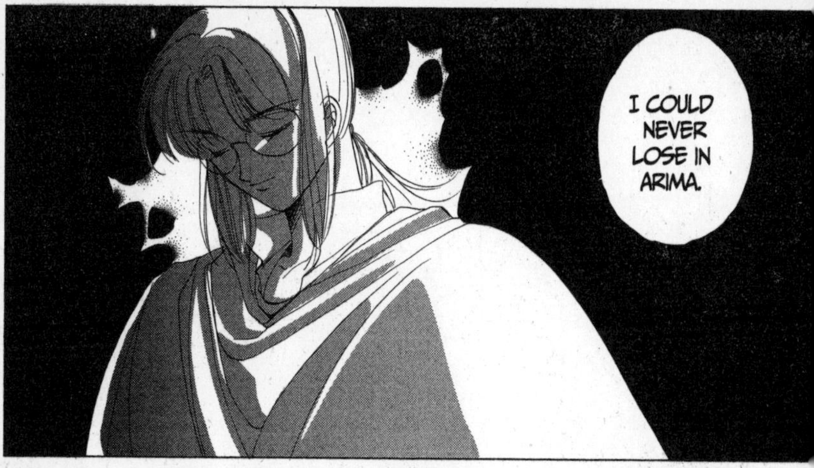
I COULD NEVER LOSE IN ARIMA.

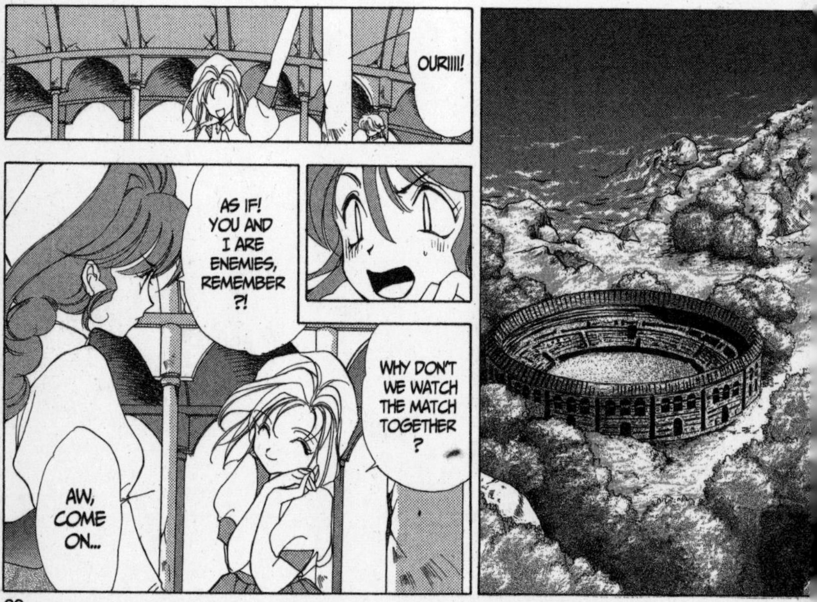
OURIIII!
WHY DON'T WE WATCH THE MATCH TOGETHER?
AS IF! YOU AND I ARE ENEMIES, REMEMBER?!
AW, COME ON...

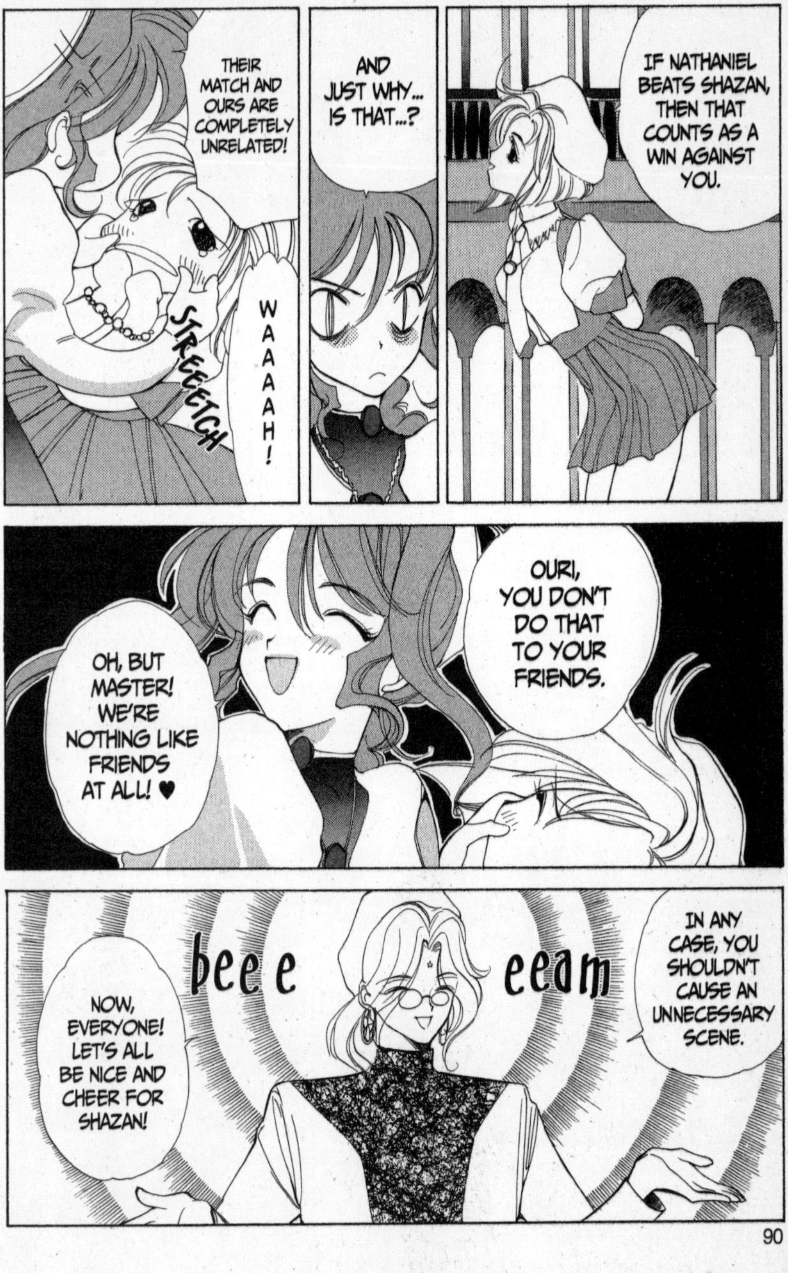
IF NATHANIEL BEATS SHAZAN, THEN THAT COUNTS AS A WIN AGAINST YOU.
AND JUST WHY... IS THAT...?
THEIR MATCH AND OURS ARE COMPLETELY UNRELATED!
WAAAAAH!
STREEETCH
OURI, YOU DON'T DO THAT TO YOUR FRIENDS.
OH, BUT MASTER! WE'RE NOTHING LIKE FRIENDS AT ALL! ♥
IN ANY CASE, YOU SHOULDN'T CAUSE AN UNNECESSARY SCENE.
bee e eeam
NOW, EVERYONE! LET'S ALL BE NICE AND CHEER FOR SHAZAN!

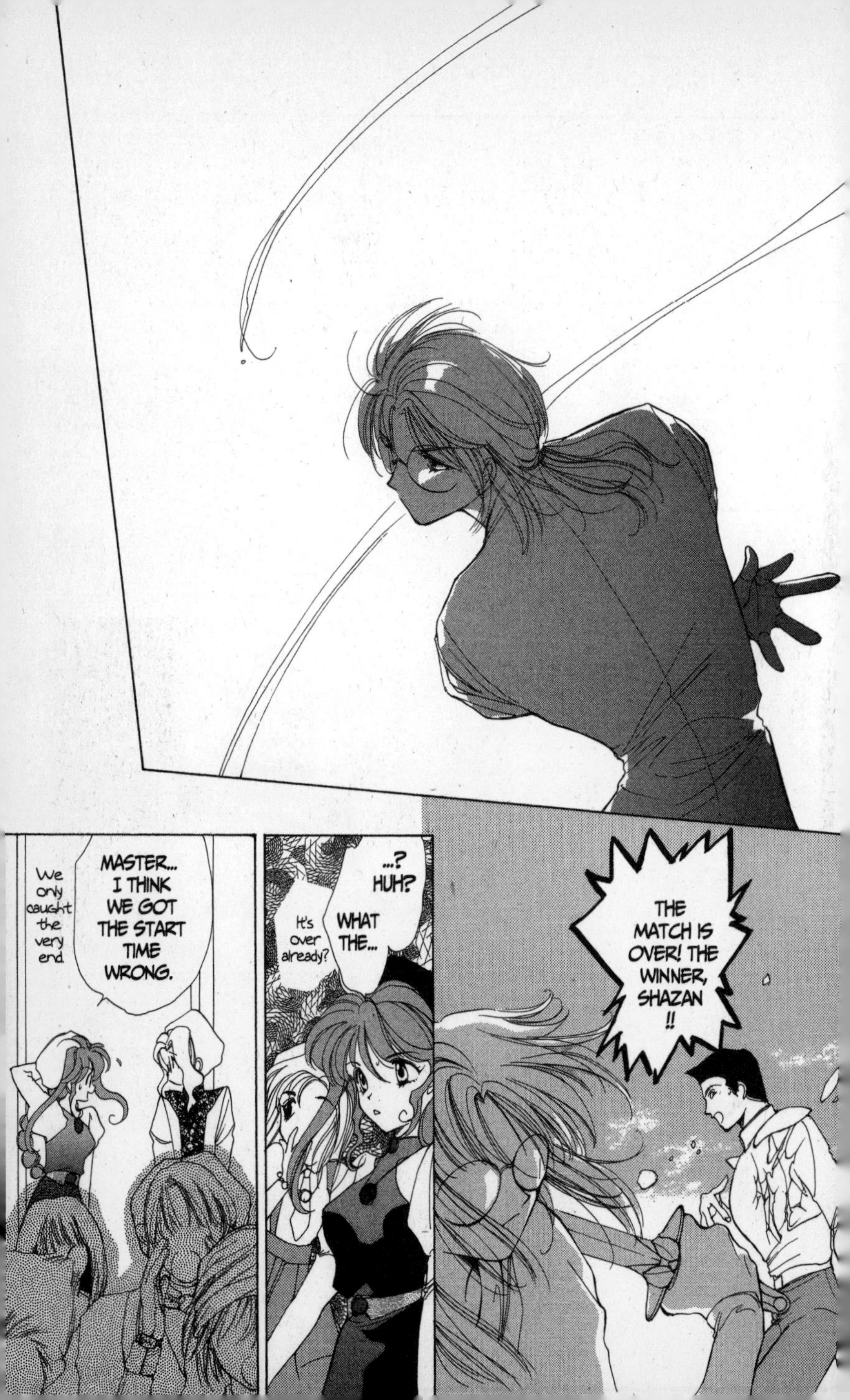
THE MATCH IS OVER! THE WINNER, SHAZAN !!
...? HUH? WHAT THE...
It's over already?
MASTER... I THINK WE GOT THE START TIME WRONG.
We only caught the very end.

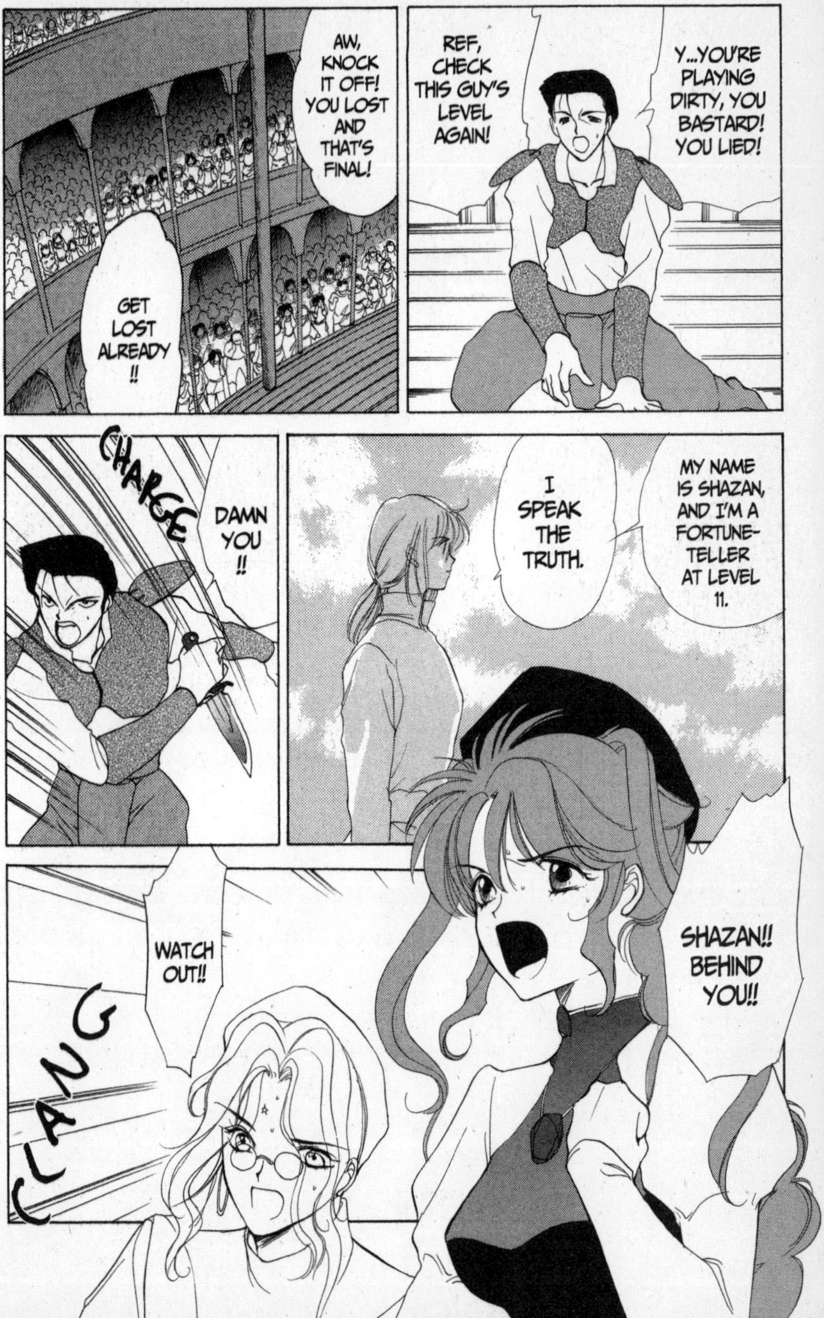
Y...YOU'RE PLAYING DIRTY, YOU BASTARD! YOU LIED!
REF, CHECK THIS GUY'S LEVEL AGAIN!
AW, KNOCK IT OFF! YOU LOST AND THAT'S FINAL!
GET LOST ALREADY !!
MY NAME IS SHAZAN, AND I'M A FORTUNE-TELLER AT LEVEL 11.
I SPEAK THE TRUTH.
DAMN YOU !!
CHARGE
SHAZAN!! BEHIND YOU!!
WATCH OUT!!
CLANG

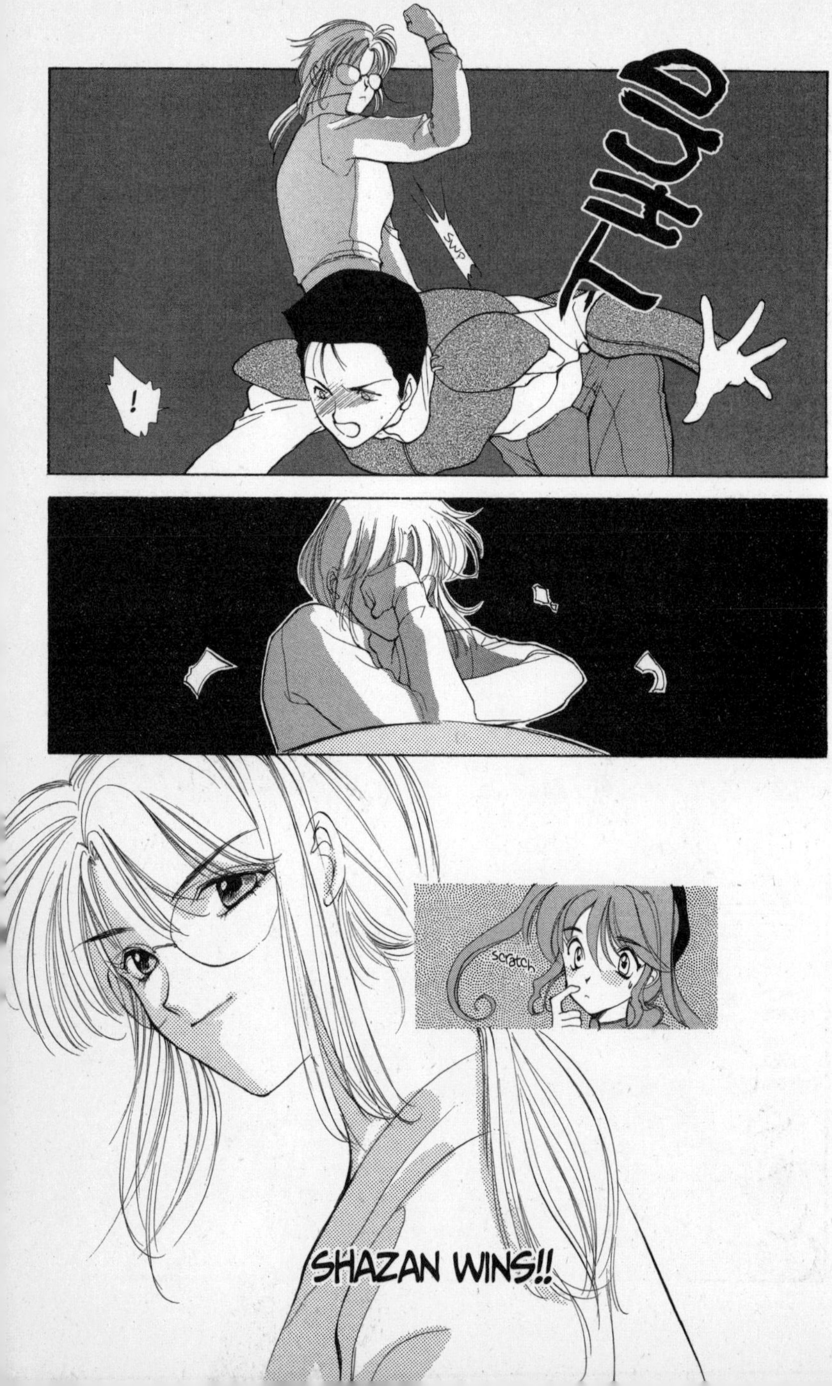
THUD
SWP
!
scratch
SHAZAN WINS!!

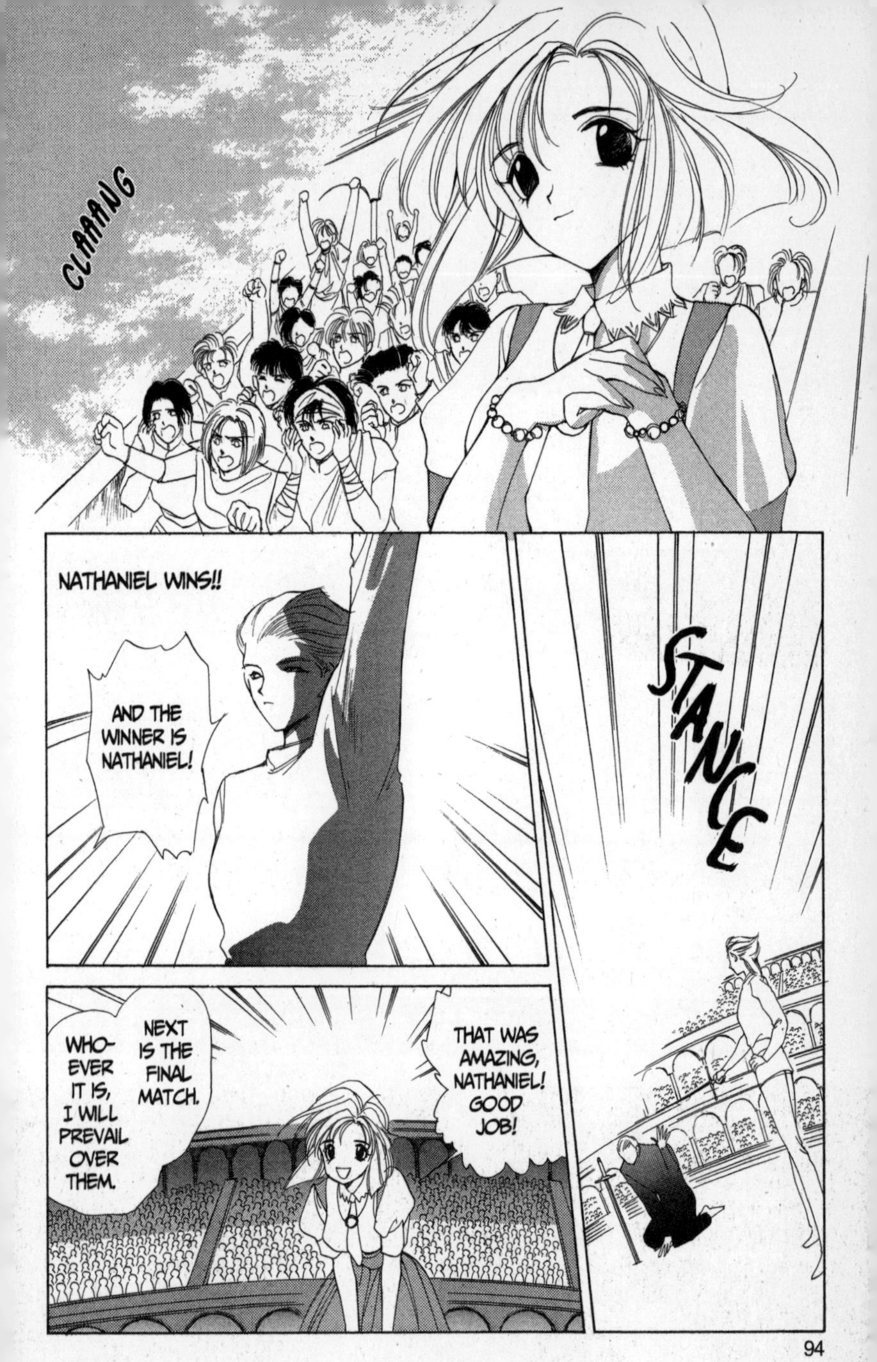
CLAAANG
STANCE
NATHANIEL WINS!!
AND THE WINNER IS NATHANIEL!
THAT WAS AMAZING, NATHANIEL! GOOD JOB!
NEXT IS THE FINAL MATCH.
WHO-EVER IT IS, I WILL PREVAIL OVER THEM.

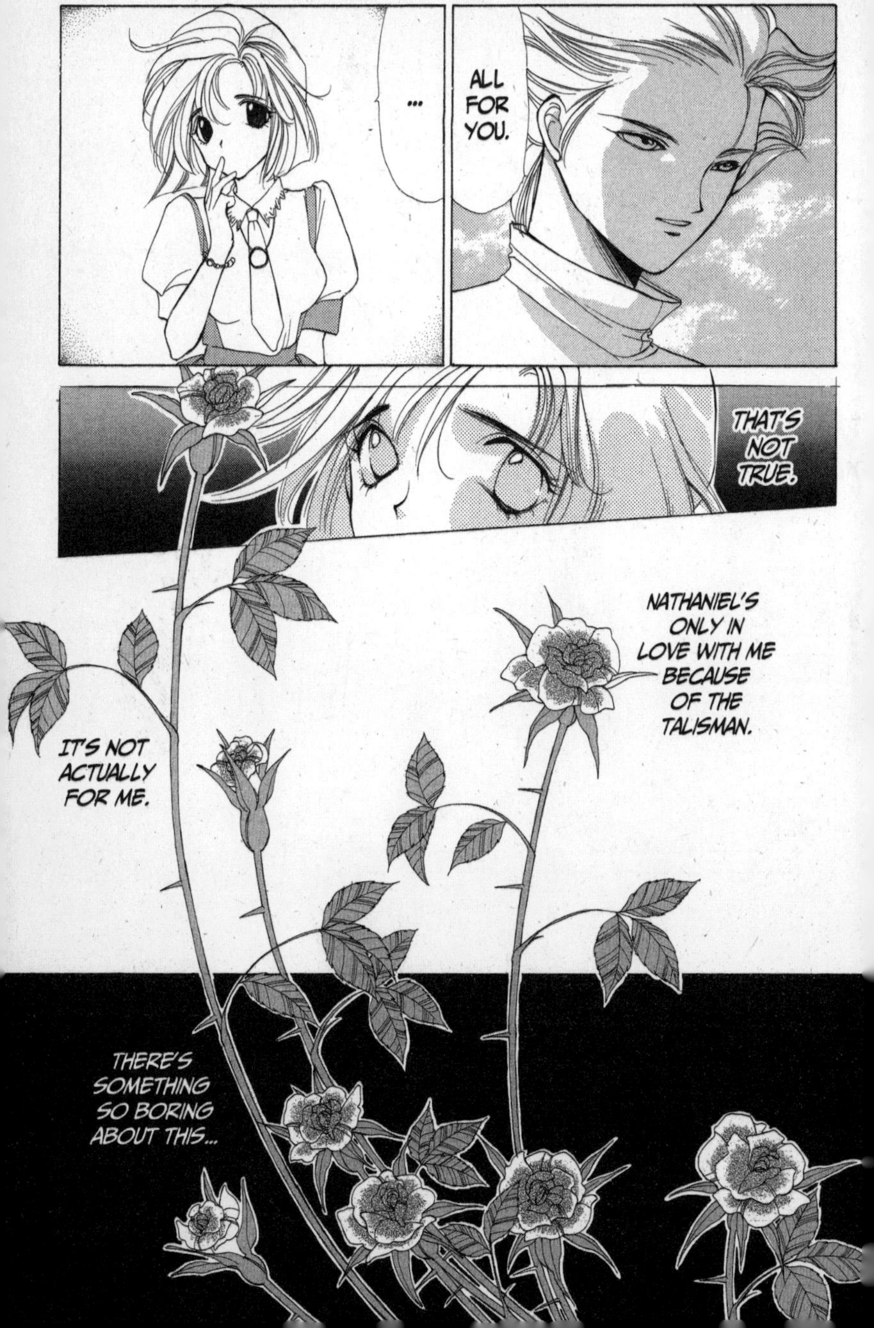
ALL FOR YOU.
...
THAT'S NOT TRUE.
NATHANIEL'S ONLY IN LOVE WITH ME BECAUSE OF THE TALISMAN.
IT'S NOT ACTUALLY FOR ME.
THERE'S SOMETHING SO BORING ABOUT THIS...

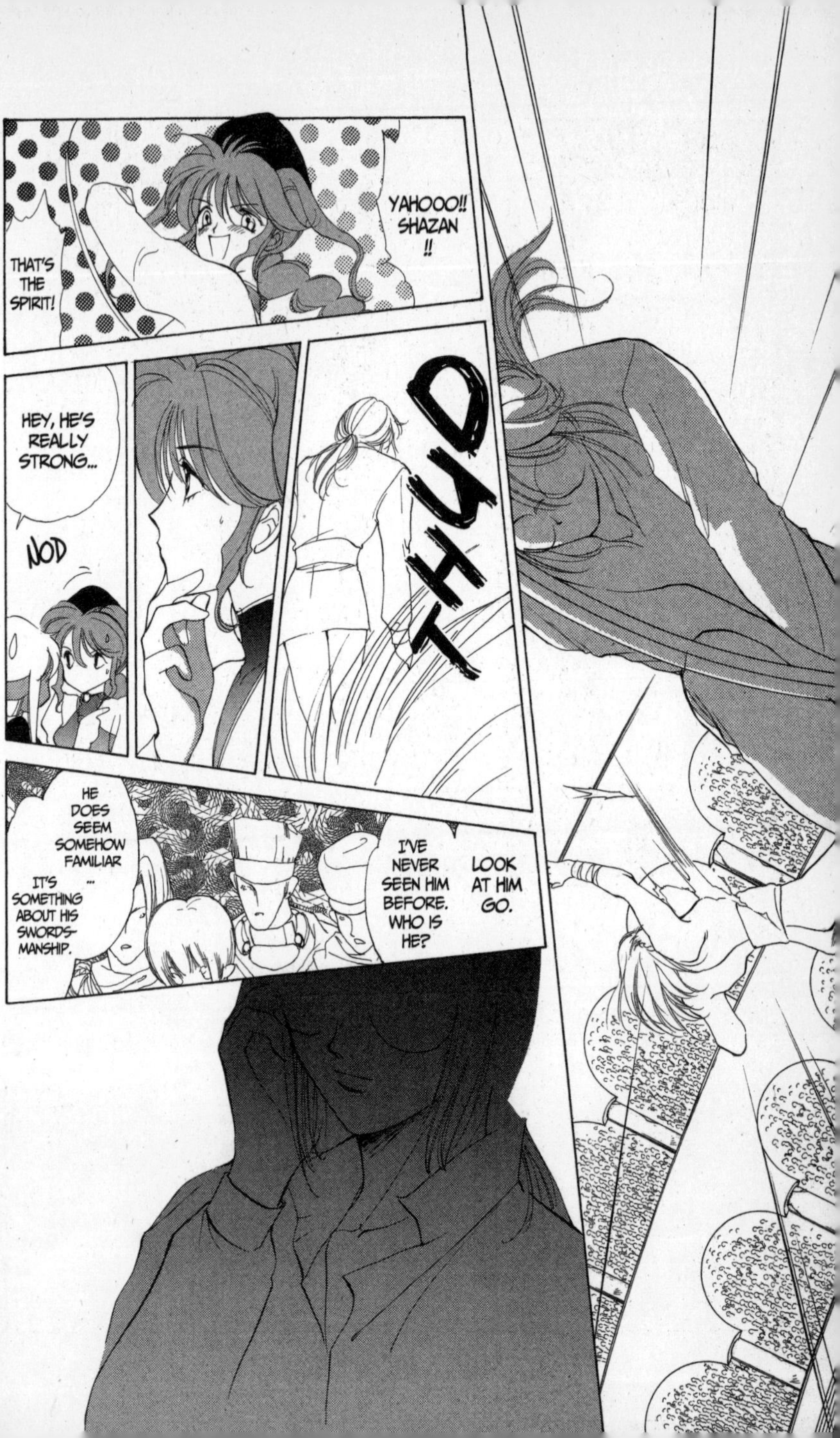
YAHOOO!! SHAZAN !!
THAT'S THE SPIRIT!
THUD
HEY, HE'S REALLY STRONG...
NOD
LOOK AT HIM GO.
I'VE NEVER SEEN HIM BEFORE. WHO IS HE?
HE DOES SEEM SOMEHOW FAMILIAR ...
IT'S SOMETHING ABOUT HIS SWORDS-MANSHIP.

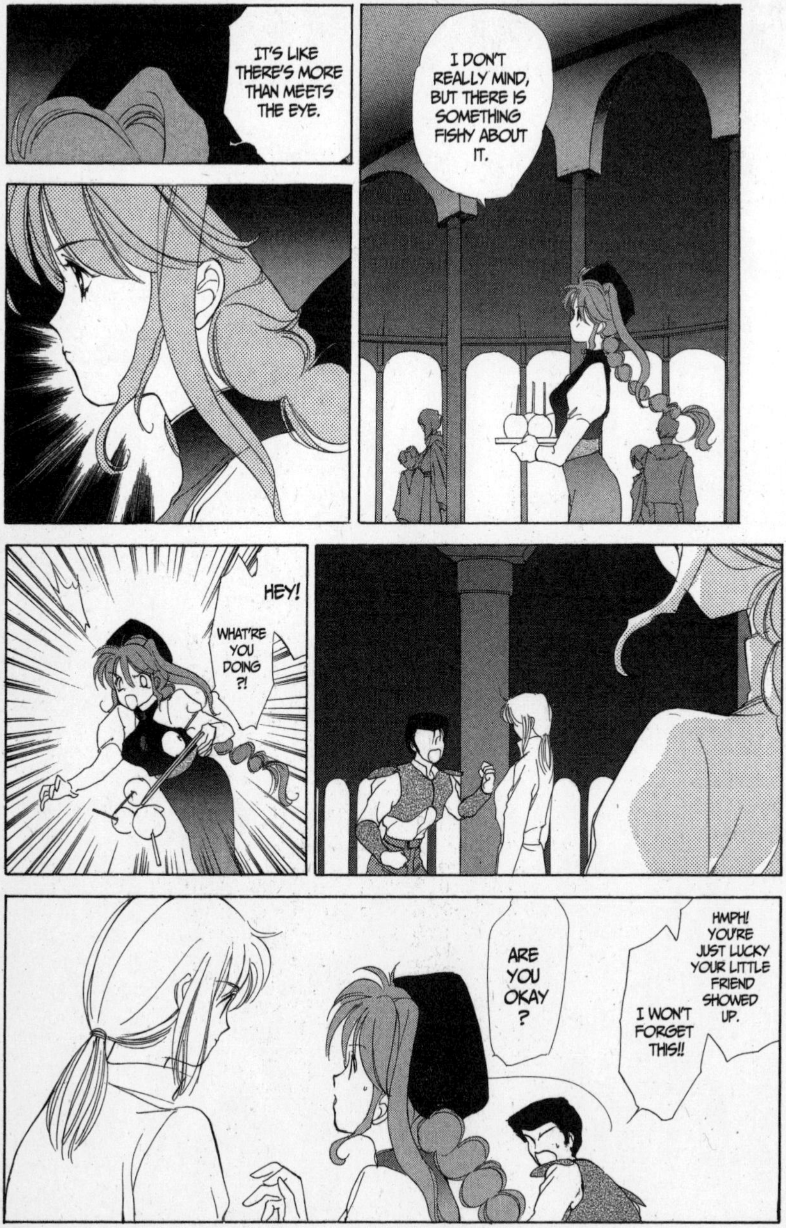
I DON'T REALLY MIND, BUT THERE IS SOMETHING FISHY ABOUT IT.
IT'S LIKE THERE'S MORE THAN MEETS THE EYE.
HEY!
WHAT'RE YOU DOING ?!
HMPH! YOU'RE JUST LUCKY YOUR LITTLE FRIEND SHOWED UP.
I WON'T FORGET THIS!!
ARE YOU OKAY ?

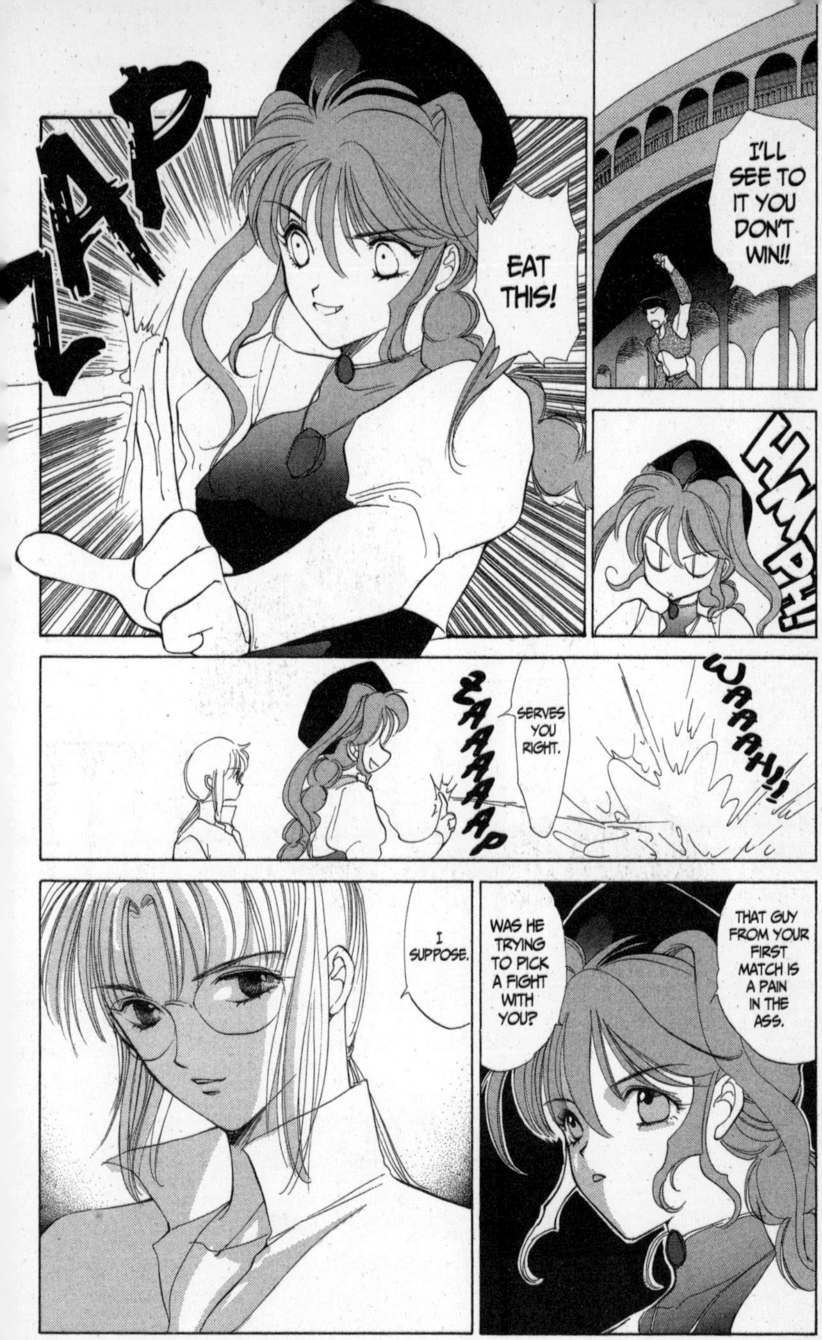
I'LL SEE TO IT YOU DON'T WIN!!
HMMPH!
ZAP
EAT THIS!
WAAAAH!!
SERVES YOU RIGHT.
ZAAAAAAAP
THAT GUY FROM YOUR FIRST MATCH IS A PAIN IN THE ASS.
WAS HE TRYING TO PICK A FIGHT WITH YOU?
I SUPPOSE.

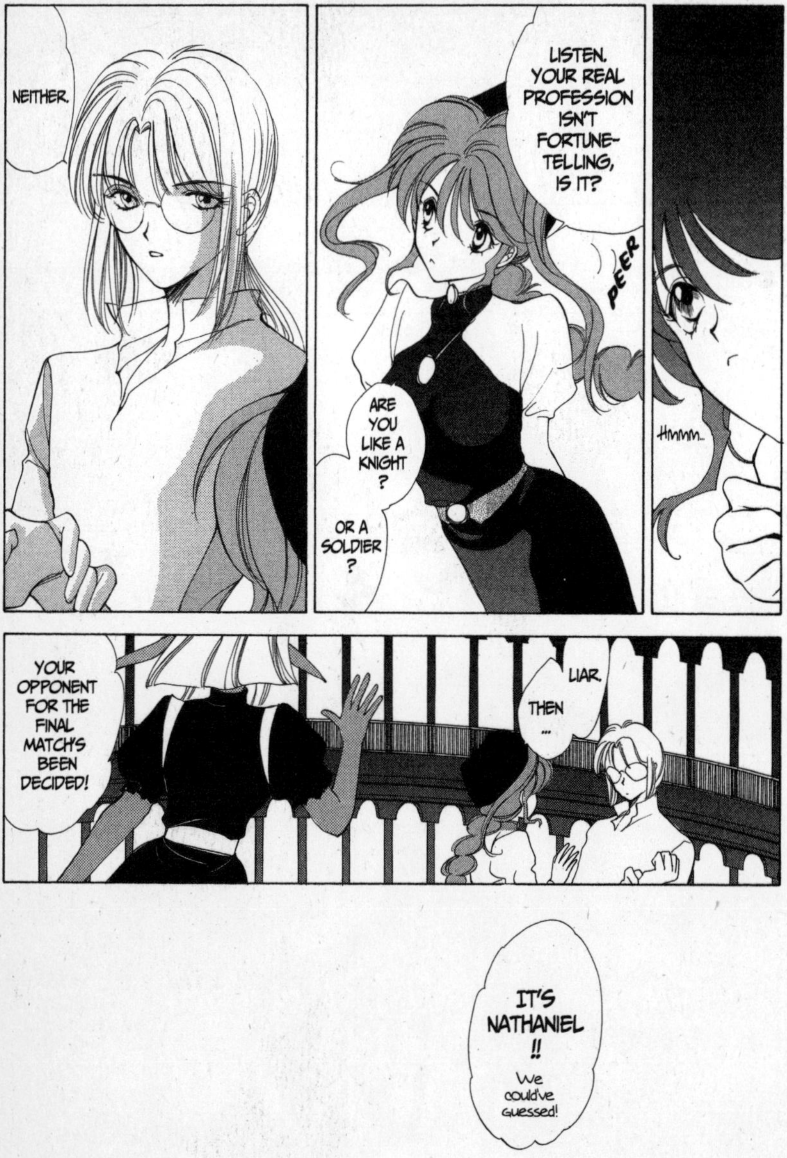
Hmmm...
LISTEN. YOUR REAL PROFESSION ISN'T FORTUNE-TELLING, IS IT?
PEER
ARE YOU LIKE A KNIGHT?
OR A SOLDIER?
NEITHER.
LIAR.
THEN ...
YOUR OPPONENT FOR THE FINAL MATCH'S BEEN DECIDED!
IT'S NATHANIEL!!
We could've guessed!

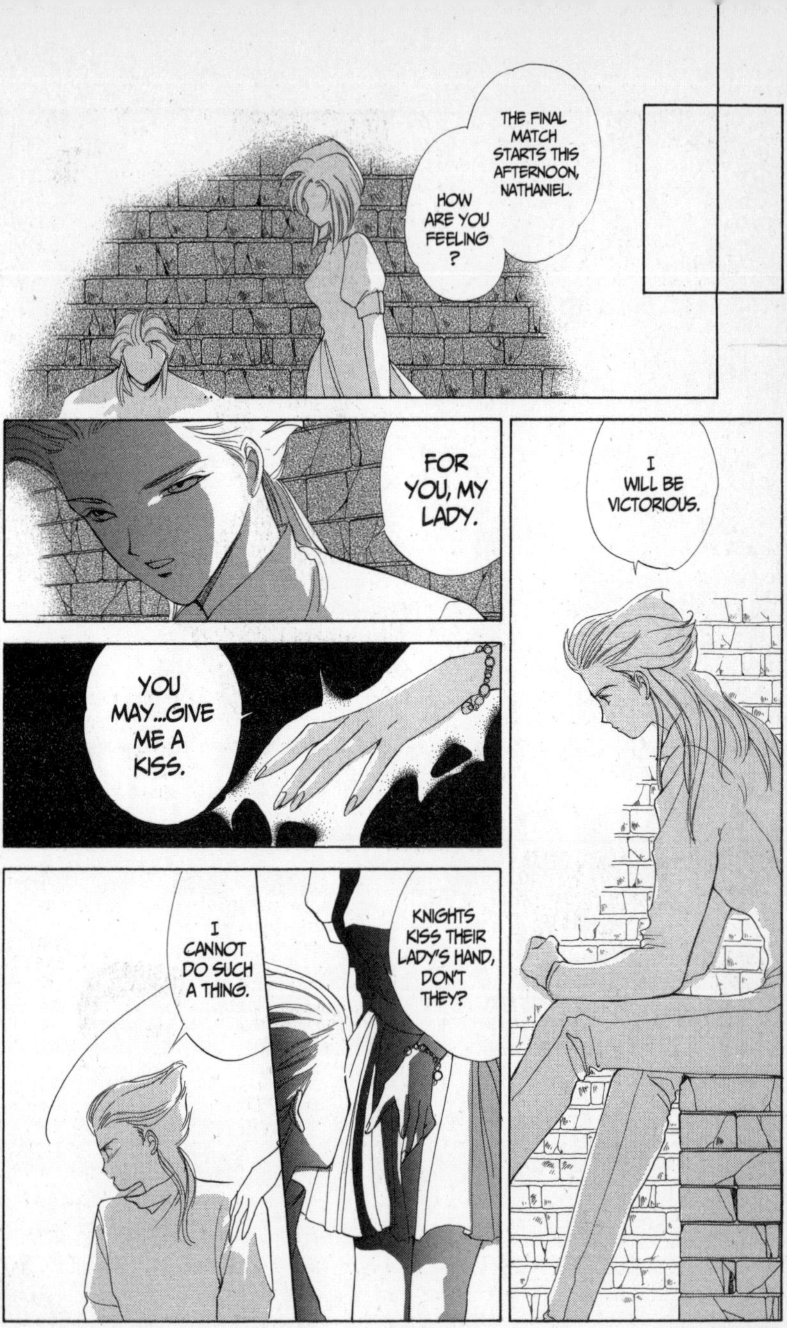
THE FINAL MATCH STARTS THIS AFTERNOON, NATHANIEL.
HOW ARE YOU FEELING?
I WILL BE VICTORIOUS.
FOR YOU, MY LADY.
YOU MAY...GIVE ME A KISS.
KNIGHTS KISS THEIR LADY'S HAND, DON'T THEY?
I CANNOT DO SUCH A THING.

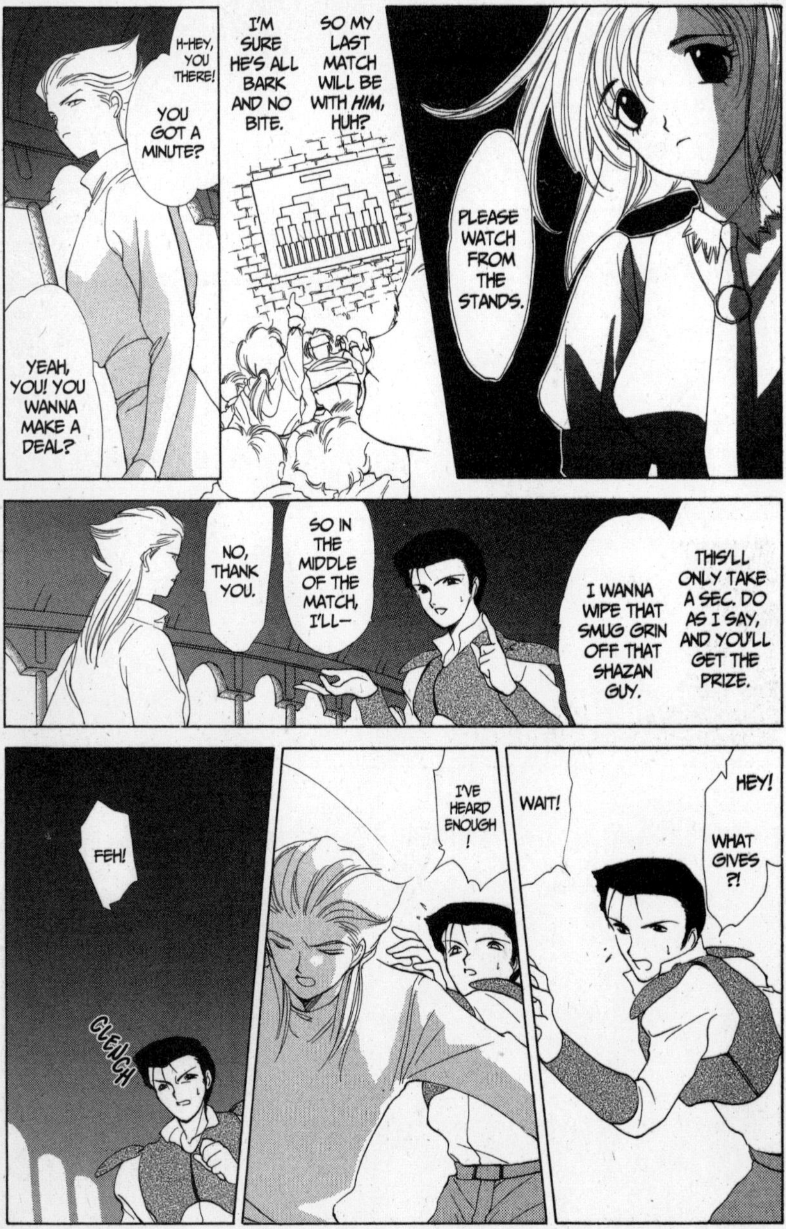
PLEASE WATCH FROM THE STANDS.
SO MY LAST MATCH WILL BE WITH *HIM*, HUH?
I'M SURE HE'S ALL BARK AND NO BITE.
H-HEY, YOU THERE!
YOU GOT A MINUTE?
YEAH, YOU! YOU WANNA MAKE A DEAL?
THIS'LL ONLY TAKE A SEC. DO AS I SAY, AND YOU'LL GET THE PRIZE.
I WANNA WIPE THAT SMUG GRIN OFF THAT SHAZAN GUY.
SO IN THE MIDDLE OF THE MATCH, I'LL—
NO, THANK YOU.
HEY!
WHAT GIVES?!
WAIT!
I'VE HEARD ENOUGH!
FEH!
CLENCH

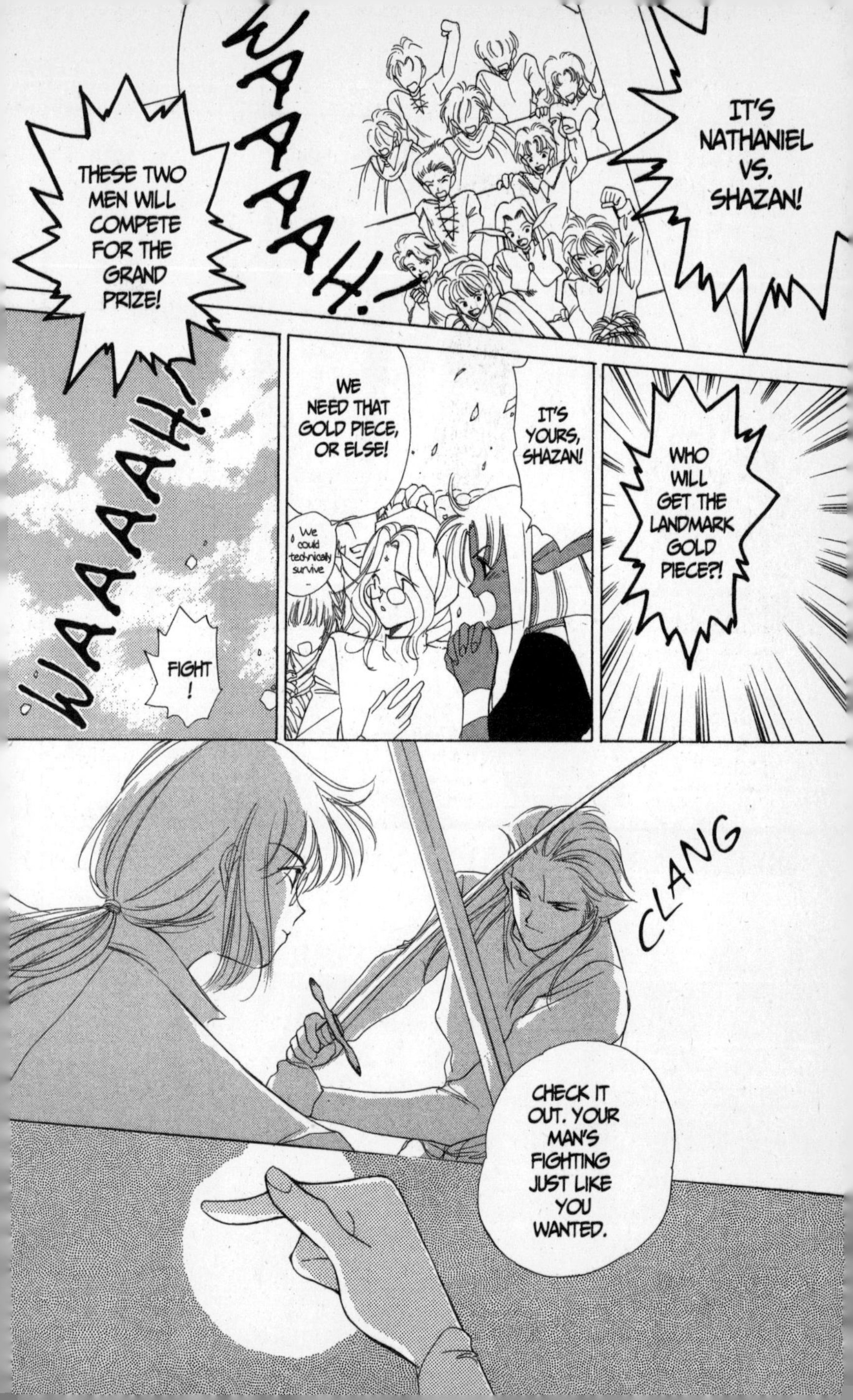

IT'S NATHANIEL VS. SHAZAN!
WAAAAH!
THESE TWO MEN WILL COMPETE FOR THE GRAND PRIZE!
WHO WILL GET THE LANDMARK GOLD PIECE?!
IT'S YOURS, SHAZAN!
WE NEED THAT GOLD PIECE, OR ELSE!
We could technically survive...
WAAAAH!
FIGHT!
CLANG
CHECK IT OUT. YOUR MAN'S FIGHTING JUST LIKE YOU WANTED.

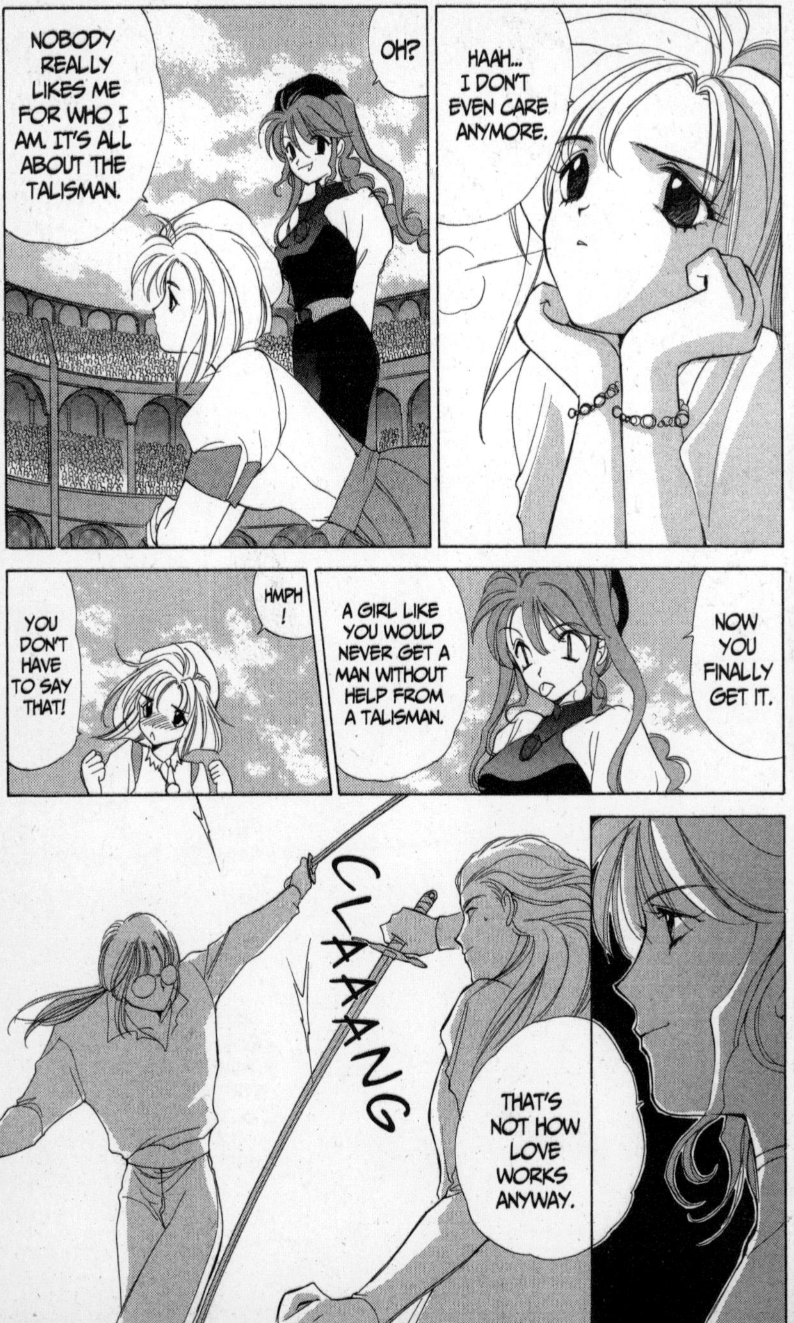
HAAH... I DON'T EVEN CARE ANYMORE.
OH?
NOBODY REALLY LIKES ME FOR WHO I AM. IT'S ALL ABOUT THE TALISMAN.
NOW YOU FINALLY GET IT.
A GIRL LIKE YOU WOULD NEVER GET A MAN WITHOUT HELP FROM A TALISMAN.
HMPH!
YOU DON'T HAVE TO SAY THAT!
THAT'S NOT HOW LOVE WORKS ANYWAY.
CLAAANG

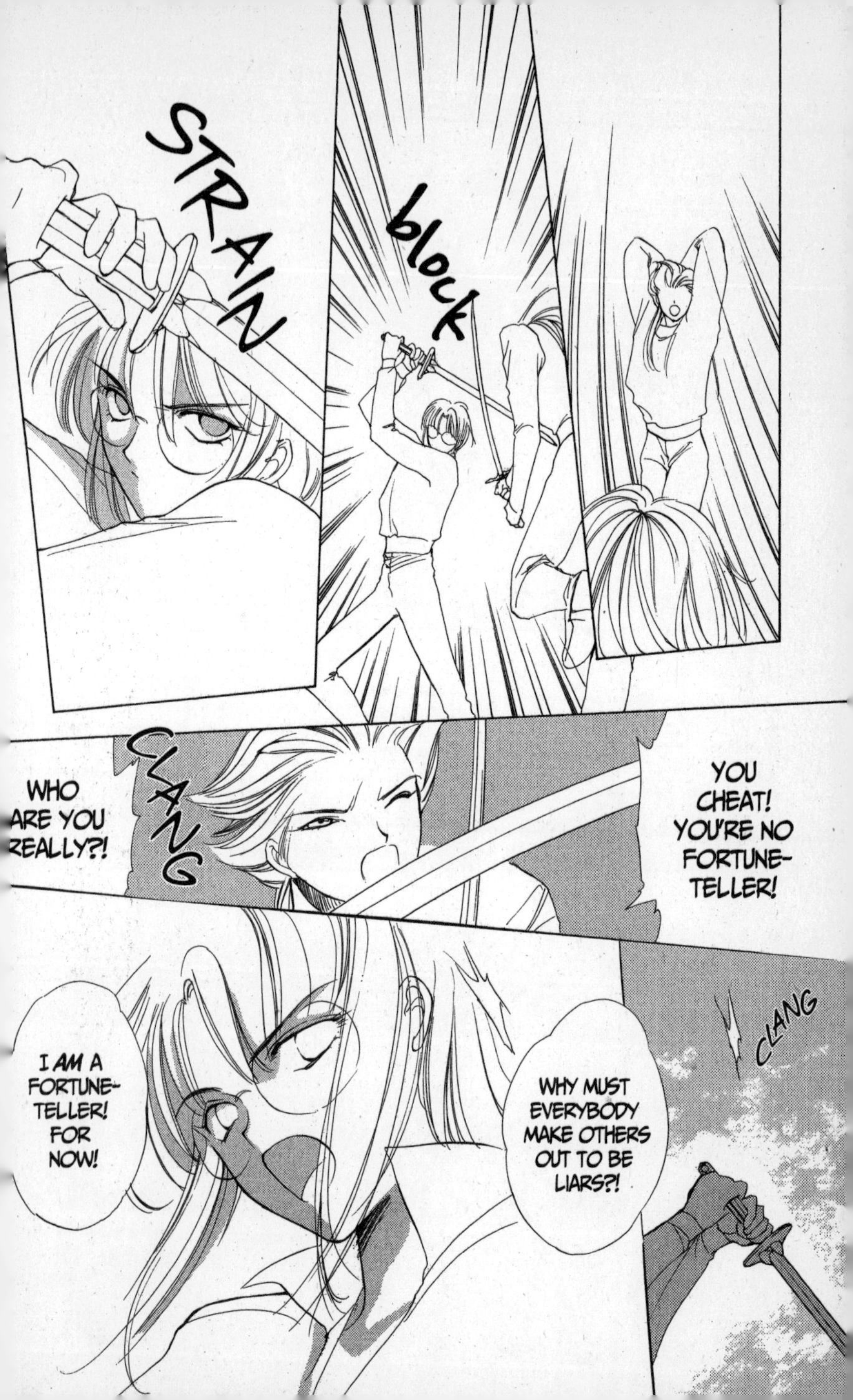
block
STRAIN
YOU CHEAT! YOU'RE NO FORTUNE-TELLER!
CLANG
WHO ARE YOU REALLY?!
CLANG
WHY MUST EVERYBODY MAKE OTHERS OUT TO BE LIARS?!
I AM A FORTUNE-TELLER! FOR NOW!

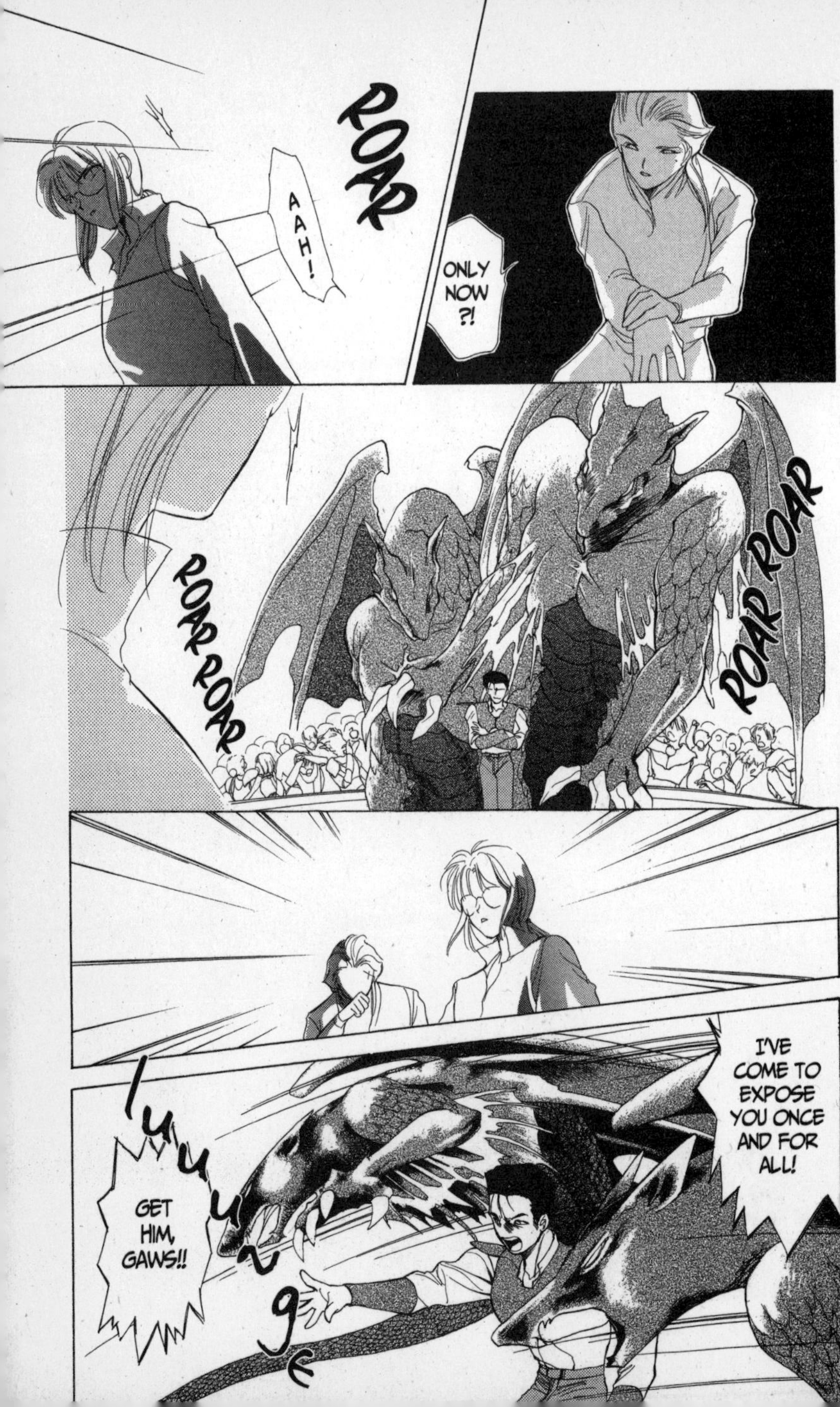
ROAR
ONLY NOW?!
AAH!
ROAR ROAR
ROAR ROAR
I'VE COME TO EXPOSE YOU ONCE AND FOR ALL!
GET HIM, GAWS!!
LUUUNGE

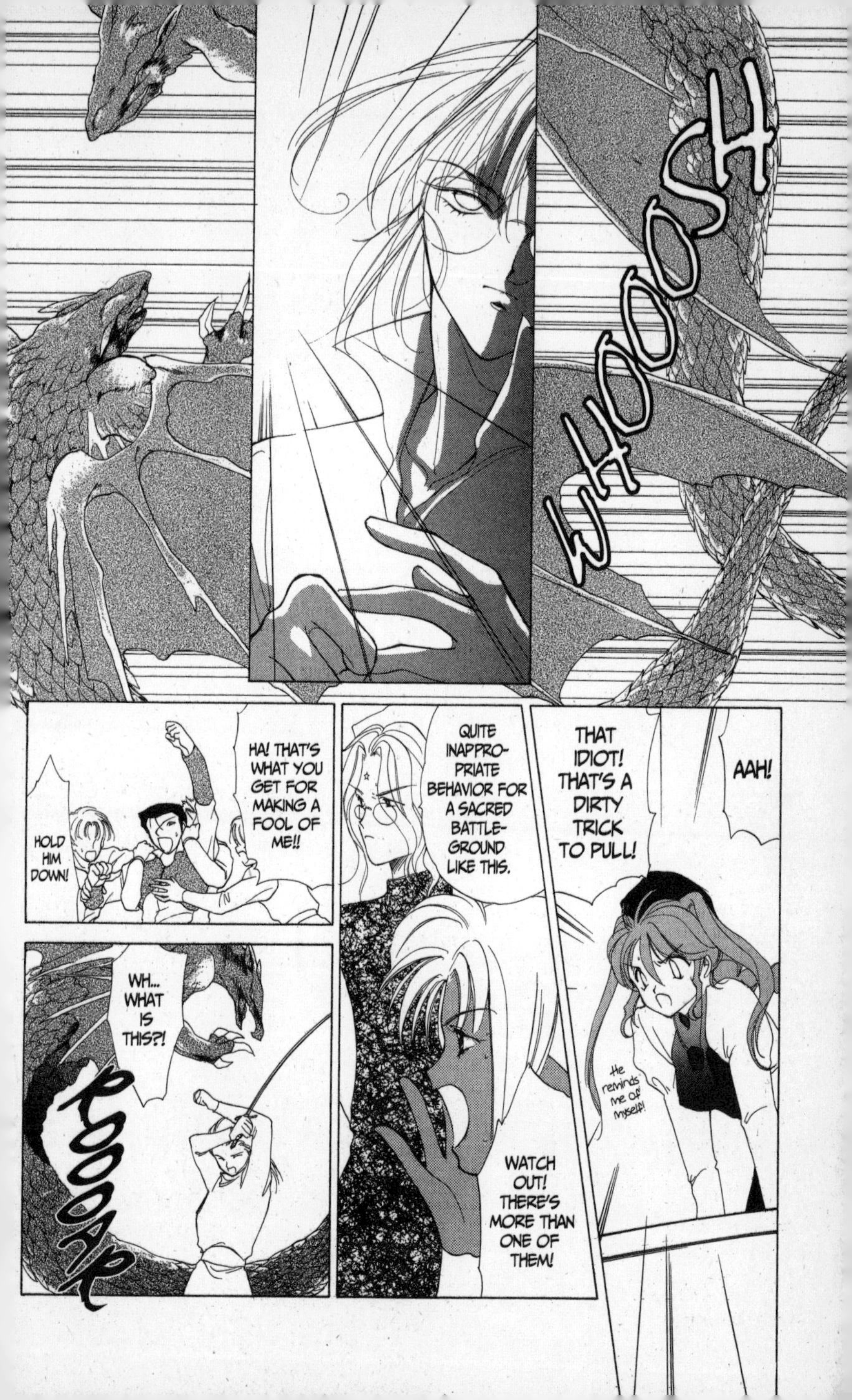
WHOOOSH
AAH!
THAT IDIOT! THAT'S A DIRTY TRICK TO PULL!
He reminds me of myself!
QUITE INAPPROPRIATE BEHAVIOR FOR A SACRED BATTLEGROUND LIKE THIS.
WATCH OUT! THERE'S MORE THAN ONE OF THEM!
HA! THAT'S WHAT YOU GET FOR MAKING A FOOL OF ME!!
HOLD HIM DOWN!
WH... WHAT IS THIS?!
ROOOAR

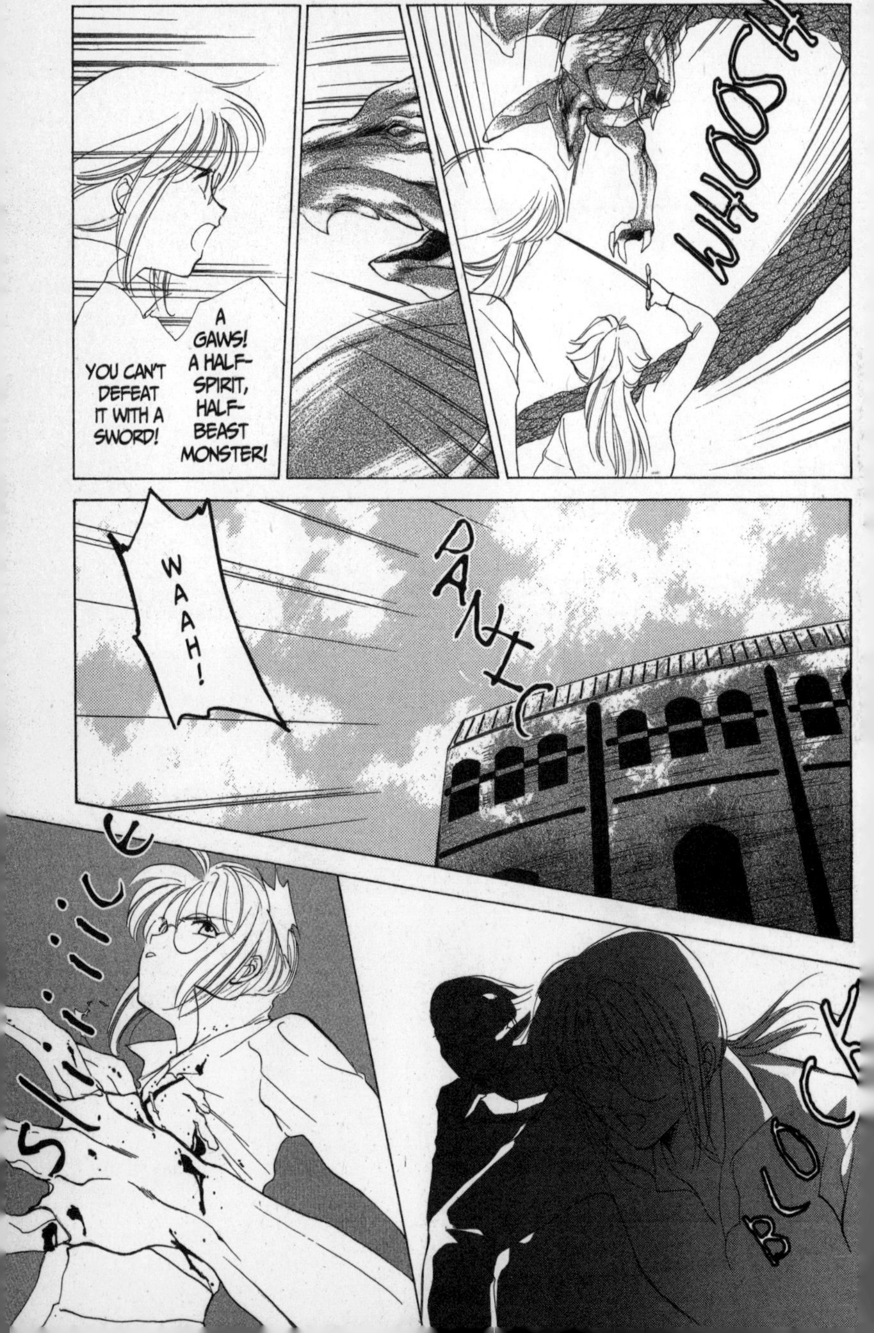
WHOOSH
A GAWS! A HALF-SPIRIT, HALF-BEAST MONSTER!
YOU CAN'T DEFEAT IT WITH A SWORD!
WAAAH!
PANIC
BLOCK
SLIIICE

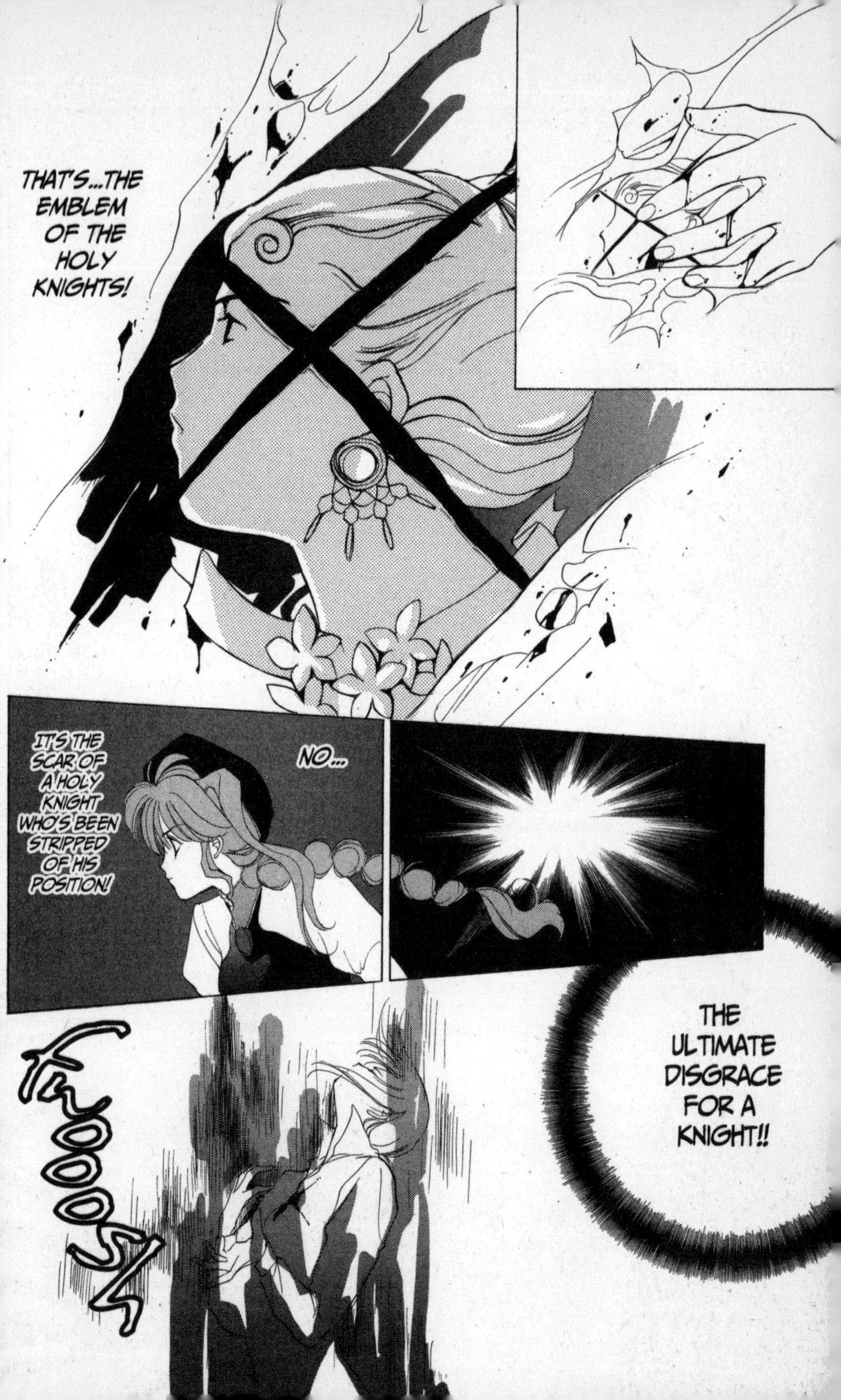
THAT'S...THE EMBLEM OF THE HOLY KNIGHTS!
NO...
IT'S THE SCAR OF A HOLY KNIGHT WHO'S BEEN STRIPPED OF HIS POSITION!
THE ULTIMATE DISGRACE FOR A KNIGHT!!
FWOOOSH

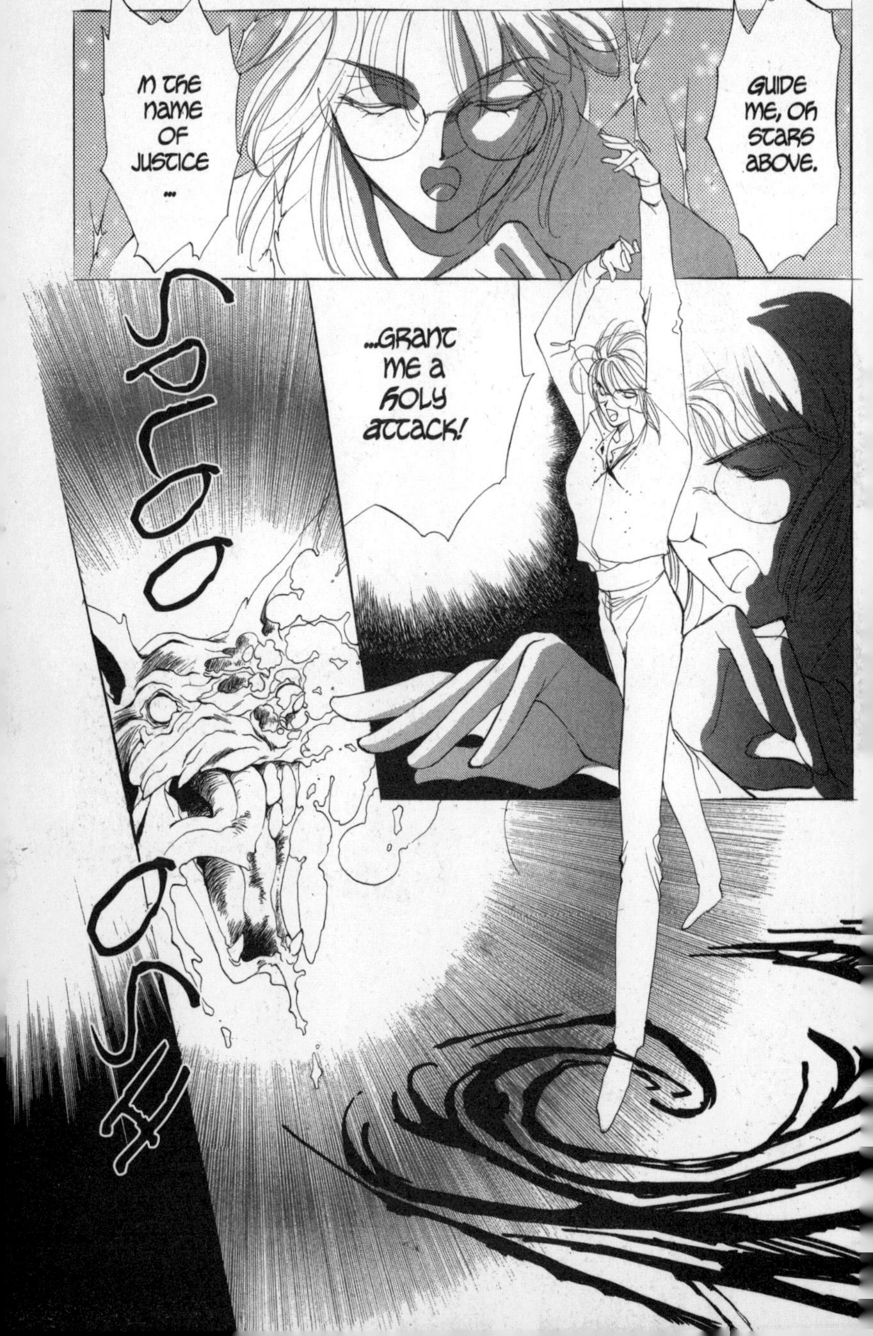
GUIDE ME, OH STARS ABOVE.
IN THE NAME OF JUSTICE ...
...GRANT ME A HOLY ATTACK!
SPLOOOSH

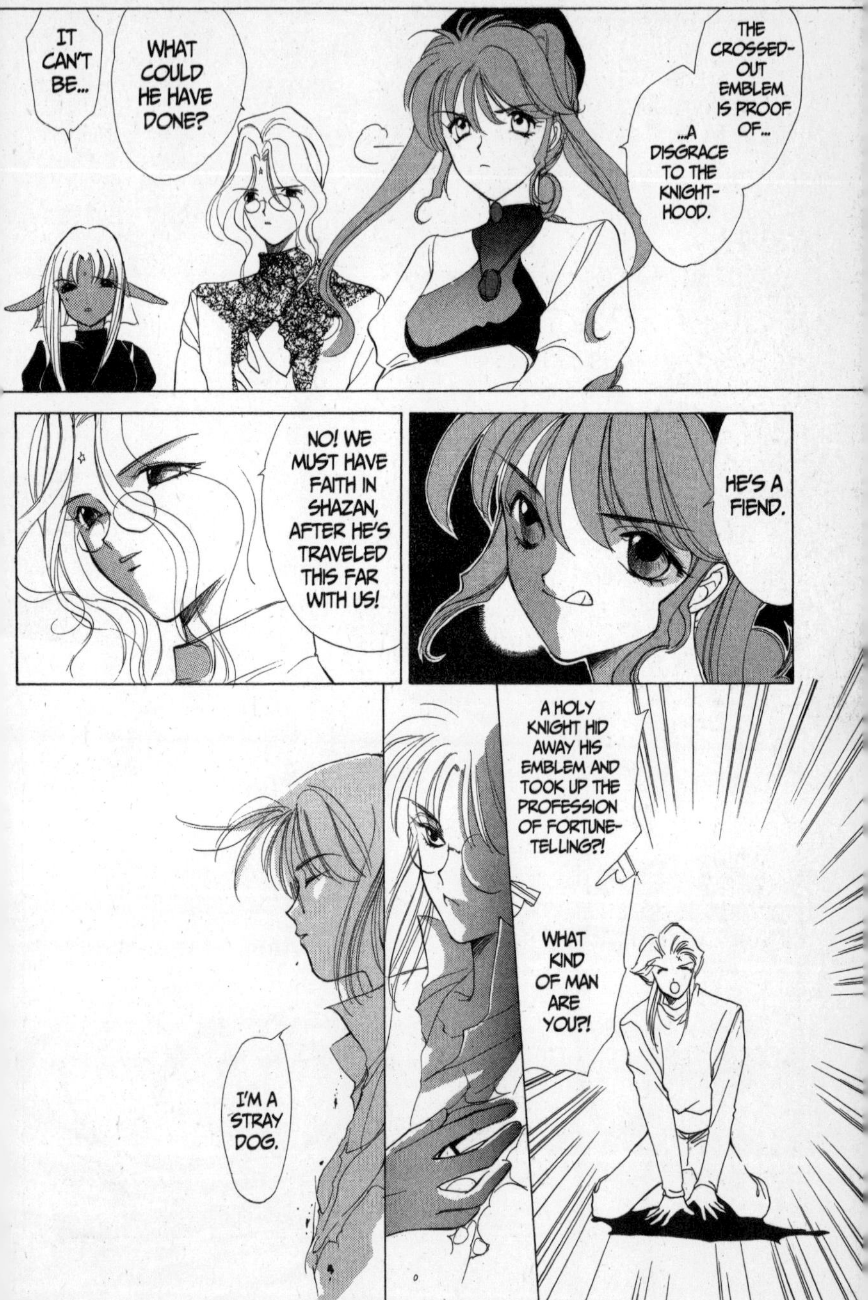
THE CROSSED-OUT EMBLEM IS PROOF OF...
...A DISGRACE TO THE KNIGHT-HOOD.
WHAT COULD HE HAVE DONE?
IT CAN'T BE...
HE'S A FIEND.
NO! WE MUST HAVE FAITH IN SHAZAN, AFTER HE'S TRAVELED THIS FAR WITH US!
A HOLY KNIGHT HID AWAY HIS EMBLEM AND TOOK UP THE PROFESSION OF FORTUNE-TELLING?!
WHAT KIND OF MAN ARE YOU?!
I'M A STRAY DOG.

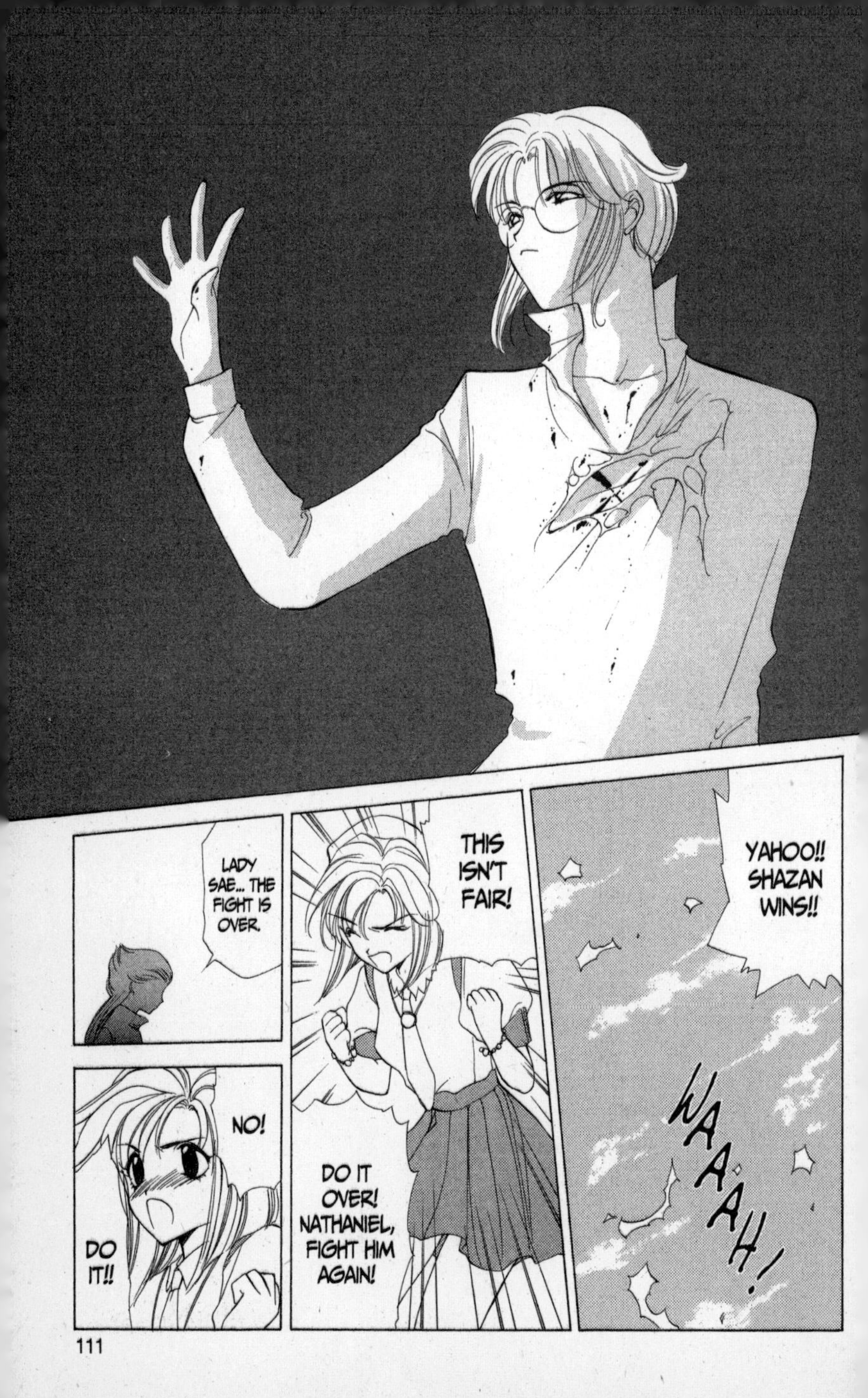
YAHOO!! SHAZAN WINS!!
WAAAH!
THIS ISN'T FAIR!
DO IT OVER! NATHANIEL, FIGHT HIM AGAIN!
LADY SAE... THE FIGHT IS OVER.
NO!
DO IT!!

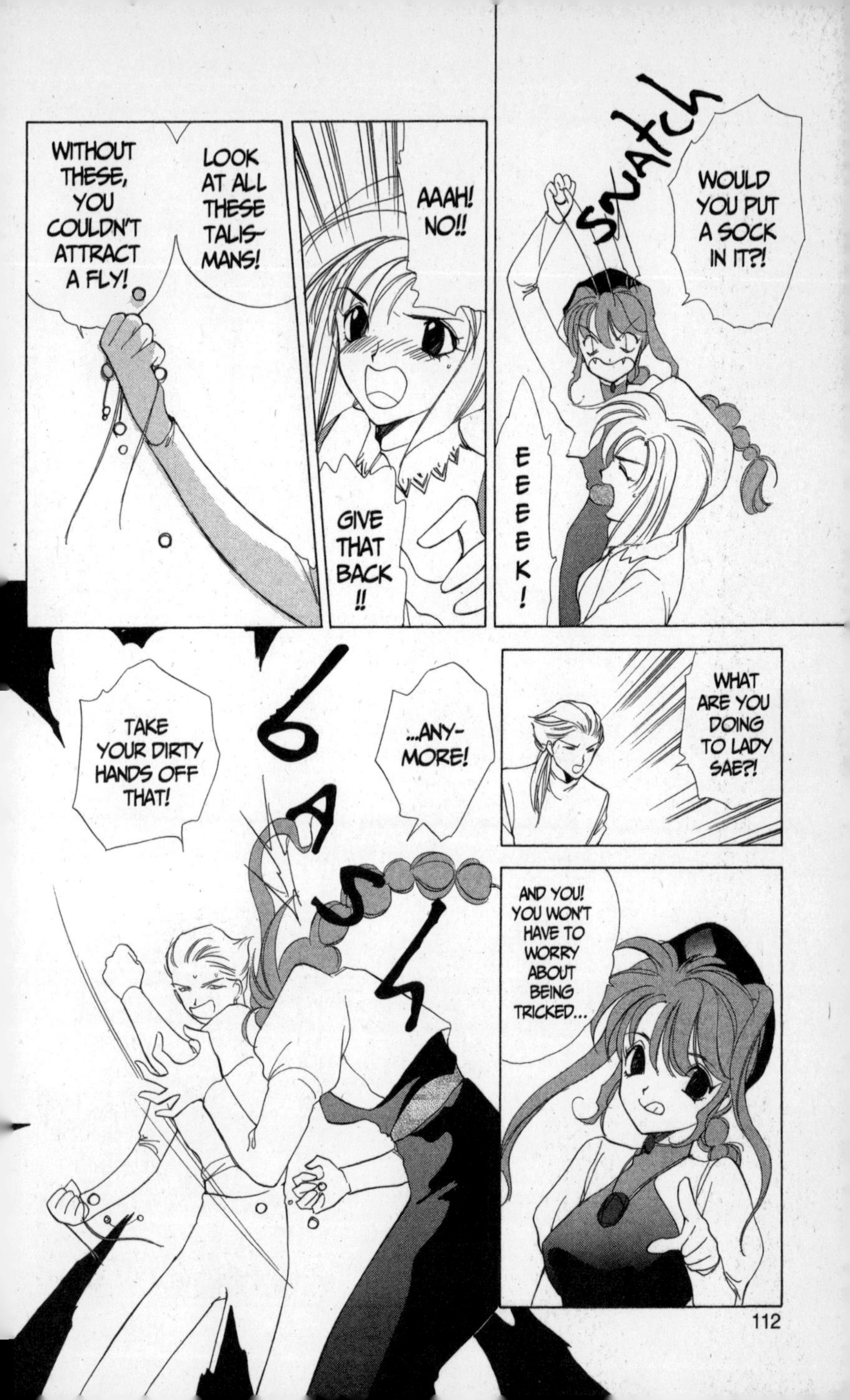
SNATCH
WOULD YOU PUT A SOCK IN IT?!
EEEEK!
AAAH! NO!!
GIVE THAT BACK!!
LOOK AT ALL THESE TALIS-MANS!
WITHOUT THESE, YOU COULDN'T ATTRACT A FLY!
WHAT ARE YOU DOING TO LADY SAE?!
AND YOU! YOU WON'T HAVE TO WORRY ABOUT BEING TRICKED...
...ANY-MORE!
TAKE YOUR DIRTY HANDS OFF THAT!
BASH

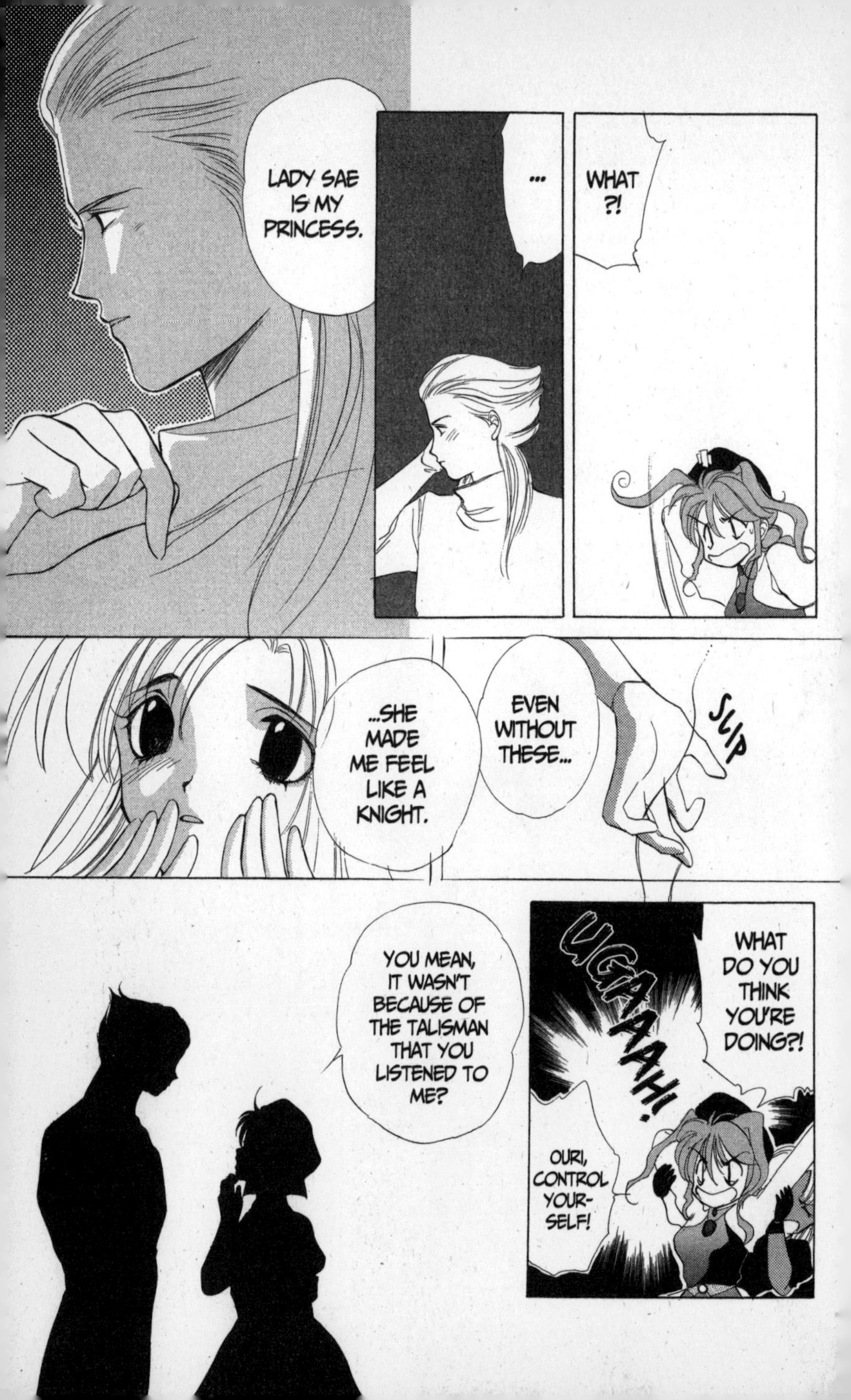
WHAT ?!
...
LADY SAE IS MY PRINCESS.
SLIP
EVEN WITHOUT THESE...
...SHE MADE ME FEEL LIKE A KNIGHT.
WHAT DO YOU THINK YOU'RE DOING?!
UGAAAH!
OURI, CONTROL YOUR-SELF!
YOU MEAN, IT WASN'T BECAUSE OF THE TALISMAN THAT YOU LISTENED TO ME?

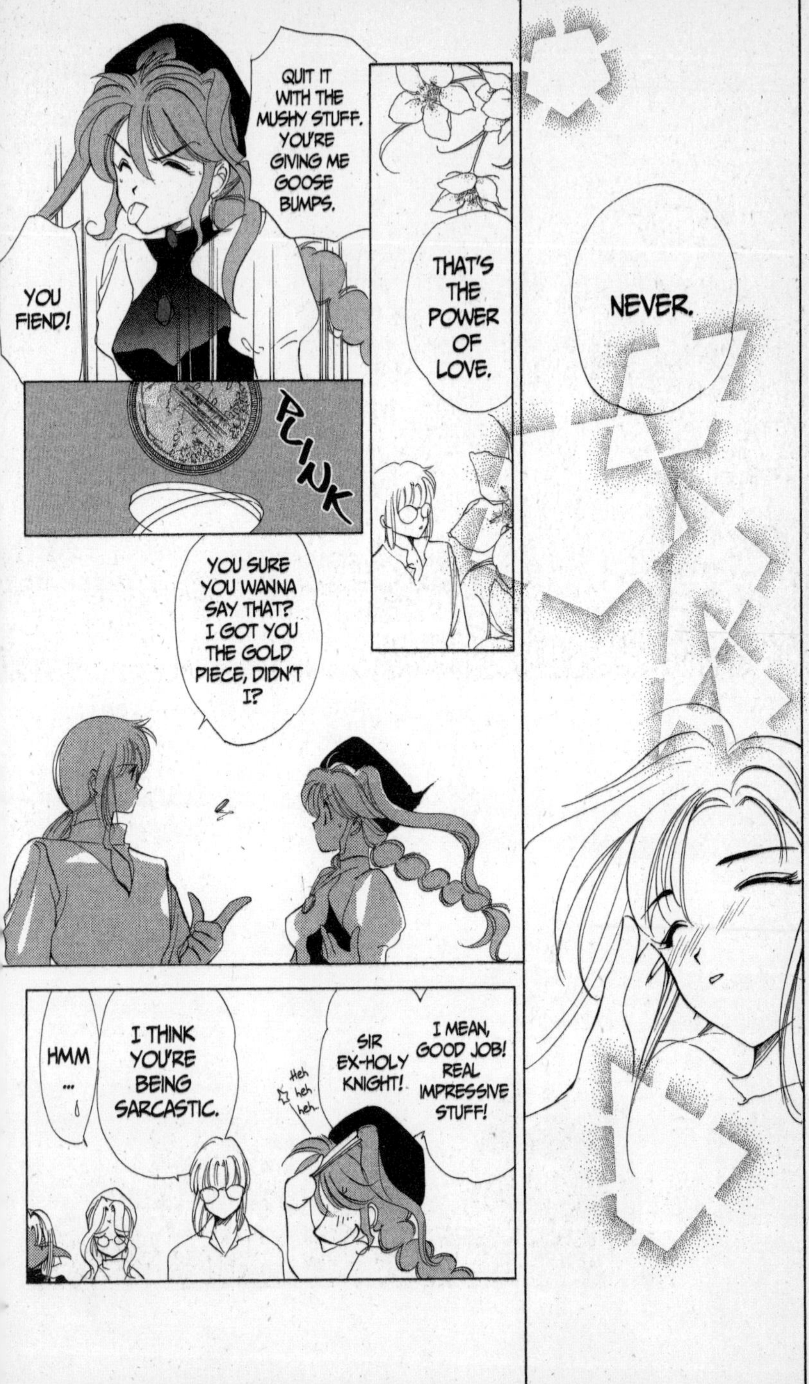
NEVER.
THAT'S THE POWER OF LOVE.
QUIT IT WITH THE MUSHY STUFF. YOU'RE GIVING ME GOOSE BUMPS.
YOU FIEND!
PLINK
YOU SURE YOU WANNA SAY THAT? I GOT YOU THE GOLD PIECE, DIDN'T I?
I MEAN, GOOD JOB! REAL IMPRESSIVE STUFF!
SIR EX-HOLY KNIGHT!
Heh heh heh..
I THINK YOU'RE BEING SARCASTIC.
HMM ...

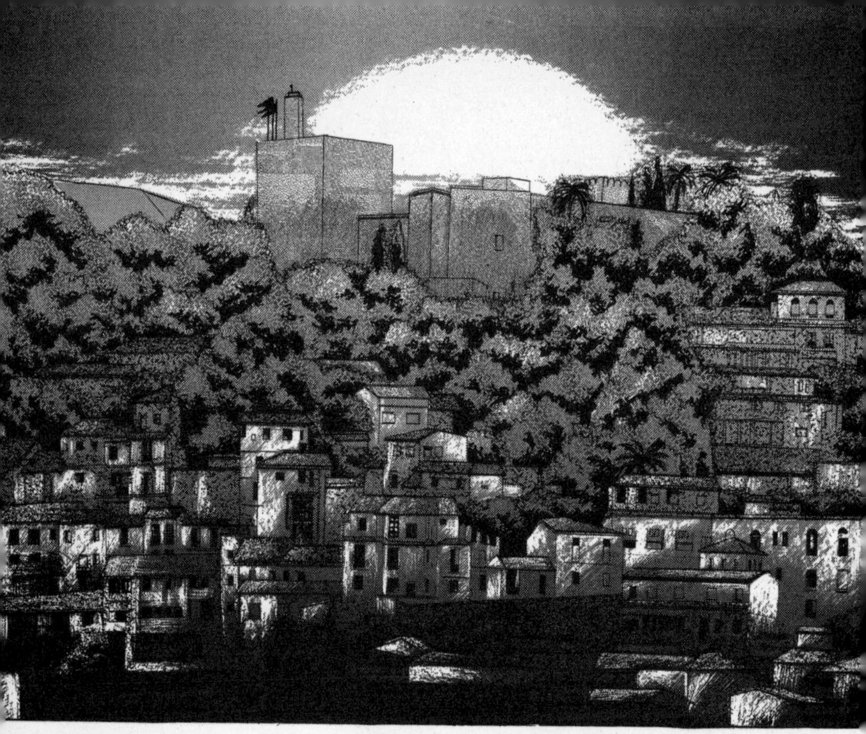

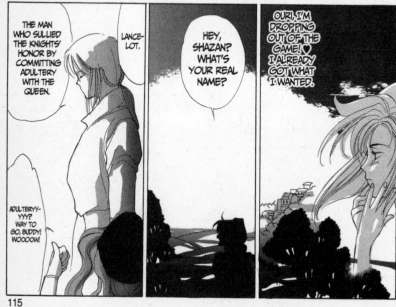

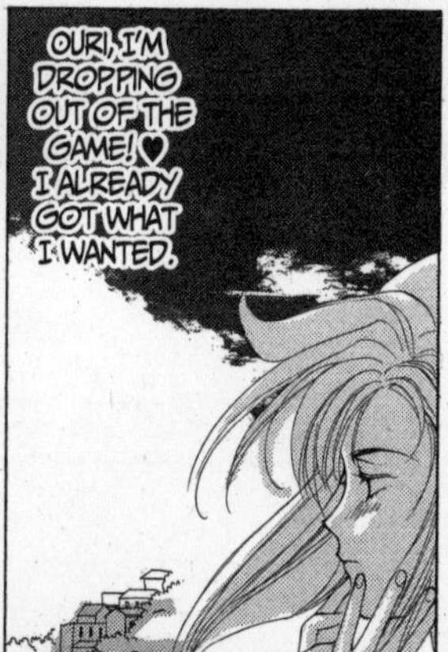
OURI, I'M DROPPING OUT OF THE GAME! ♥ I ALREADY GOT WHAT I WANTED.

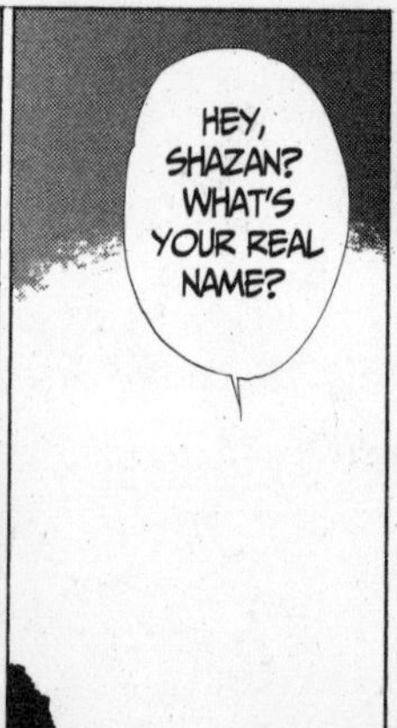
HEY, SHAZAN? WHAT'S YOUR REAL NAME?

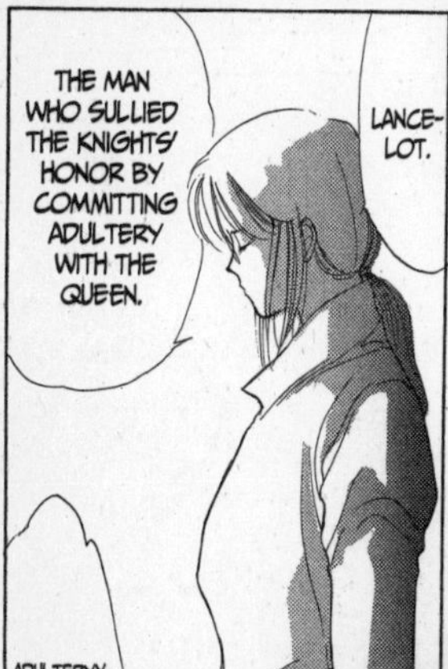
LANCE-LOT.
THE MAN WHO SULLIED THE KNIGHTS' HONOR BY COMMITTING ADULTERY WITH THE QUEEN.
ADULTERYY-YYY? WAY TO GO, BUDDY! WOOOOW!

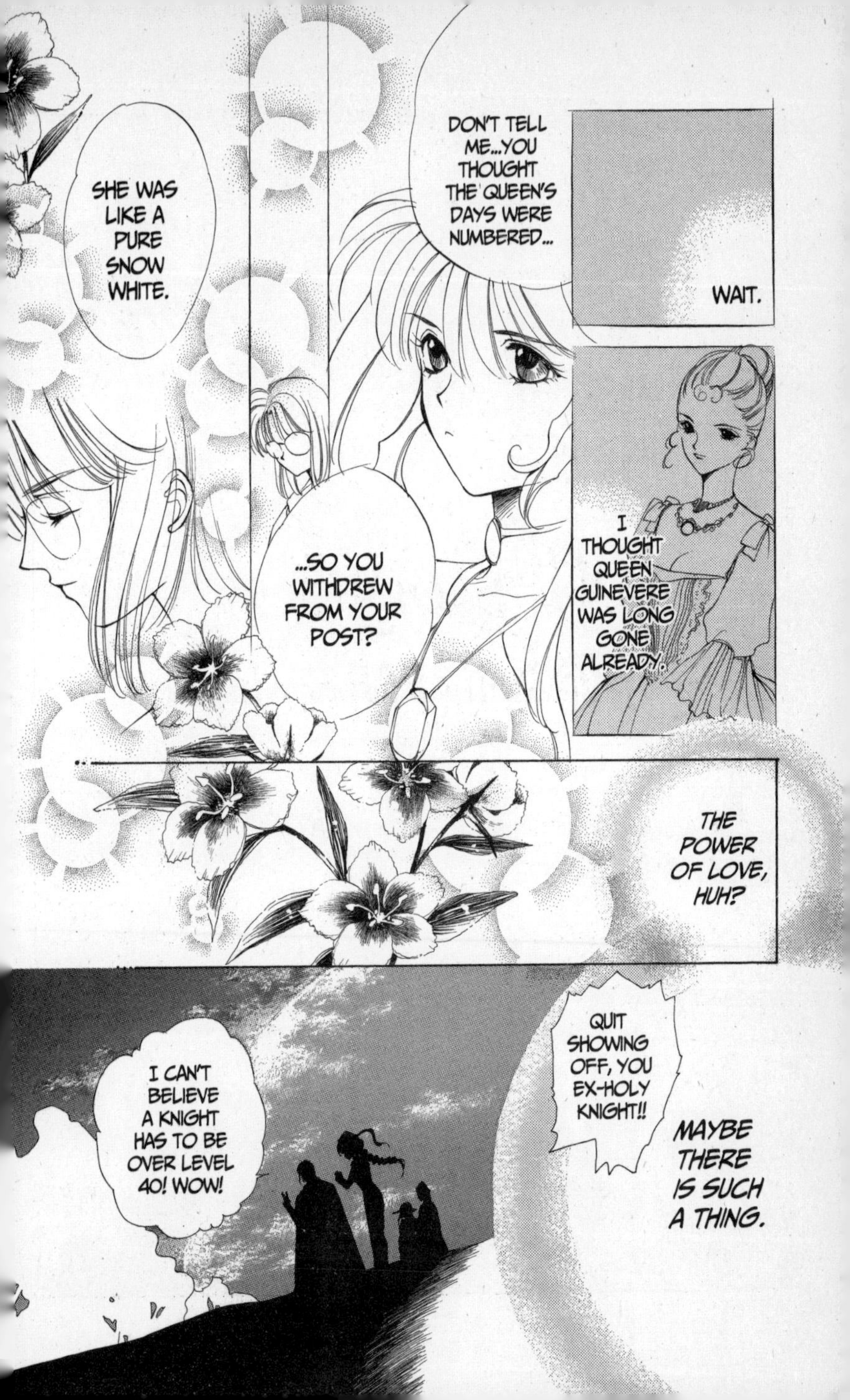
WAIT.
I THOUGHT QUEEN GUINEVERE WAS LONG GONE ALREADY.
DON'T TELL ME...YOU THOUGHT THE QUEEN'S DAYS WERE NUMBERED...
...SO YOU WITHDREW FROM YOUR POST?
SHE WAS LIKE A PURE SNOW WHITE.
THE POWER OF LOVE, HUH?
QUIT SHOWING OFF, YOU EX-HOLY KNIGHT!!
MAYBE THERE IS SUCH A THING.
I CAN'T BELIEVE A KNIGHT HAS TO BE OVER LEVEL 40! WOW!

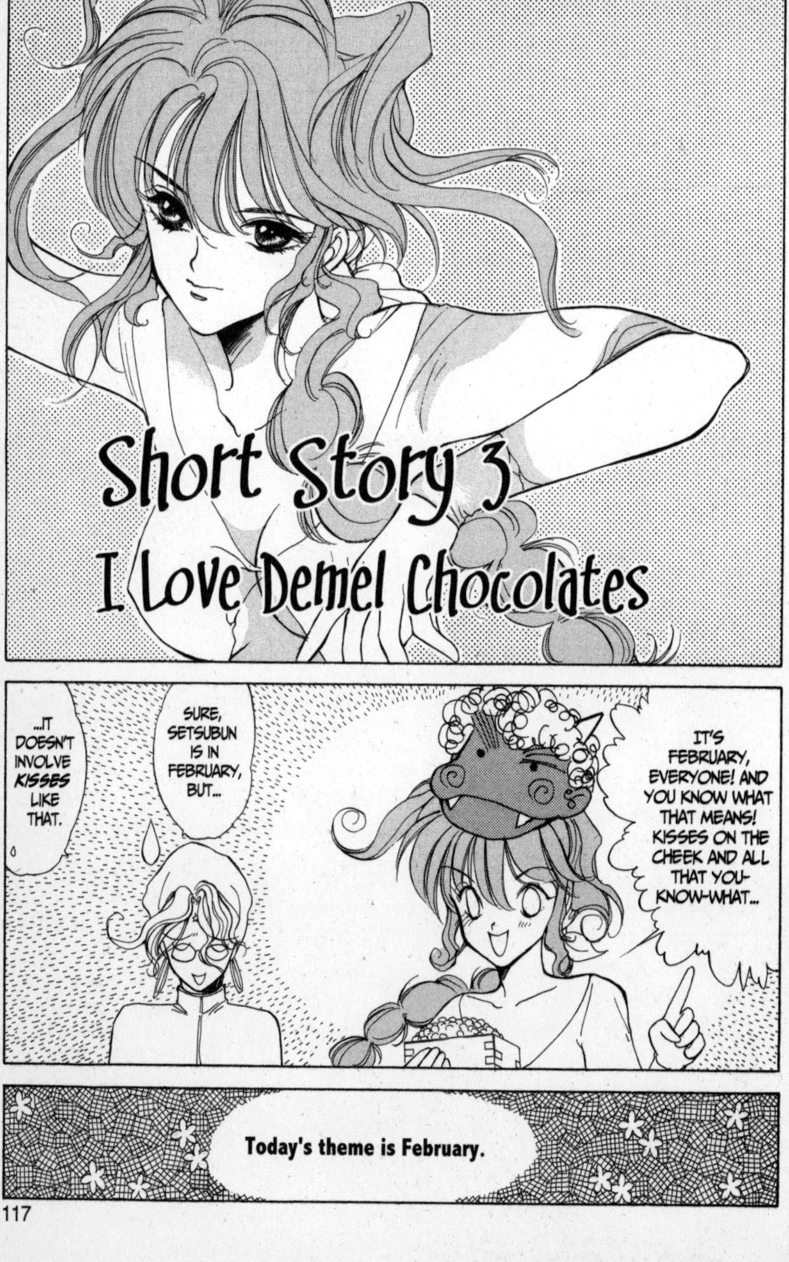
Short Story 3
I Love Demel Chocolates
IT'S FEBRUARY, EVERYONE! AND YOU KNOW WHAT THAT MEANS! KISSES ON THE CHEEK AND ALL THAT YOU-KNOW-WHAT...
SURE, SETSUBUN IS IN FEBRUARY, BUT...
...IT DOESN'T INVOLVE *KISSES* LIKE THAT.
Today's theme is February.

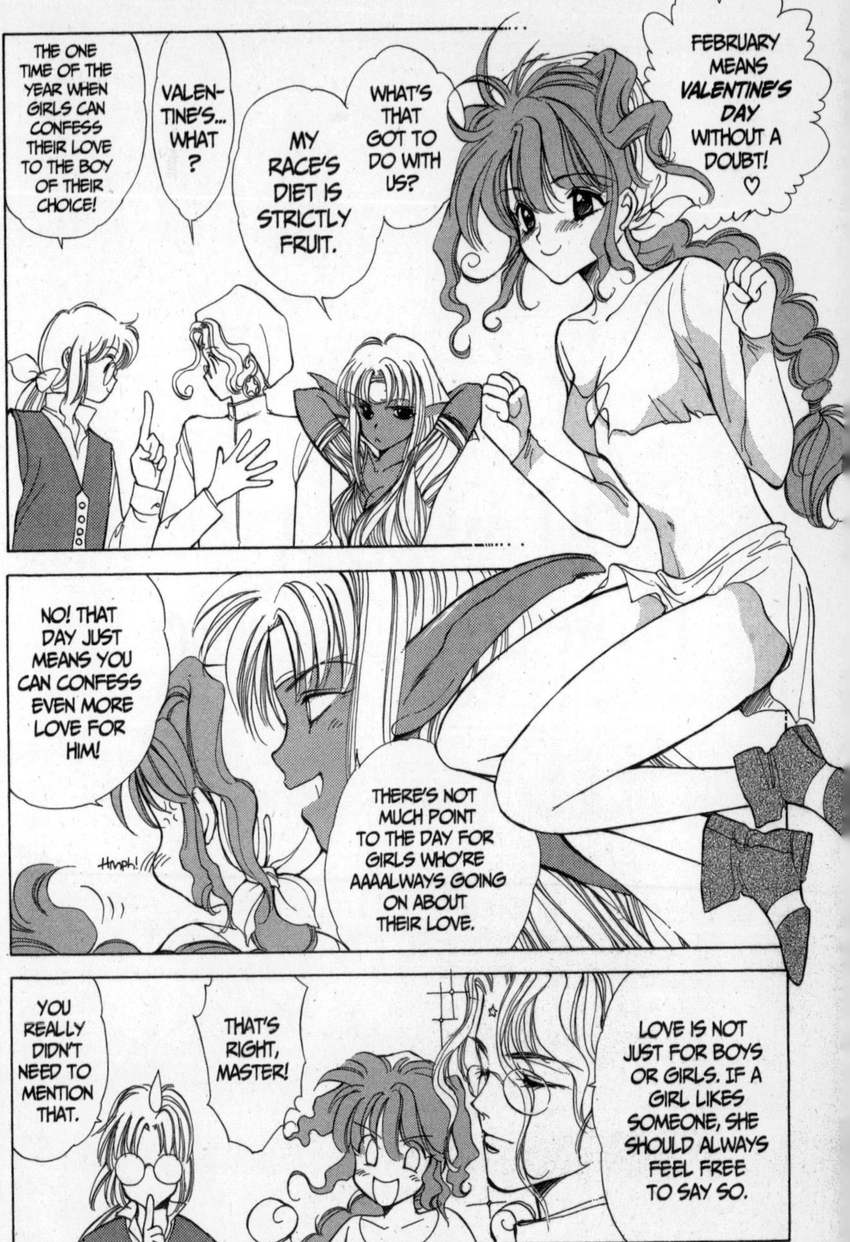
FEBRUARY MEANS VALENTINE'S DAY WITHOUT A DOUBT! ♡
WHAT'S THAT GOT TO DO WITH US?
MY RACE'S DIET IS STRICTLY FRUIT.
VALEN-TINE'S... WHAT ?
THE ONE TIME OF THE YEAR WHEN GIRLS CAN CONFESS THEIR LOVE TO THE BOY OF THEIR CHOICE!
THERE'S NOT MUCH POINT TO THE DAY FOR GIRLS WHO'RE AAAALWAYS GOING ON ABOUT THEIR LOVE.
NO! THAT DAY JUST MEANS YOU CAN CONFESS EVEN MORE LOVE FOR HIM!
Hmph!
LOVE IS NOT JUST FOR BOYS OR GIRLS. IF A GIRL LIKES SOMEONE, SHE SHOULD ALWAYS FEEL FREE TO SAY SO.
THAT'S RIGHT, MASTER!
YOU REALLY DIDN'T NEED TO MENTION THAT.

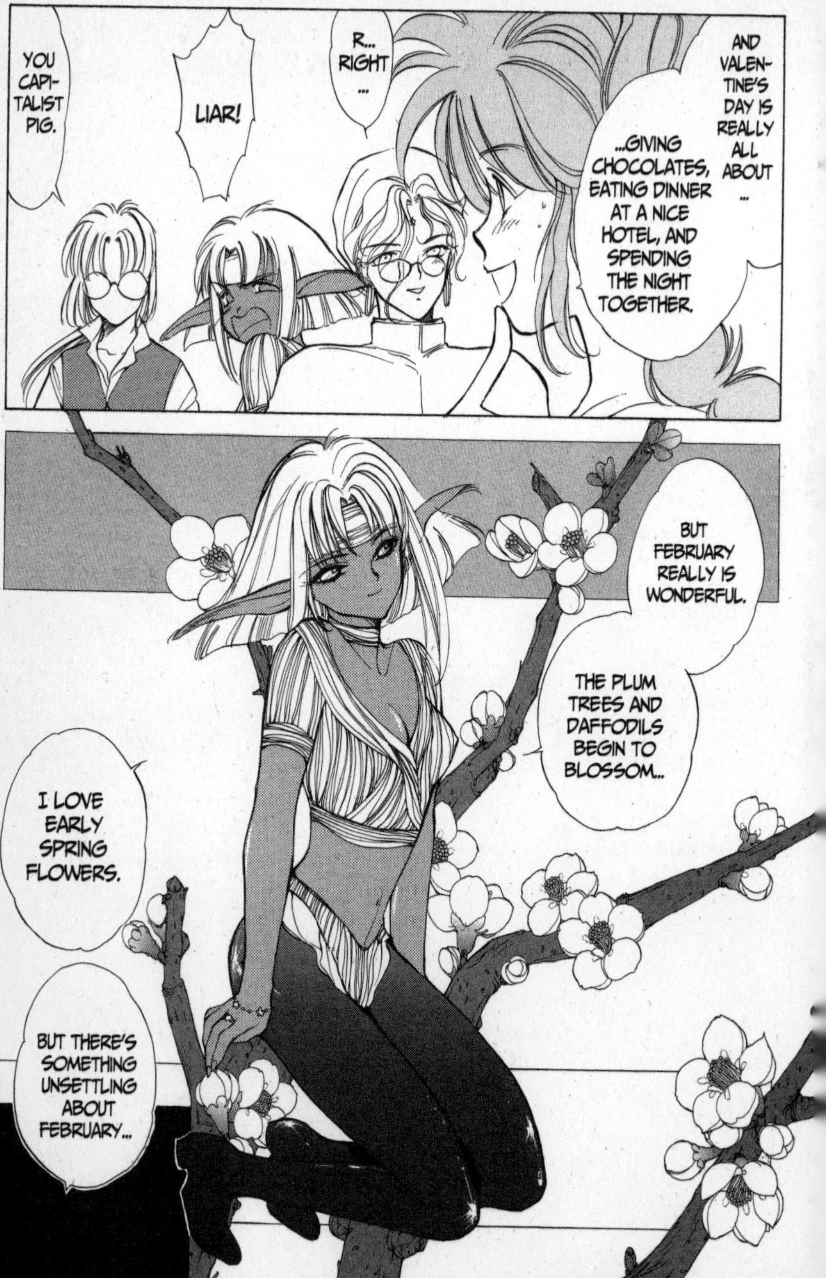
AND VALENTINE'S DAY IS REALLY ALL ABOUT...
...GIVING CHOCOLATES, EATING DINNER AT A NICE HOTEL, AND SPENDING THE NIGHT TOGETHER.
R... RIGHT...
LIAR!
YOU CAPITALIST PIG.
BUT FEBRUARY REALLY IS WONDERFUL.
THE PLUM TREES AND DAFFODILS BEGIN TO BLOSSOM...
I LOVE EARLY SPRING FLOWERS.
BUT THERE'S SOMETHING UNSETTLING ABOUT FEBRUARY...

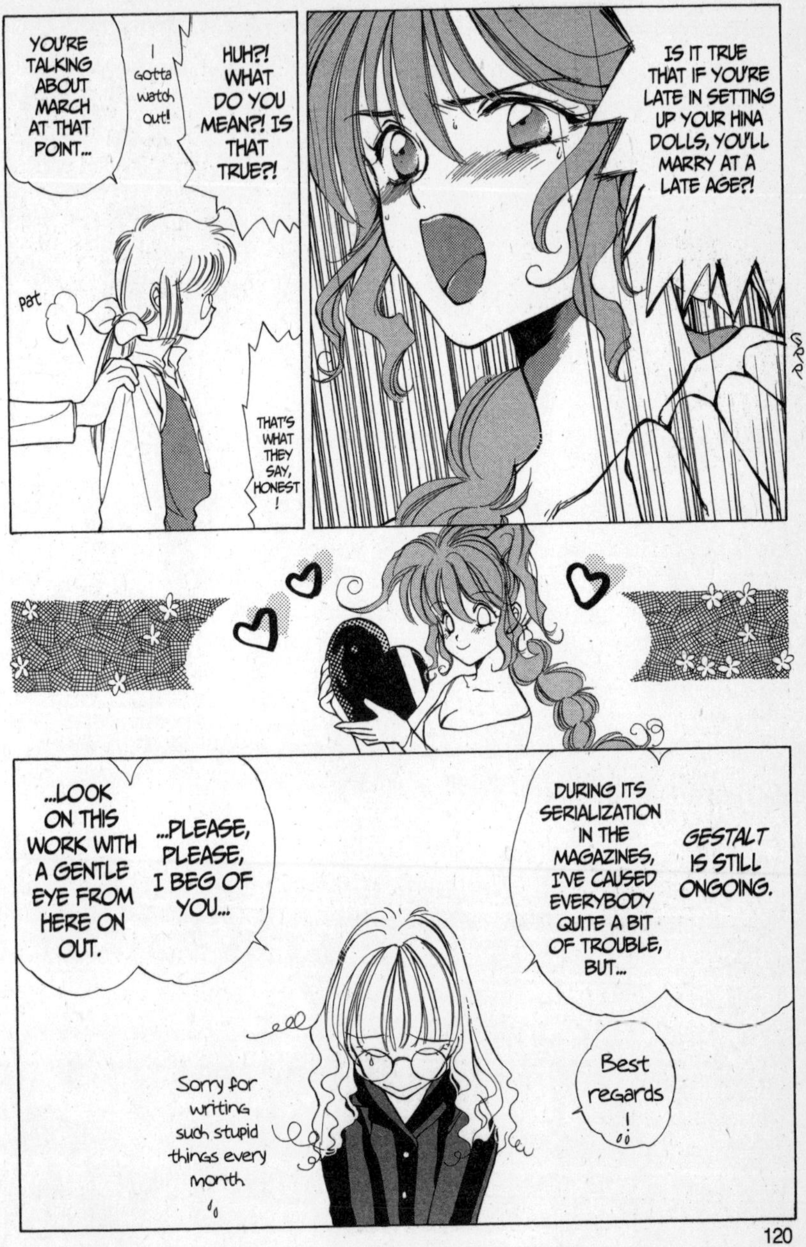
IS IT TRUE THAT IF YOU'RE LATE IN SETTING UP YOUR HINA DOLLS, YOU'LL MARRY AT A LATE AGE?!
GRR
HUH?! WHAT DO YOU MEAN?! IS THAT TRUE?!
I gotta watch out!
YOU'RE TALKING ABOUT MARCH AT THAT POINT...
THAT'S WHAT THEY SAY, HONEST!
pat
GESTALT IS STILL ONGOING.
DURING ITS SERIALIZATION IN THE MAGAZINES, I'VE CAUSED EVERYBODY QUITE A BIT OF TROUBLE, BUT...
...PLEASE, PLEASE, I BEG OF YOU...
...LOOK ON THIS WORK WITH A GENTLE EYE FROM HERE ON OUT.
Best regards!
Sorry for writing such stupid things every month.

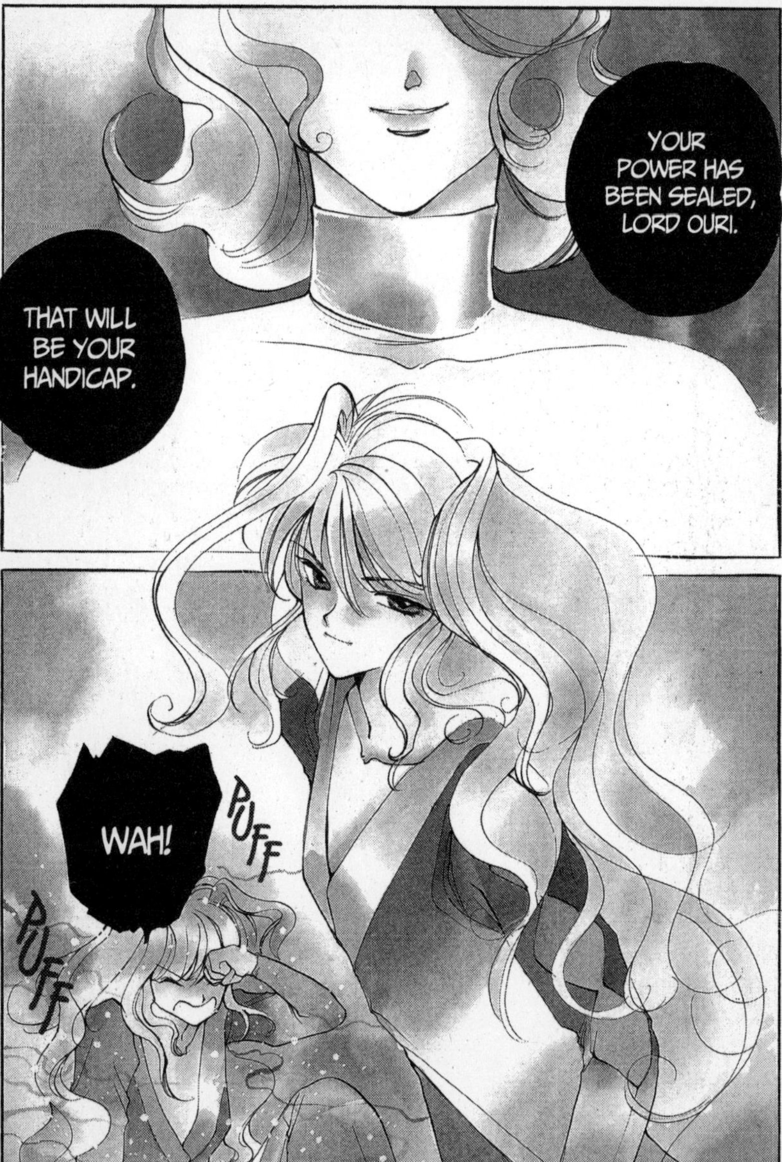
YOUR POWER HAS BEEN SEALED, LORD OURI.
THAT WILL BE YOUR HANDICAP.
WAH!
PUFF
PUFF

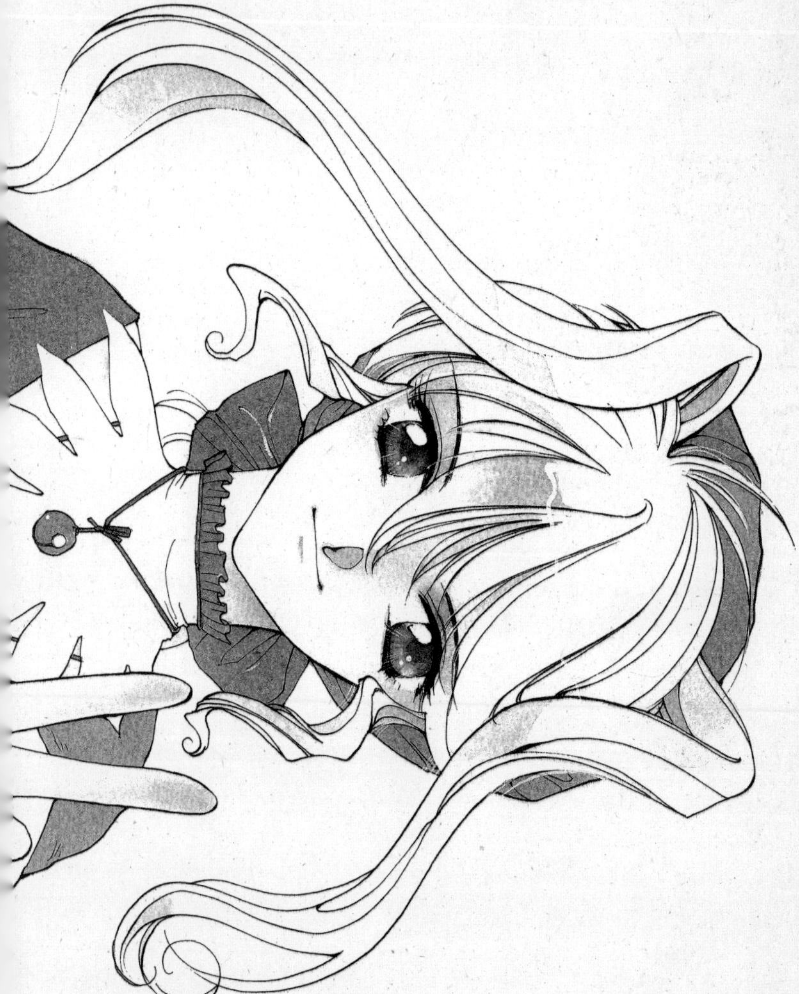

Chapter 10
Steamy Yearning Pt. I

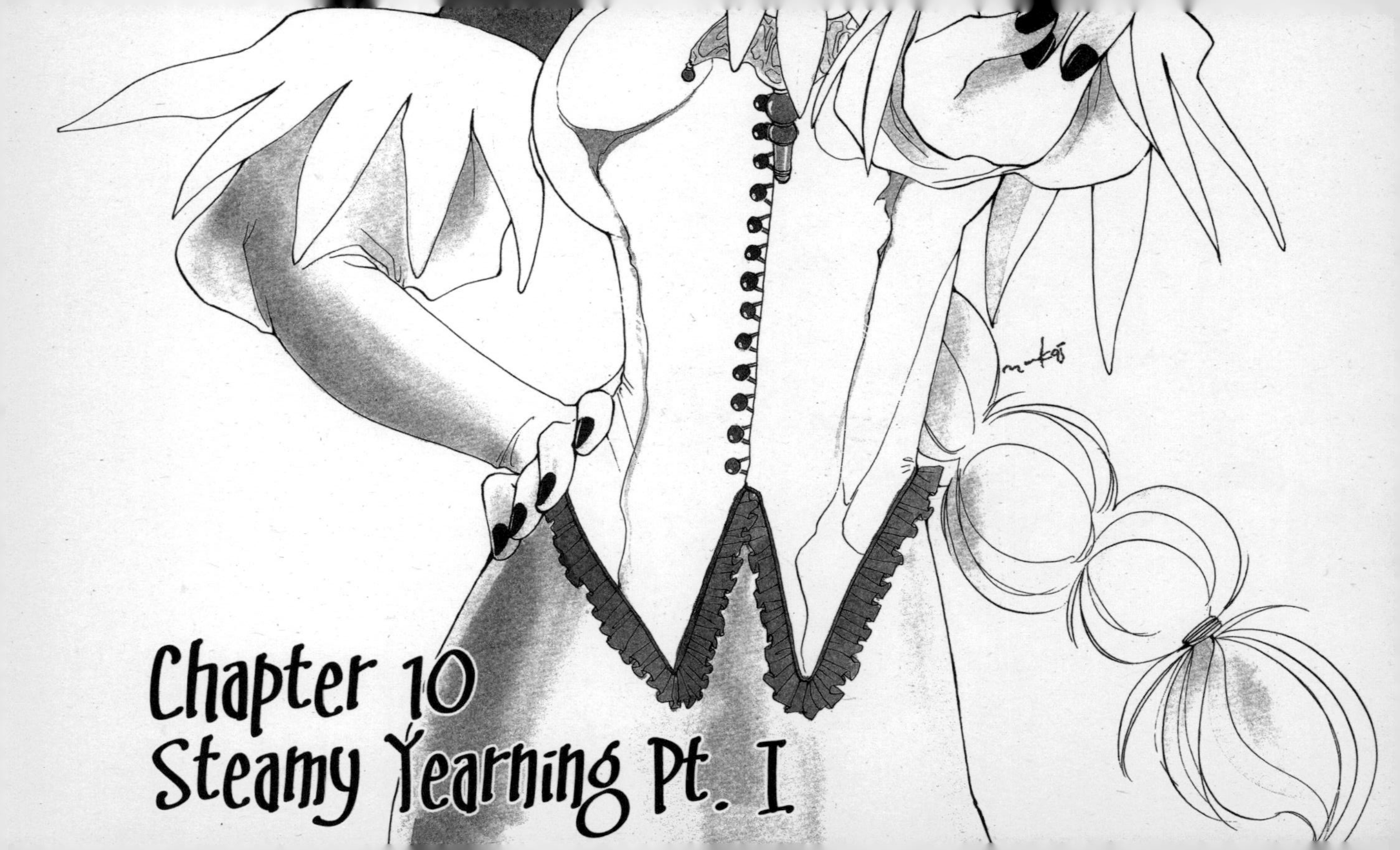

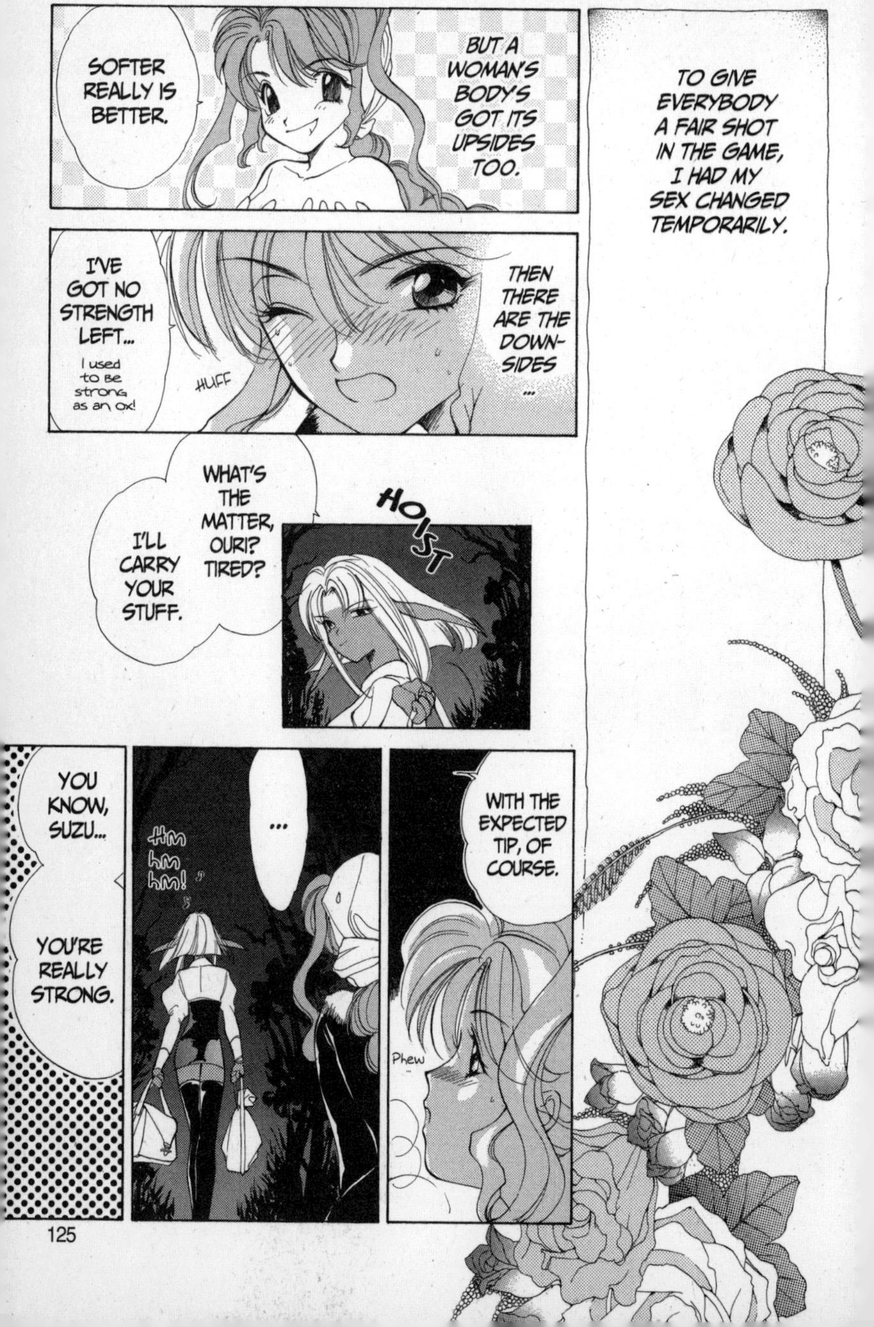
TO GIVE EVERYBODY A FAIR SHOT IN THE GAME, I HAD MY SEX CHANGED TEMPORARILY.
BUT A WOMAN'S BODY'S GOT ITS UPSIDES TOO.
SOFTER REALLY IS BETTER.
THEN THERE ARE THE DOWNSIDES ...
I'VE GOT NO STRENGTH LEFT...
I used to be strong as an ox!
HUFF
HOIST
WHAT'S THE MATTER, OURI? TIRED?
I'LL CARRY YOUR STUFF.
WITH THE EXPECTED TIP, OF COURSE.
Phew ...
...
hm hm hm!
YOU KNOW, SUZU...
YOU'RE REALLY STRONG.

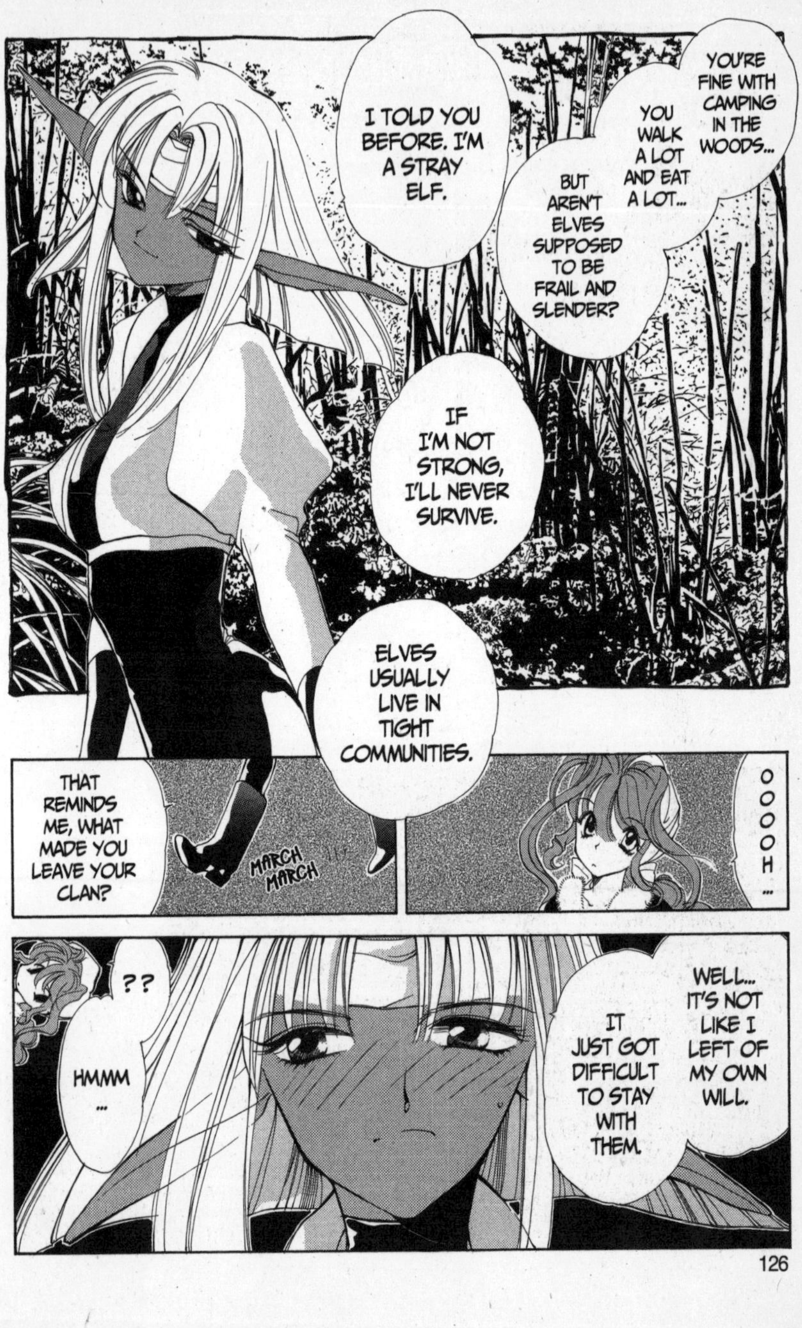
YOU'RE FINE WITH CAMPING IN THE WOODS...
YOU WALK A LOT AND EAT A LOT...
BUT AREN'T ELVES SUPPOSED TO BE FRAIL AND SLENDER?
I TOLD YOU BEFORE. I'M A STRAY ELF.
IF I'M NOT STRONG, I'LL NEVER SURVIVE.
ELVES USUALLY LIVE IN TIGHT COMMUNITIES.
OOOOH...
THAT REMINDS ME, WHAT MADE YOU LEAVE YOUR CLAN?
MARCH MARCH
WELL... IT'S NOT LIKE I LEFT OF MY OWN WILL.
IT JUST GOT DIFFICULT TO STAY WITH THEM.
??
HMMM...

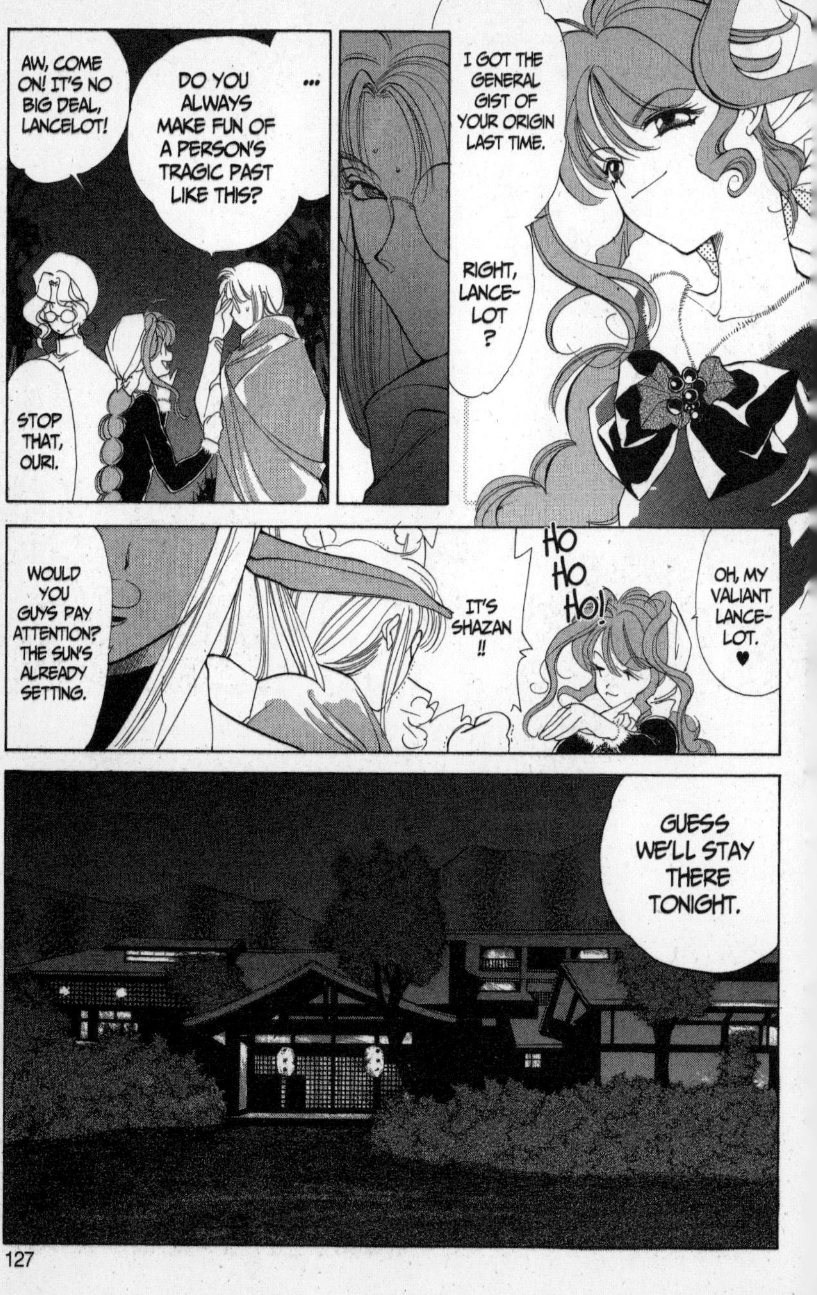
I GOT THE GENERAL GIST OF YOUR ORIGIN LAST TIME.
RIGHT, LANCE-LOT?
...
DO YOU ALWAYS MAKE FUN OF A PERSON'S TRAGIC PAST LIKE THIS?
AW, COME ON! IT'S NO BIG DEAL, LANCELOT!
STOP THAT, OURI.
OH, MY VALIANT LANCE-LOT. ♥
HO HO HO!
IT'S SHAZAN !!
WOULD YOU GUYS PAY ATTENTION? THE SUN'S ALREADY SETTING.
GUESS WE'LL STAY THERE TONIGHT.

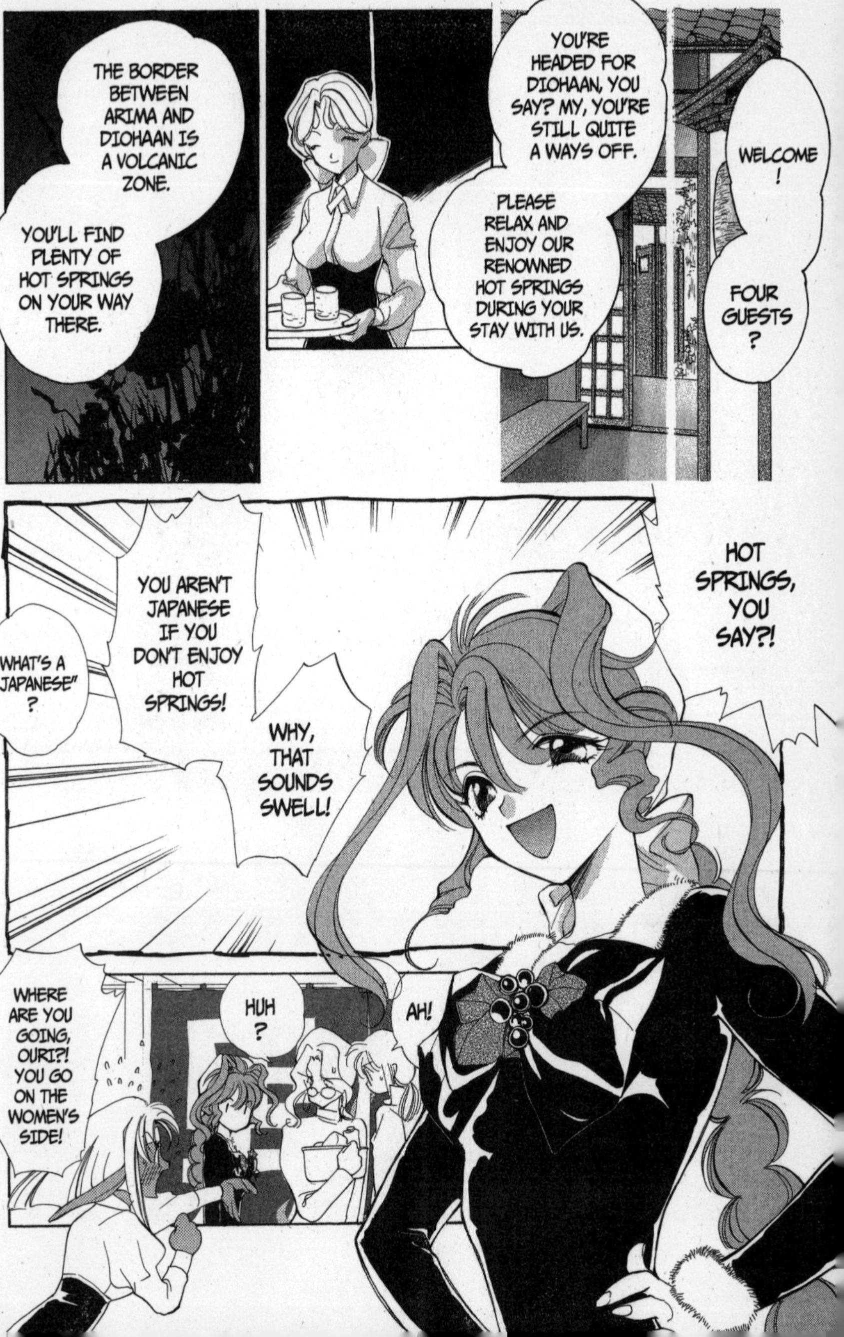
WELCOME!
FOUR GUESTS?
YOU'RE HEADED FOR DIOHAAN, YOU SAY? MY, YOU'RE STILL QUITE A WAYS OFF.
PLEASE RELAX AND ENJOY OUR RENOWNED HOT SPRINGS DURING YOUR STAY WITH US.
THE BORDER BETWEEN ARIMA AND DIOHAAN IS A VOLCANIC ZONE.
YOU'LL FIND PLENTY OF HOT SPRINGS ON YOUR WAY THERE.
HOT SPRINGS, YOU SAY?!
WHY, THAT SOUNDS SWELL!
YOU AREN'T JAPANESE IF YOU DON'T ENJOY HOT SPRINGS!
WHAT'S A "JAPANESE"?
AH!
HUH?
WHERE ARE YOU GOING, OURI?! YOU GO ON THE WOMEN'S SIDE!

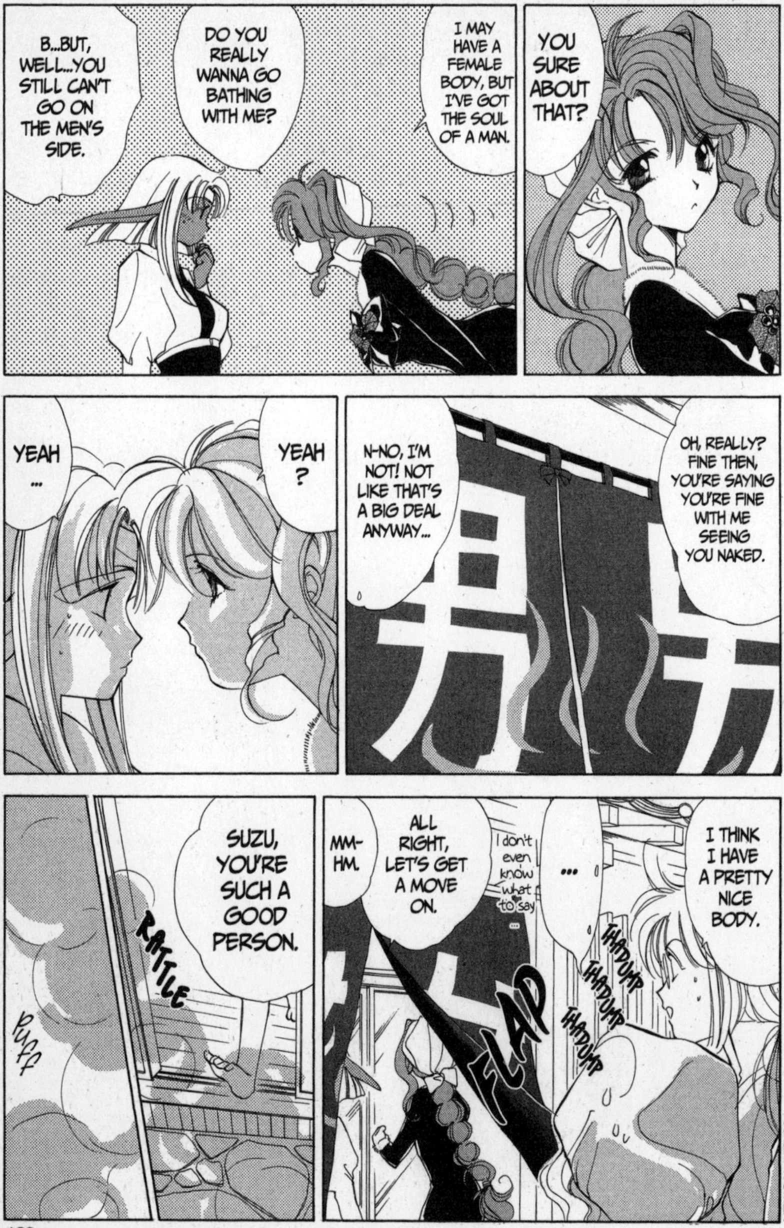
YOU SURE ABOUT THAT?
I MAY HAVE A FEMALE BODY, BUT I'VE GOT THE SOUL OF A MAN.
DO YOU REALLY WANNA GO BATHING WITH ME?
B...BUT, WELL...YOU STILL CAN'T GO ON THE MEN'S SIDE.
OH, REALLY? FINE THEN, YOU'RE SAYING YOU'RE FINE WITH ME SEEING YOU NAKED.
N-NO, I'M NOT! NOT LIKE THAT'S A BIG DEAL ANYWAY...
YEAH?
YEAH...
I THINK I HAVE A PRETTY NICE BODY.
...
I don't even know what to say...
THADUMP THADUMP THADUMP
ALL RIGHT, LET'S GET A MOVE ON.
MM-HM.
FLAP
SUZU, YOU'RE SUCH A GOOD PERSON.
RATTLE
PUFF

Curtain: 'MEN'

Curtain: 'WOMEN'

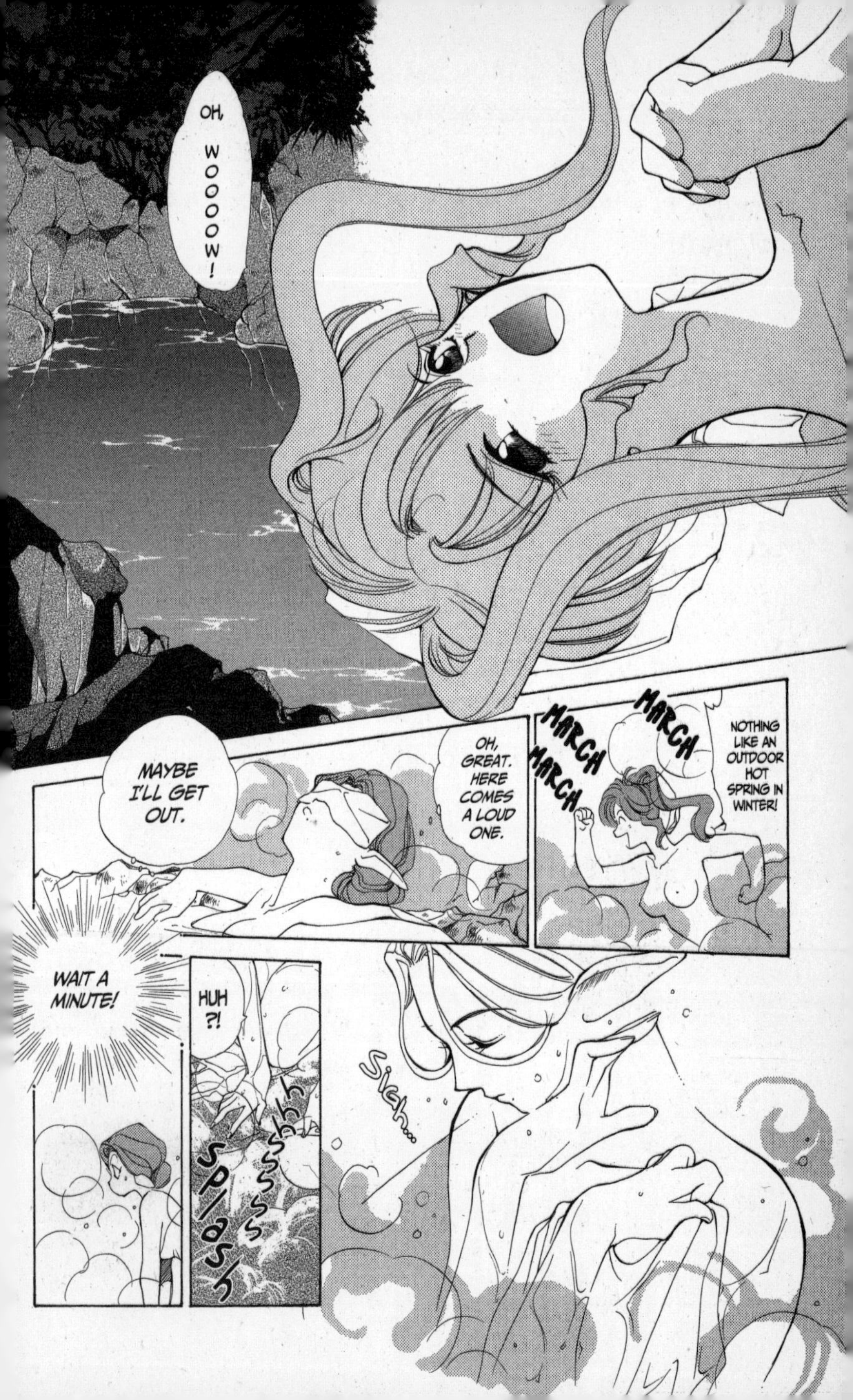
OH, WOOOOW!
MARCH MARCH MARCH
NOTHING LIKE AN OUTDOOR HOT SPRING IN WINTER!
OH, GREAT. HERE COMES A LOUD ONE.
MAYBE I'LL GET OUT.
Sigh...
HUH ?!
SSSShhh
splash
WAIT A MINUTE!

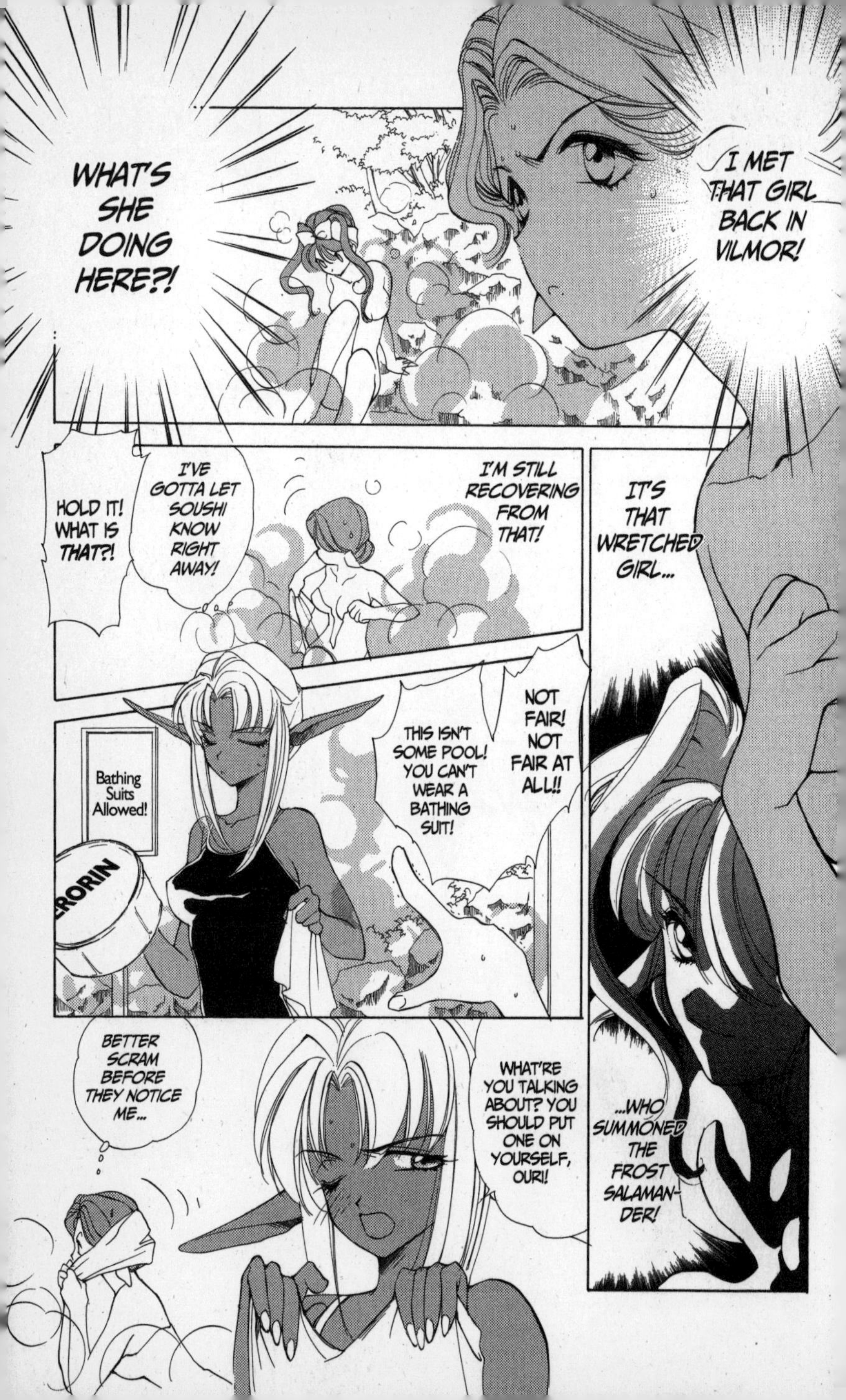
I MET THAT GIRL BACK IN VILMOR!
WHAT'S SHE DOING HERE?!
IT'S THAT WRETCHED GIRL...
...WHO SUMMONED THE FROST SALAMANDER!
I'M STILL RECOVERING FROM THAT!
I'VE GOTTA LET SOUSHI KNOW RIGHT AWAY!
HOLD IT! WHAT IS THAT?!
NOT FAIR! NOT FAIR AT ALL!!
THIS ISN'T SOME POOL! YOU CAN'T WEAR A BATHING SUIT!
Bathing Suits Allowed!
ERORIN
WHAT'RE YOU TALKING ABOUT? YOU SHOULD PUT ONE ON YOURSELF, OURI!
BETTER SCRAM BEFORE THEY NOTICE ME...

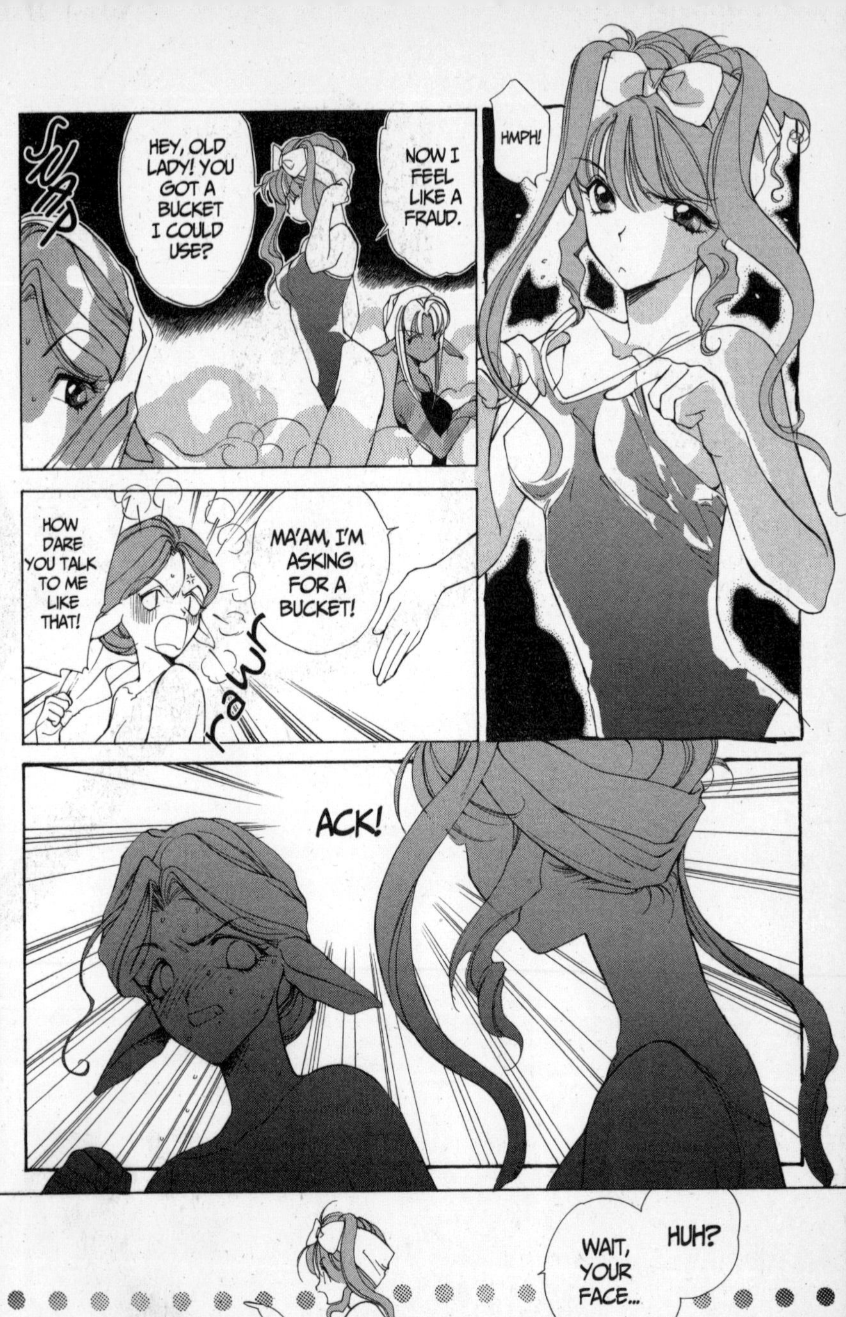
HMPH!
NOW I FEEL LIKE A FRAUD.
HEY, OLD LADY! YOU GOT A BUCKET I COULD USE?
SLAP
MA'AM, I'M ASKING FOR A BUCKET!
HOW DARE YOU TALK TO ME LIKE THAT!
rawr
ACK!
HUH?
WAIT, YOUR FACE...

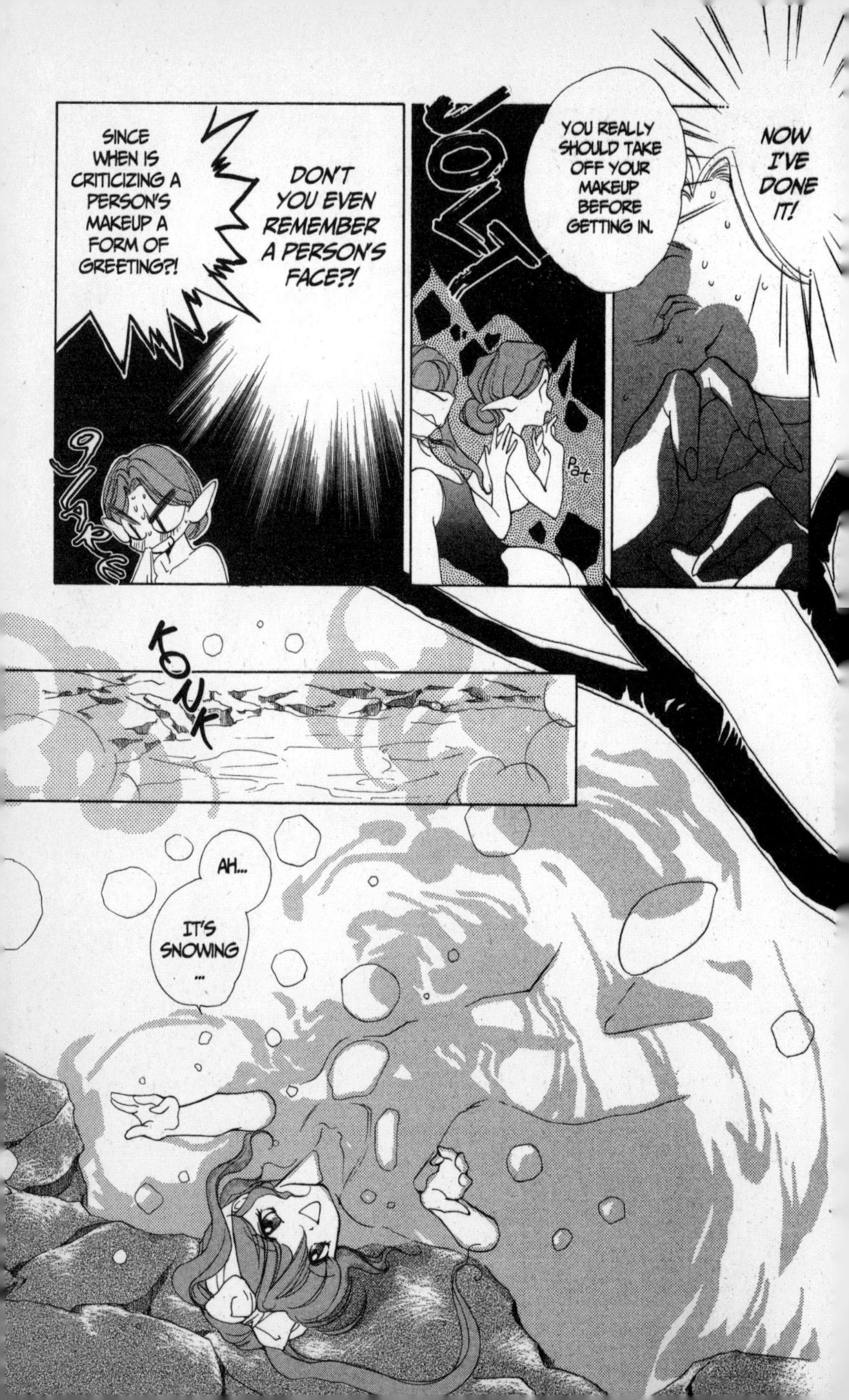
NOW I'VE DONE IT!
YOU REALLY SHOULD TAKE OFF YOUR MAKEUP BEFORE GETTING IN.
JOLT
Pat
DON'T YOU EVEN REMEMBER A PERSON'S FACE?!
SINCE WHEN IS CRITICIZING A PERSON'S MAKEUP A FORM OF GREETING?!
GLARE
KONK
AH...
IT'S SNOWING ...

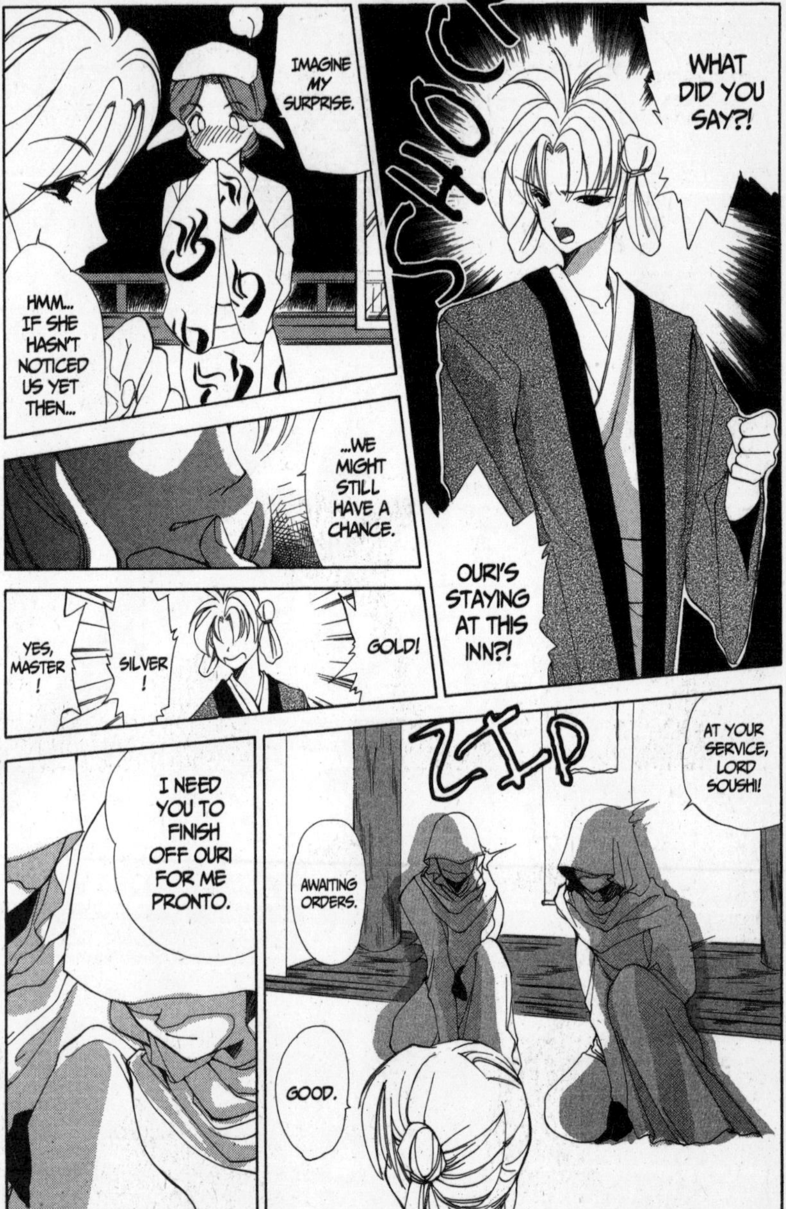
SHOCK
WHAT DID YOU SAY?!
OURI'S STAYING AT THIS INN?!
IMAGINE MY SURPRISE.
HMM... IF SHE HASN'T NOTICED US YET THEN...
...WE MIGHT STILL HAVE A CHANCE.
GOLD!
SILVER!
YES, MASTER!
ZIP
AT YOUR SERVICE, LORD SOUSHI!
AWAITING ORDERS.
GOOD.
I NEED YOU TO FINISH OFF OURI FOR ME PRONTO.

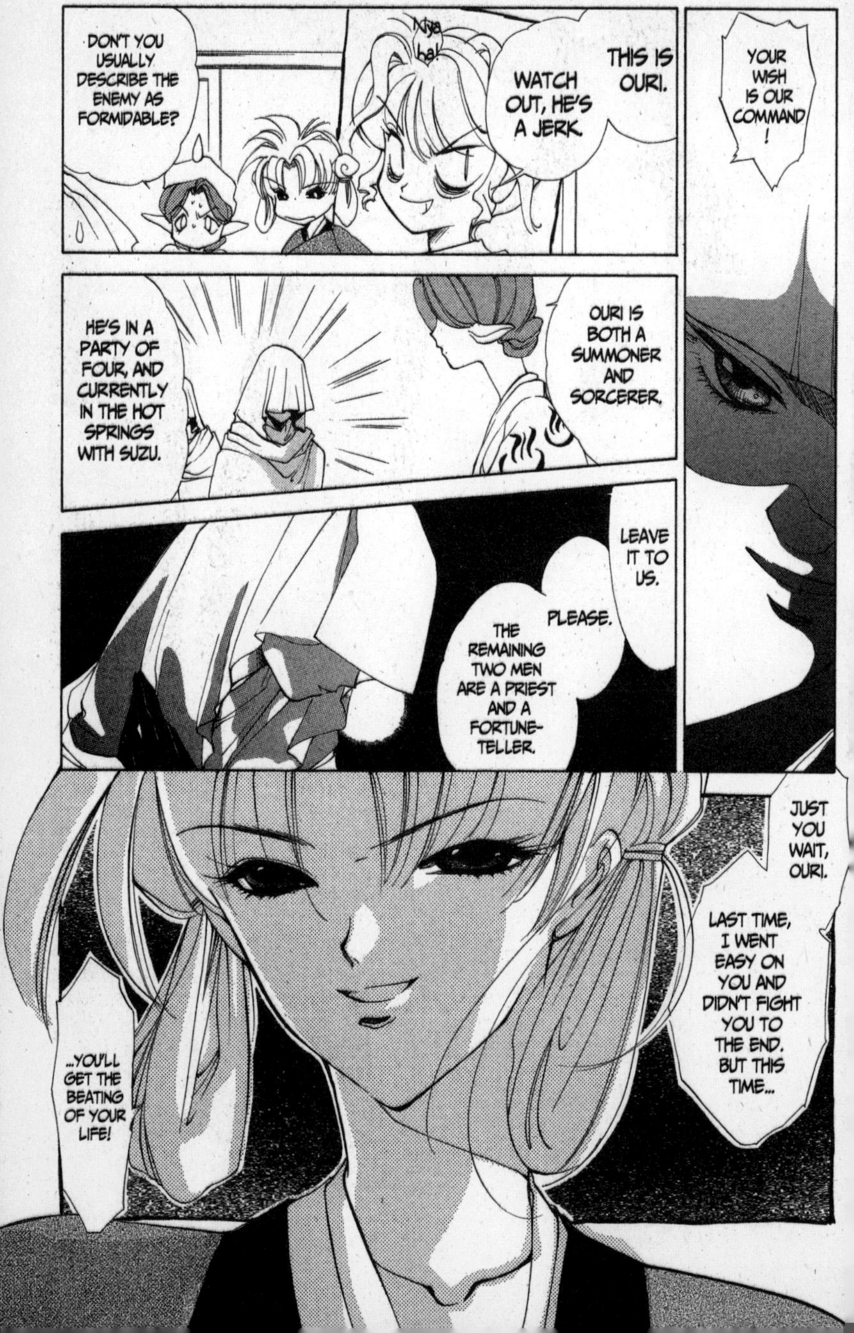
YOUR WISH IS OUR COMMAND!
THIS IS OURI.
WATCH OUT, HE'S A JERK.
Nya ha!
DON'T YOU USUALLY DESCRIBE THE ENEMY AS FORMIDABLE?
OURI IS BOTH A SUMMONER AND SORCERER.
HE'S IN A PARTY OF FOUR, AND CURRENTLY IN THE HOT SPRINGS WITH SUZU.
LEAVE IT TO US.
PLEASE.
THE REMAINING TWO MEN ARE A PRIEST AND A FORTUNE-TELLER.
JUST YOU WAIT, OURI.
LAST TIME, I WENT EASY ON YOU AND DIDN'T FIGHT YOU TO THE END. BUT THIS TIME...
...YOU'LL GET THE BEATING OF YOUR LIFE!

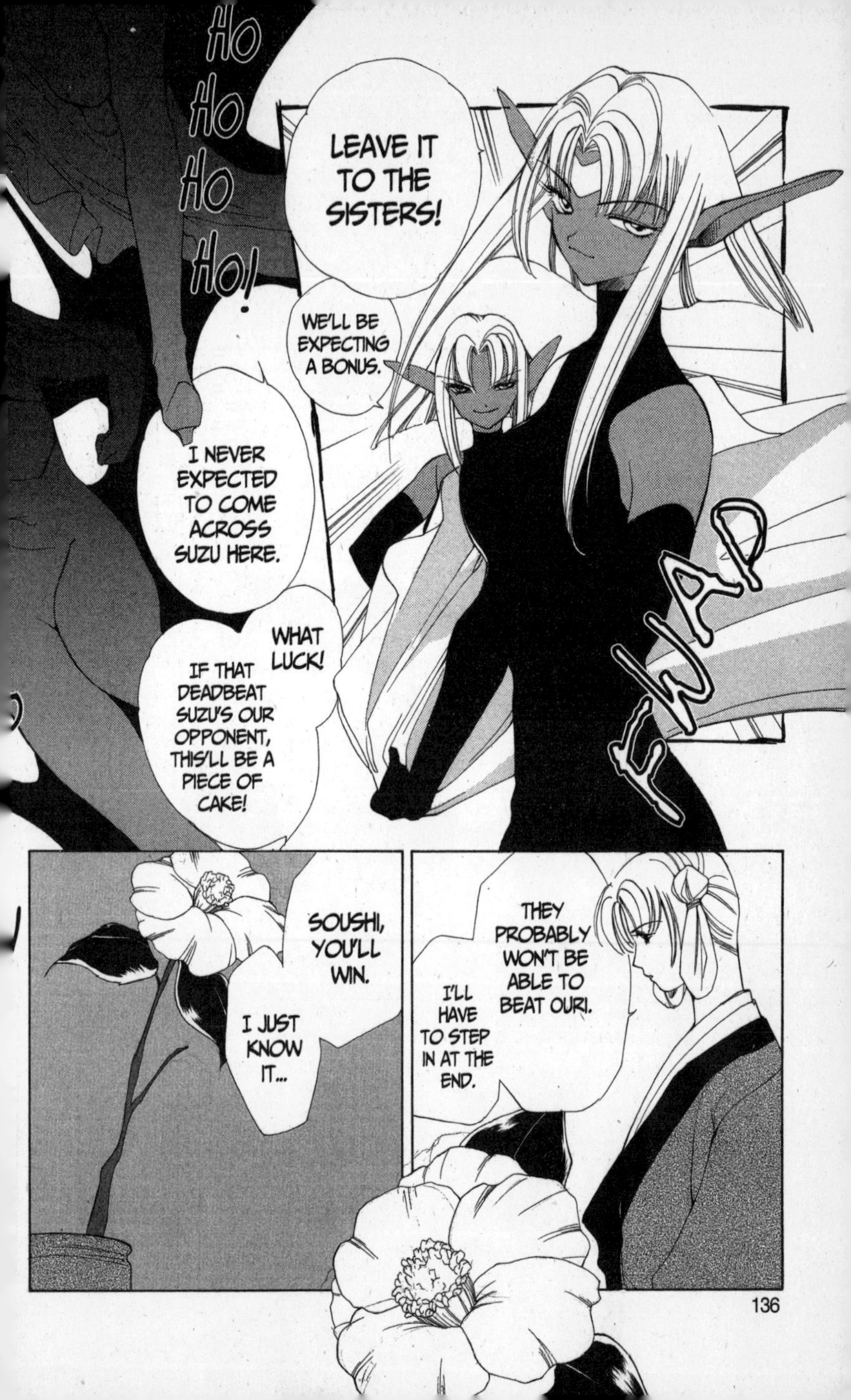
LEAVE IT TO THE SISTERS!
HO HO HO HO!
WE'LL BE EXPECTING A BONUS.
FWAP
I NEVER EXPECTED TO COME ACROSS SUZU HERE.
WHAT LUCK!
IF THAT DEADBEAT SUZU'S OUR OPPONENT, THIS'LL BE A PIECE OF CAKE!
THEY PROBABLY WON'T BE ABLE TO BEAT OURI.
I'LL HAVE TO STEP IN AT THE END.
SOUSHI, YOU'LL WIN.
I JUST KNOW IT...

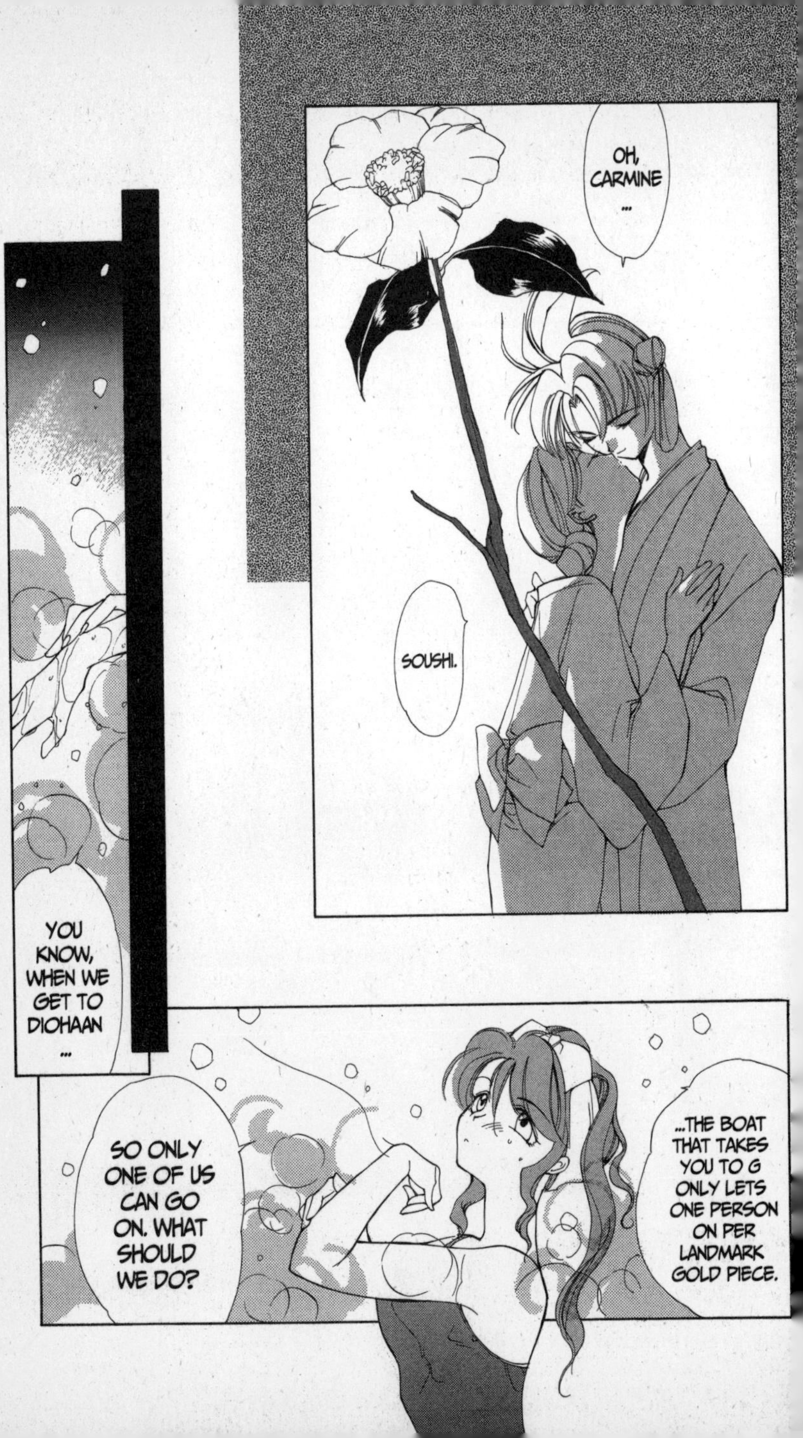
OH, CARMINE ...
SOUSHI.
YOU KNOW, WHEN WE GET TO DIOHAAN ...
...THE BOAT THAT TAKES YOU TO G ONLY LETS ONE PERSON ON PER LANDMARK GOLD PIECE.
SO ONLY ONE OF US CAN GO ON. WHAT SHOULD WE DO?

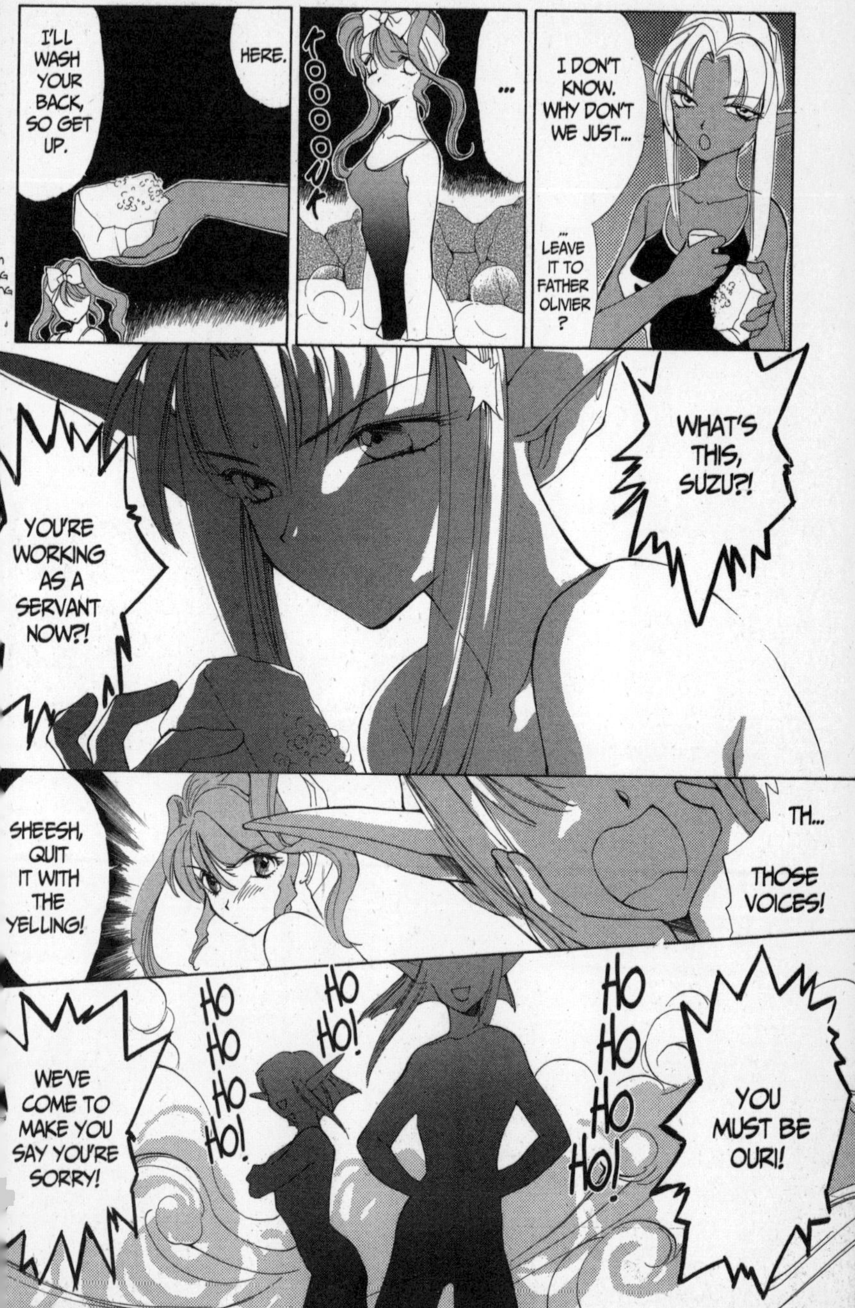
I DON'T KNOW. WHY DON'T WE JUST...
... LEAVE IT TO FATHER OLIVIER?
...
HERE.
I'LL WASH YOUR BACK, SO GET UP.
WHAT'S THIS, SUZU?!
YOU'RE WORKING AS A SERVANT NOW?!
TH...
THOSE VOICES!
SHEESH, QUIT IT WITH THE YELLING!
YOU MUST BE OURI!
HO HO HO HO HO!
HO HO!
HO HO HO HO!
WE'VE COME TO MAKE YOU SAY YOU'RE SORRY!

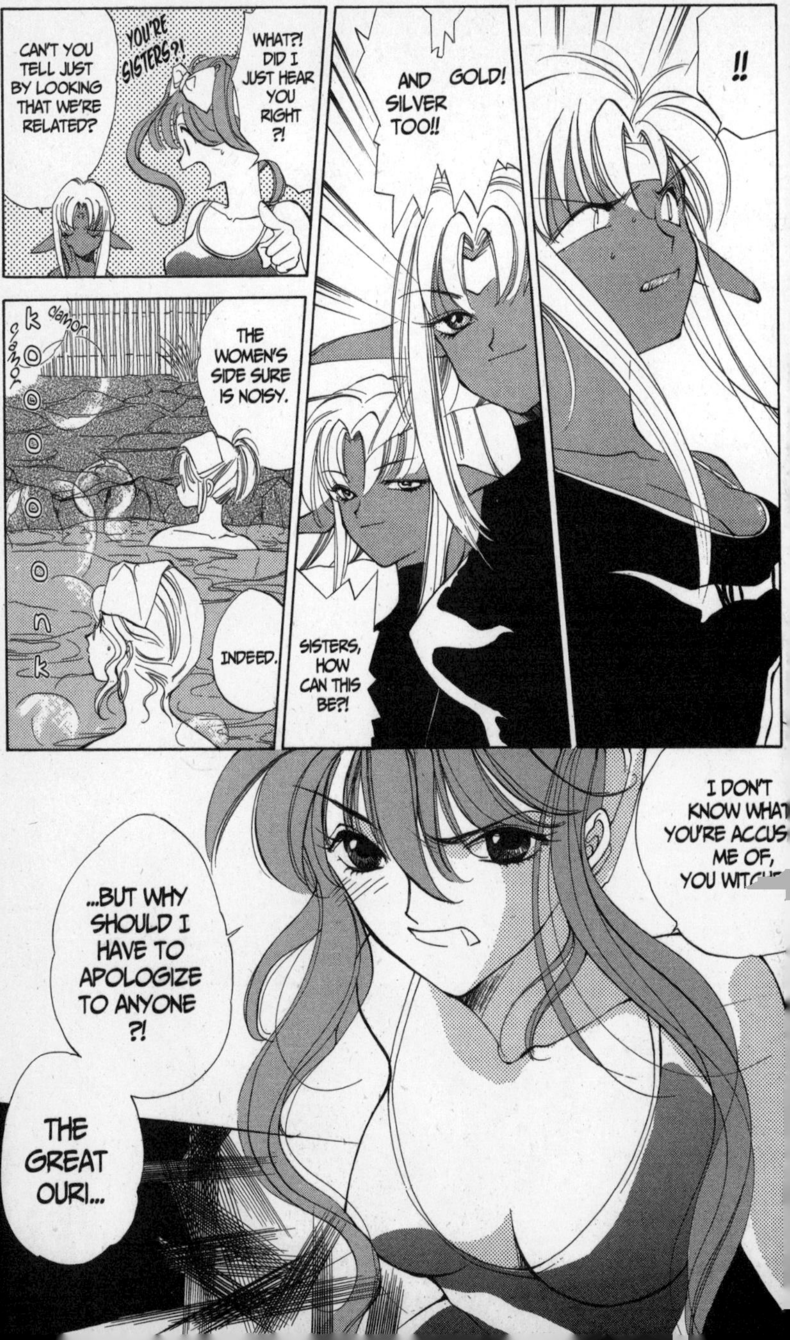
!!
GOLD!
AND SILVER TOO!!
SISTERS, HOW CAN THIS BE?!
WHAT?! DID I JUST HEAR YOU RIGHT ?!
YOU'RE SISTERS?!
CAN'T YOU TELL JUST BY LOOKING THAT WE'RE RELATED?
clamor
clamor
kooooonk
THE WOMEN'S SIDE SURE IS NOISY.
INDEED.
I DON'T KNOW WHAT YOU'RE ACCUS
ME OF,
YOU WITC
...BUT WHY SHOULD I HAVE TO APOLOGIZE TO ANYONE ?!
THE GREAT OURI...

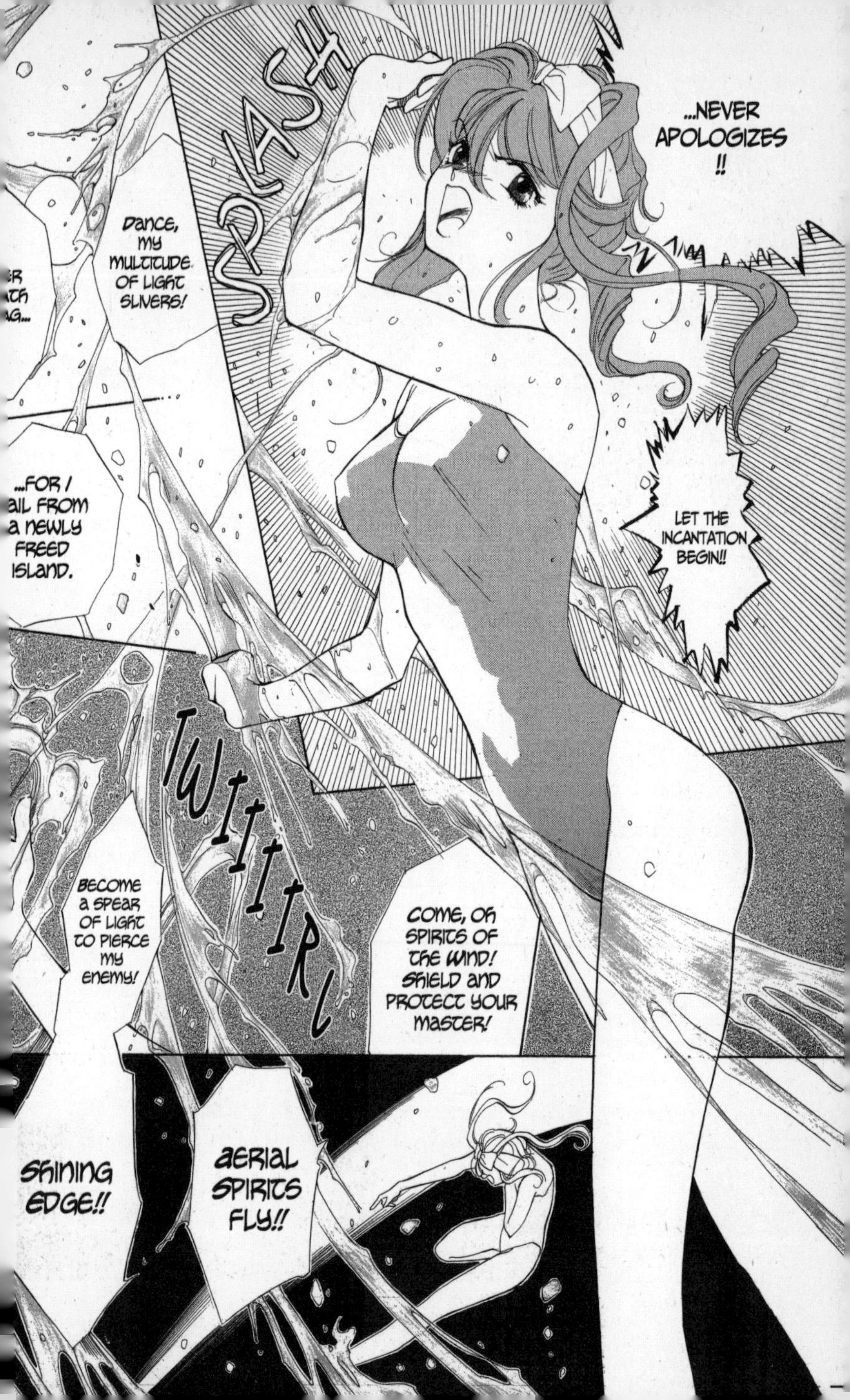

...NEVER APOLOGIZES!!
LET THE INCANTATION BEGIN!!
SPLASH
DANCE, MY MULTITUDE OF LIGHT SLIVERS!
...FOR I HAIL FROM A NEWLY FREED ISLAND.
COME, OH SPIRITS OF THE WIND! SHIELD AND PROTECT YOUR MASTER!
TWIIIIRL
BECOME A SPEAR OF LIGHT TO PIERCE MY ENEMY!
AERIAL SPIRITS FLY!!
SHINING EDGE!!

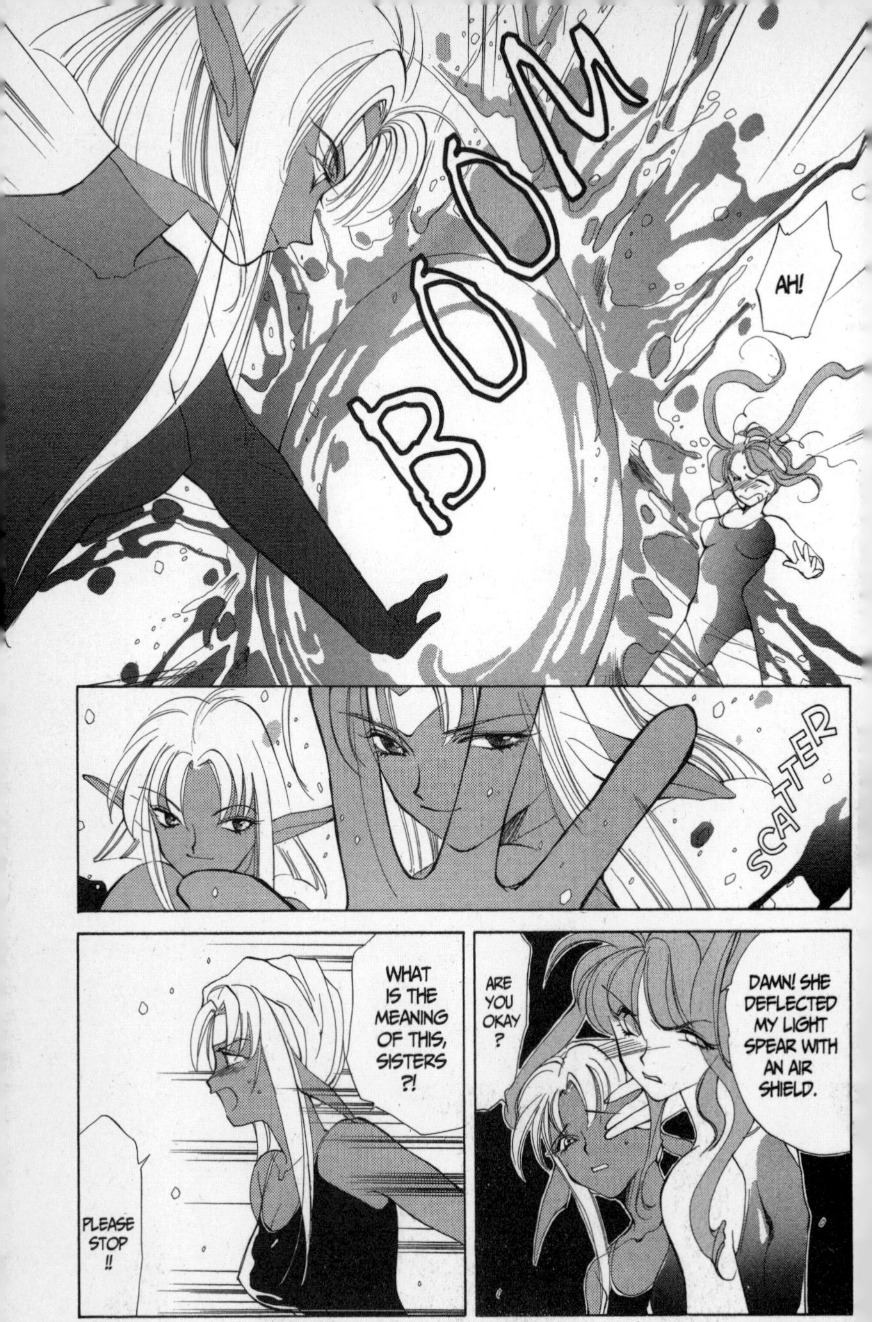
BOOM
AH!
SCATTER
DAMN! SHE DEFLECTED MY LIGHT SPEAR WITH AN AIR SHIELD.
ARE YOU OKAY?
WHAT IS THE MEANING OF THIS, SISTERS?!
PLEASE STOP!!

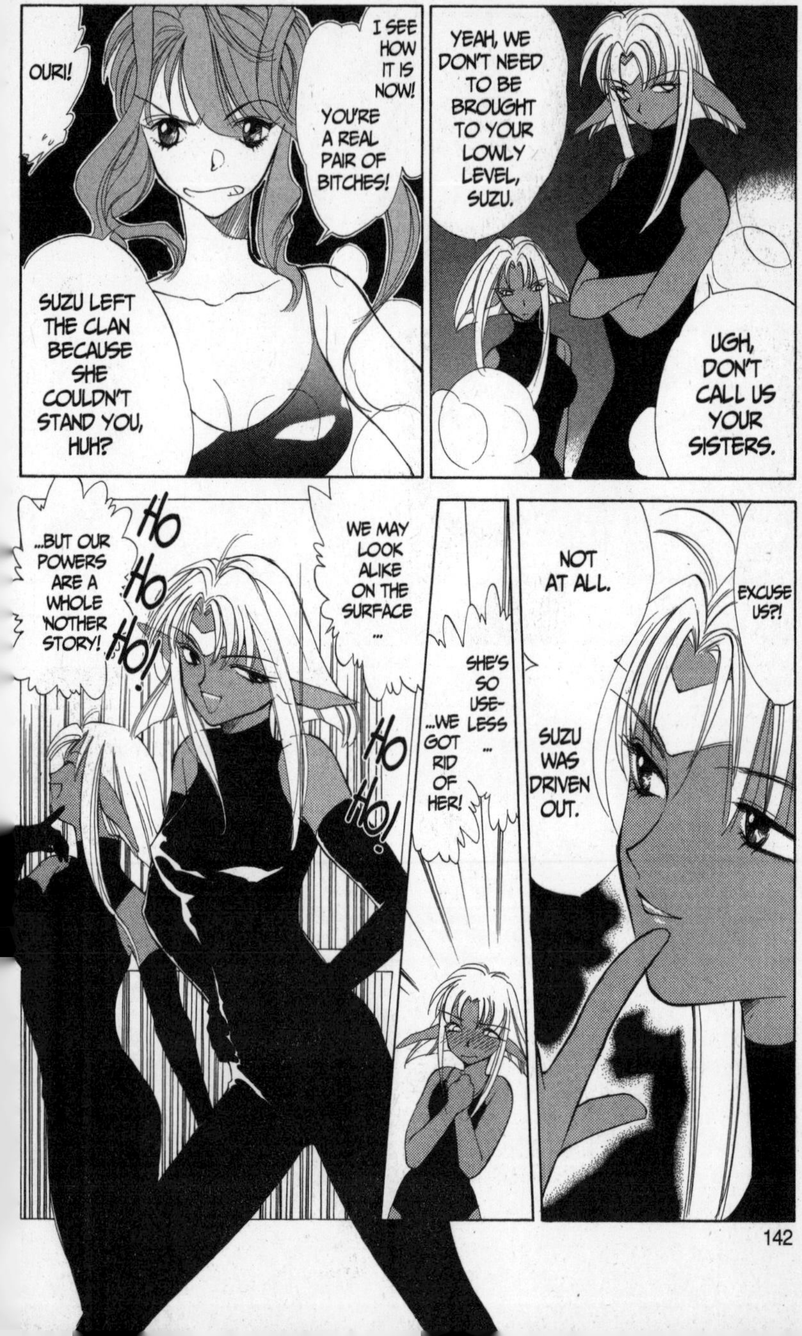
YEAH, WE DON'T NEED TO BE BROUGHT TO YOUR LOWLY LEVEL, SUZU.
UGH, DON'T CALL US YOUR SISTERS.
I SEE HOW IT IS NOW! YOU'RE A REAL PAIR OF BITCHES!
OURI!
SUZU LEFT THE CLAN BECAUSE SHE COULDN'T STAND YOU, HUH?
EXCUSE US?!
NOT AT ALL.
SUZU WAS DRIVEN OUT.
SHE'S SO USE-LESS...
...WE GOT RID OF HER!
WE MAY LOOK ALIKE ON THE SURFACE...
...BUT OUR POWERS ARE A WHOLE 'NOTHER STORY!
HO HO HO!
HO HO!

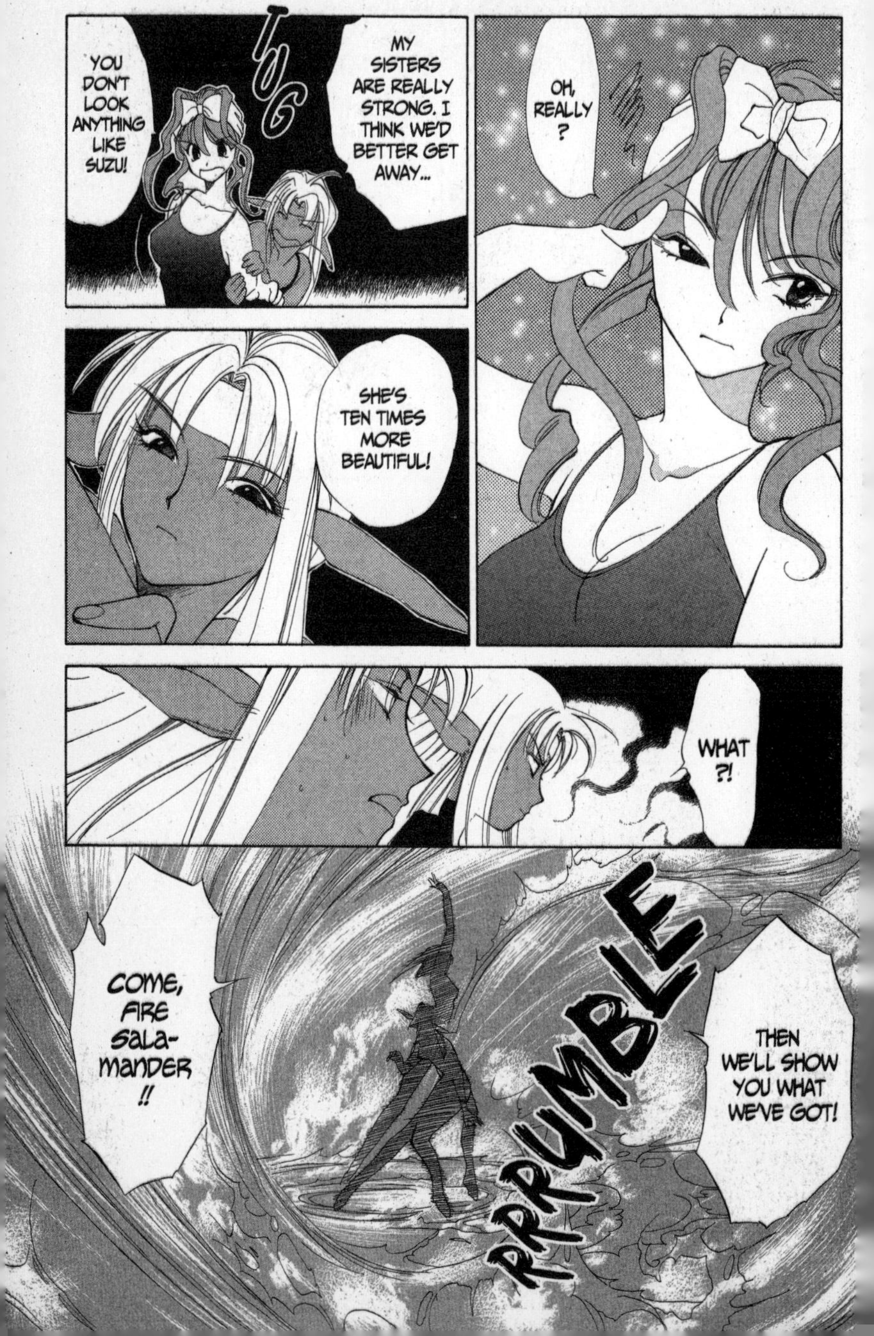
OH, REALLY ?
MY SISTERS ARE REALLY STRONG. I THINK WE'D BETTER GET AWAY...
YOU DON'T LOOK ANYTHING LIKE SUZU!
TUG
SHE'S TEN TIMES MORE BEAUTIFUL!
WHAT ?!
THEN WE'LL SHOW YOU WHAT WE'VE GOT!
RRRUMBLE
COME, FIRE Sala-mander !!

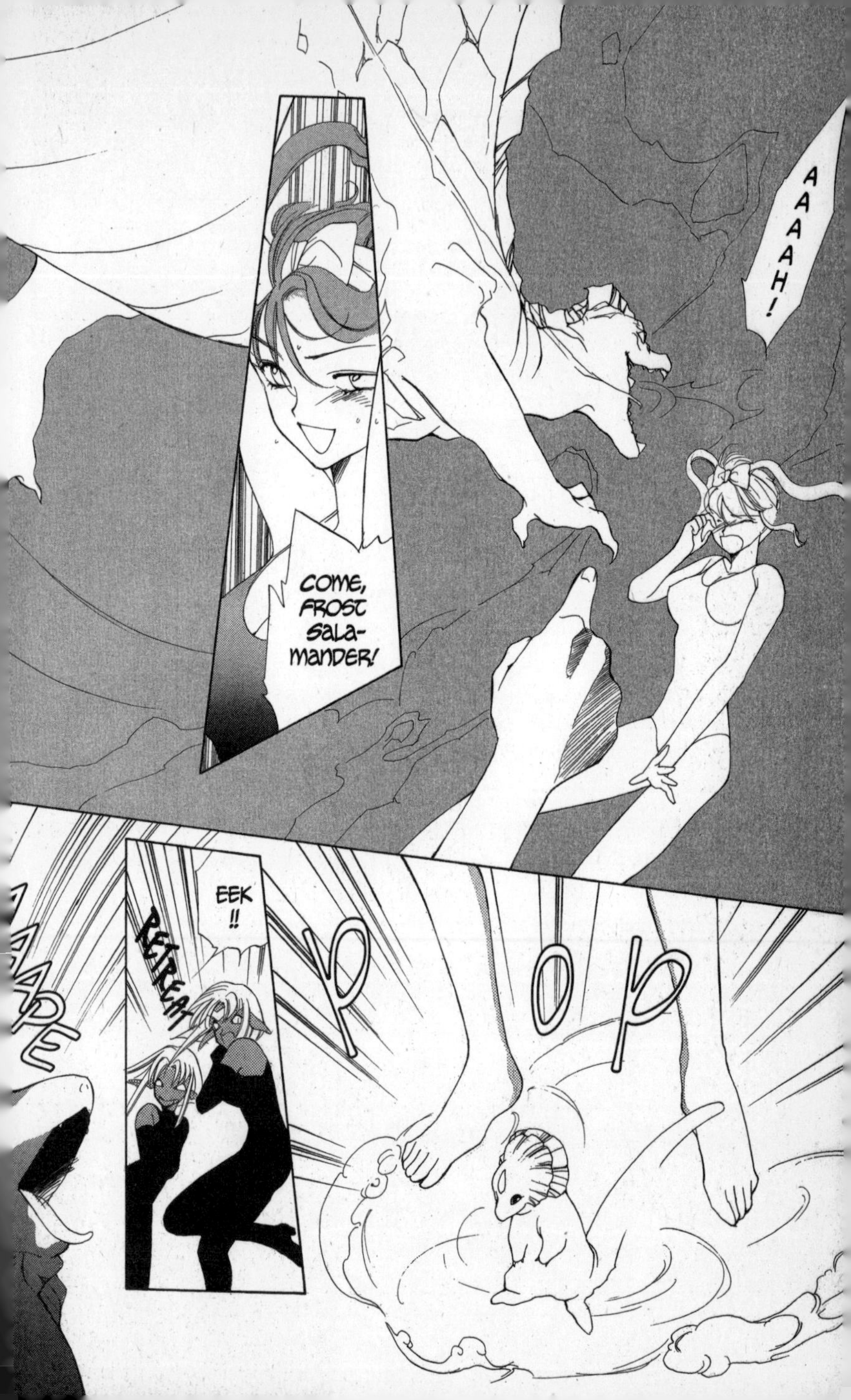
AAAAAH!
COME, FROST SALA-MANDER!
POP
EEK !!
RETREAT

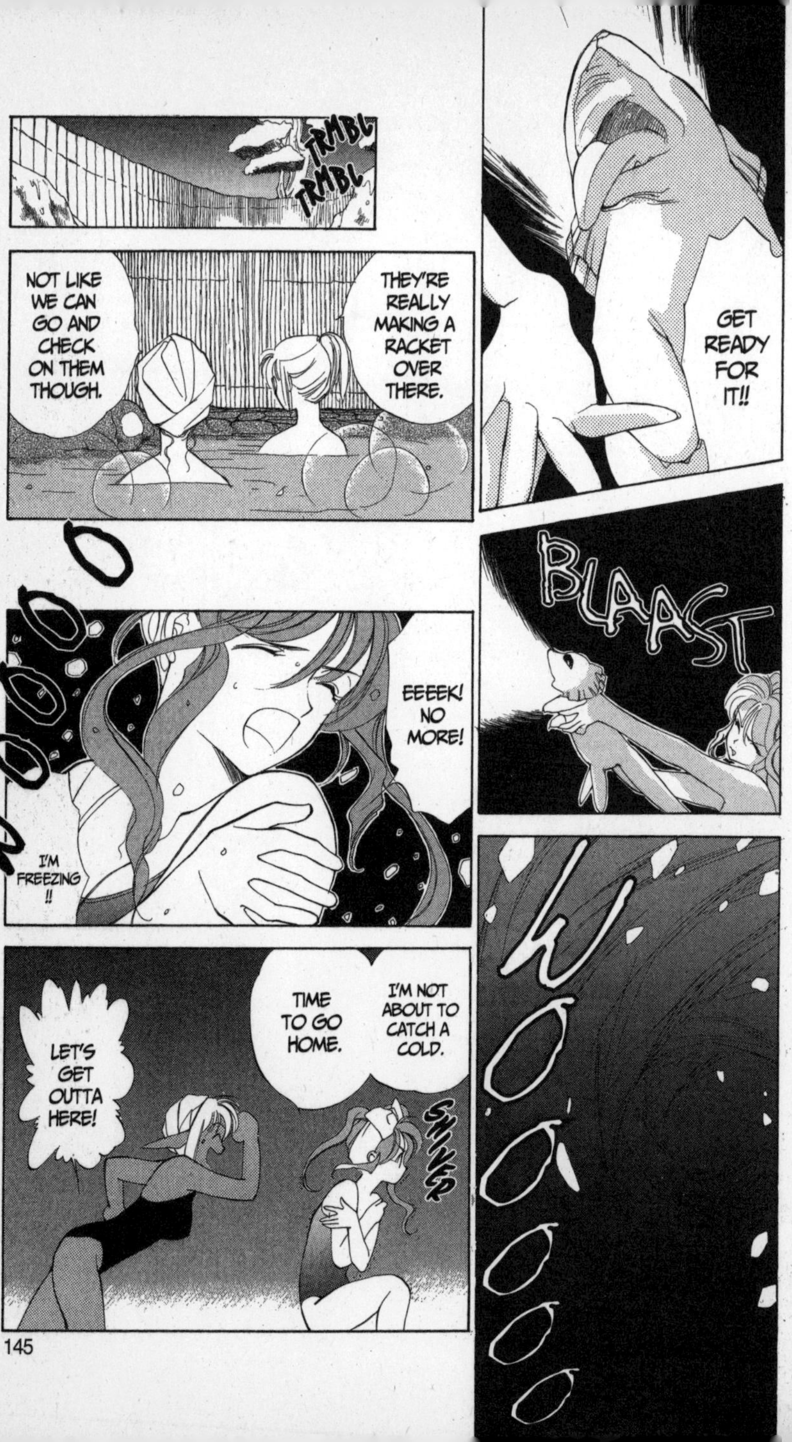
GET READY FOR IT!!
BLAAST
WOOOOOOOO
TRMBL TRMBL
THEY'RE REALLY MAKING A RACKET OVER THERE.
NOT LIKE WE CAN GO AND CHECK ON THEM THOUGH.
WOOOOOO
EEEEK! NO MORE!
I'M FREEZING !!
I'M NOT ABOUT TO CATCH A COLD.
TIME TO GO HOME.
SHIVER
LET'S GET OUTTA HERE!

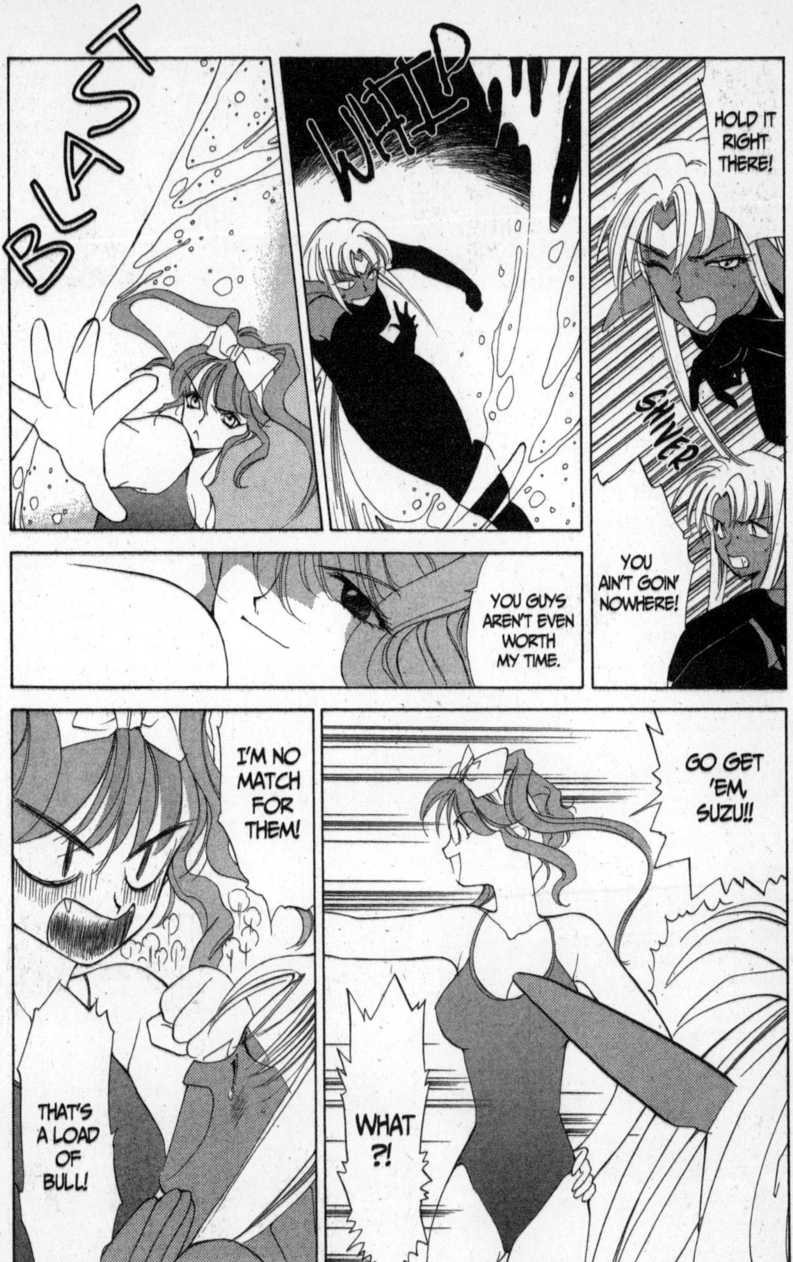
HOLD IT RIGHT THERE!
SHIVER
YOU AIN'T GOIN' NOWHERE!
WHIP
BLAST
YOU GUYS AREN'T EVEN WORTH MY TIME.
GO GET 'EM, SUZU!!
WHAT ?!
I'M NO MATCH FOR THEM!
THAT'S A LOAD OF BULL!

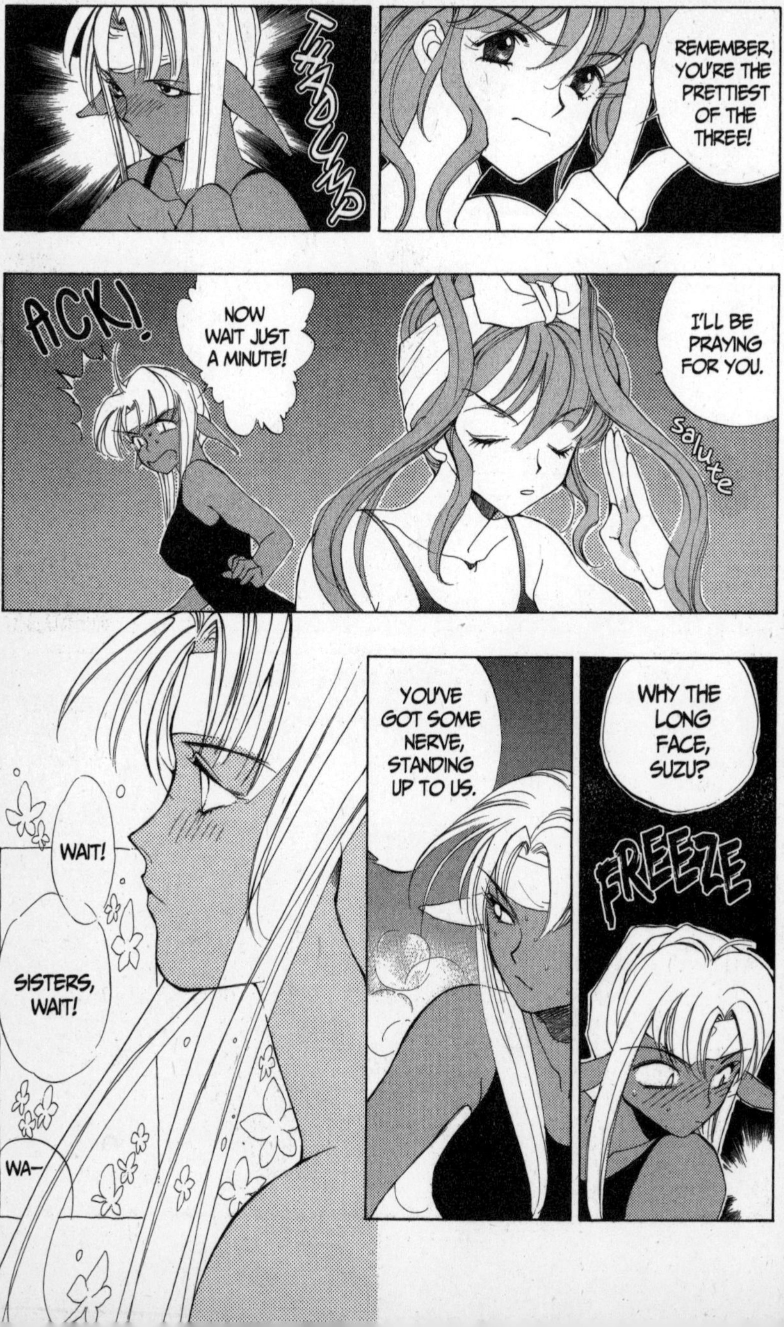
REMEMBER, YOU'RE THE PRETTIEST OF THE THREE!
THADUMP
I'LL BE PRAYING FOR YOU.
salute
NOW WAIT JUST A MINUTE!
ACK!
WHY THE LONG FACE, SUZU?
FREEZE
YOU'VE GOT SOME NERVE, STANDING UP TO US.
WAIT!
SISTERS, WAIT!
WA–

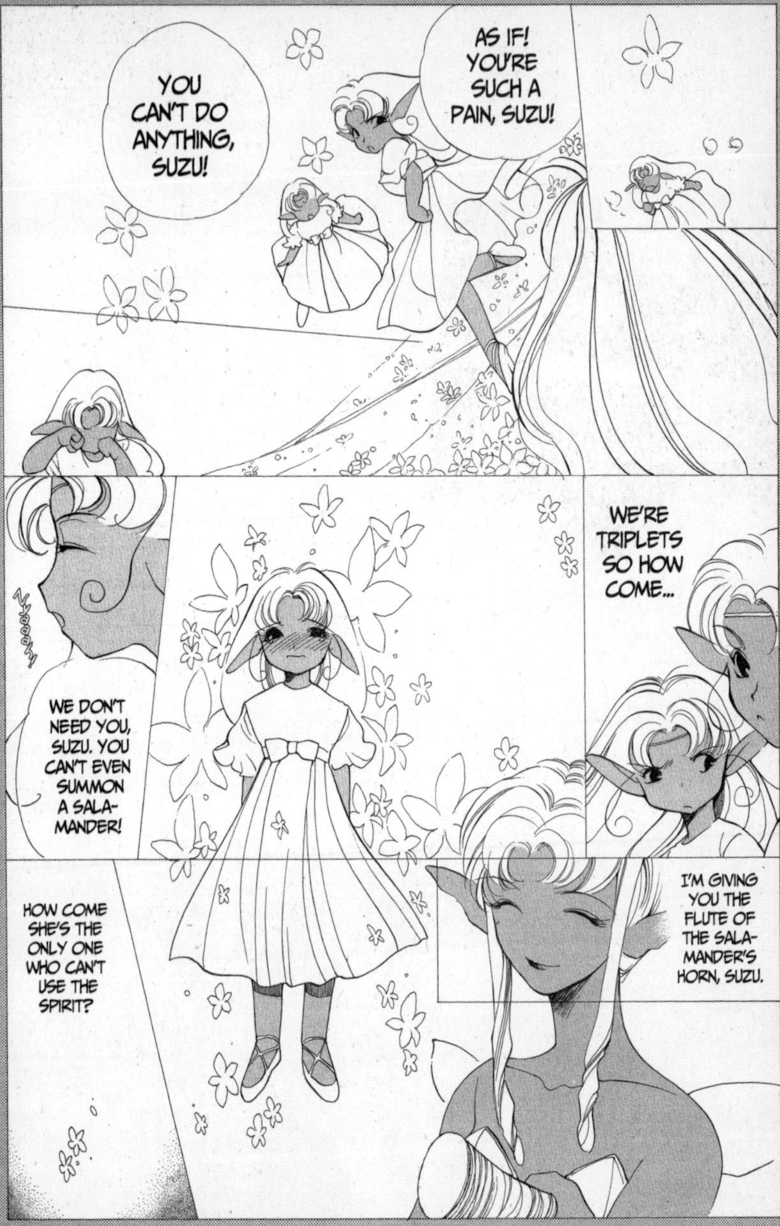
AS IF! YOU'RE SUCH A PAIN, SUZU!
YOU CAN'T DO ANYTHING, SUZU!
WE'RE TRIPLETS SO HOW COME...
WE DON'T NEED YOU, SUZU. YOU CAN'T EVEN SUMMON A SALA-MANDER!
Nyaah!
I'M GIVING YOU THE FLUTE OF THE SALA-MANDER'S HORN, SUZU.
HOW COME SHE'S THE ONLY ONE WHO CAN'T USE THE SPIRIT?

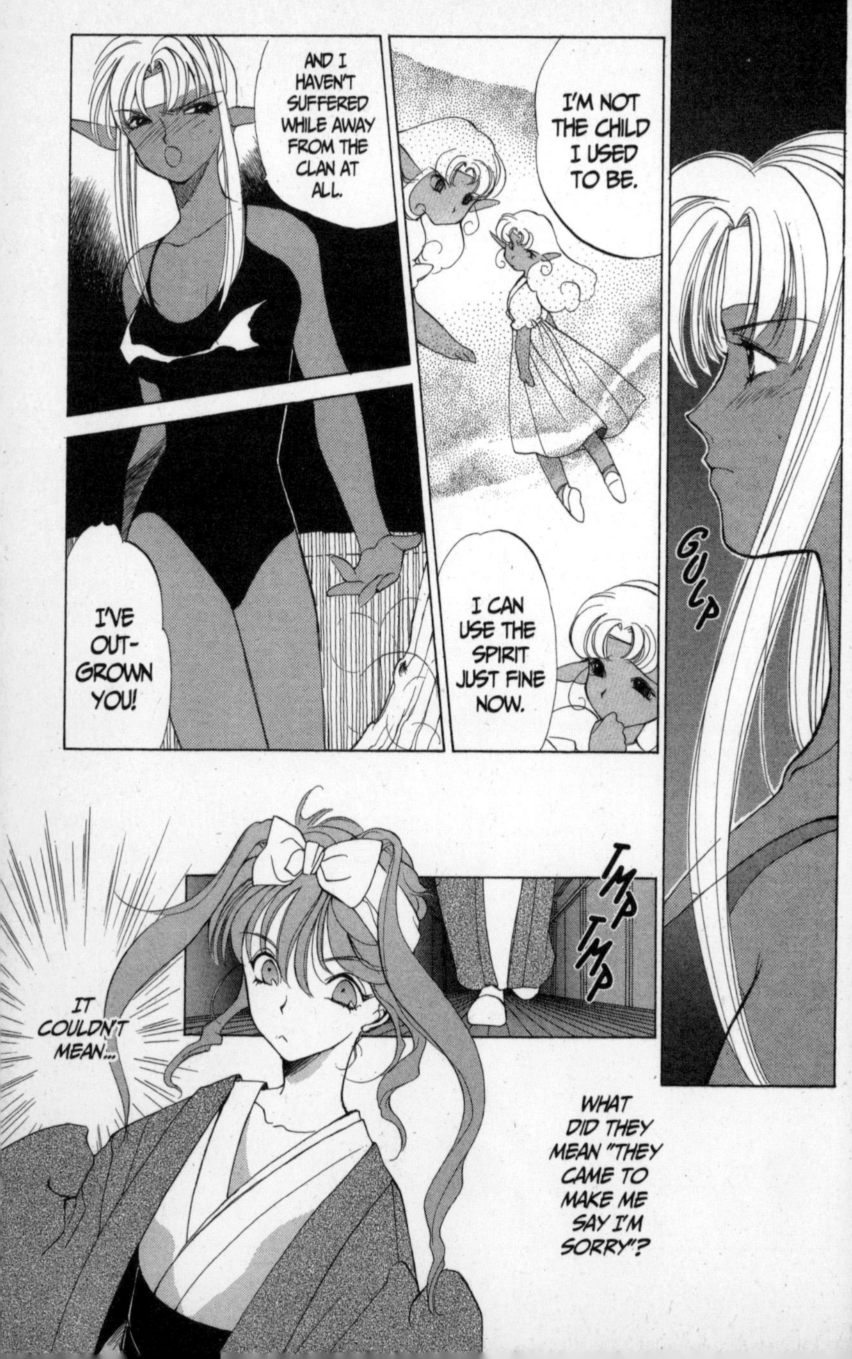
GULP
TMP TMP
I'M NOT THE CHILD I USED TO BE.
I CAN USE THE SPIRIT JUST FINE NOW.
AND I HAVEN'T SUFFERED WHILE AWAY FROM THE CLAN AT ALL.
I'VE OUT-GROWN YOU!
IT COULDN'T MEAN...
WHAT DID THEY MEAN "THEY CAME TO MAKE ME SAY I'M SORRY"?

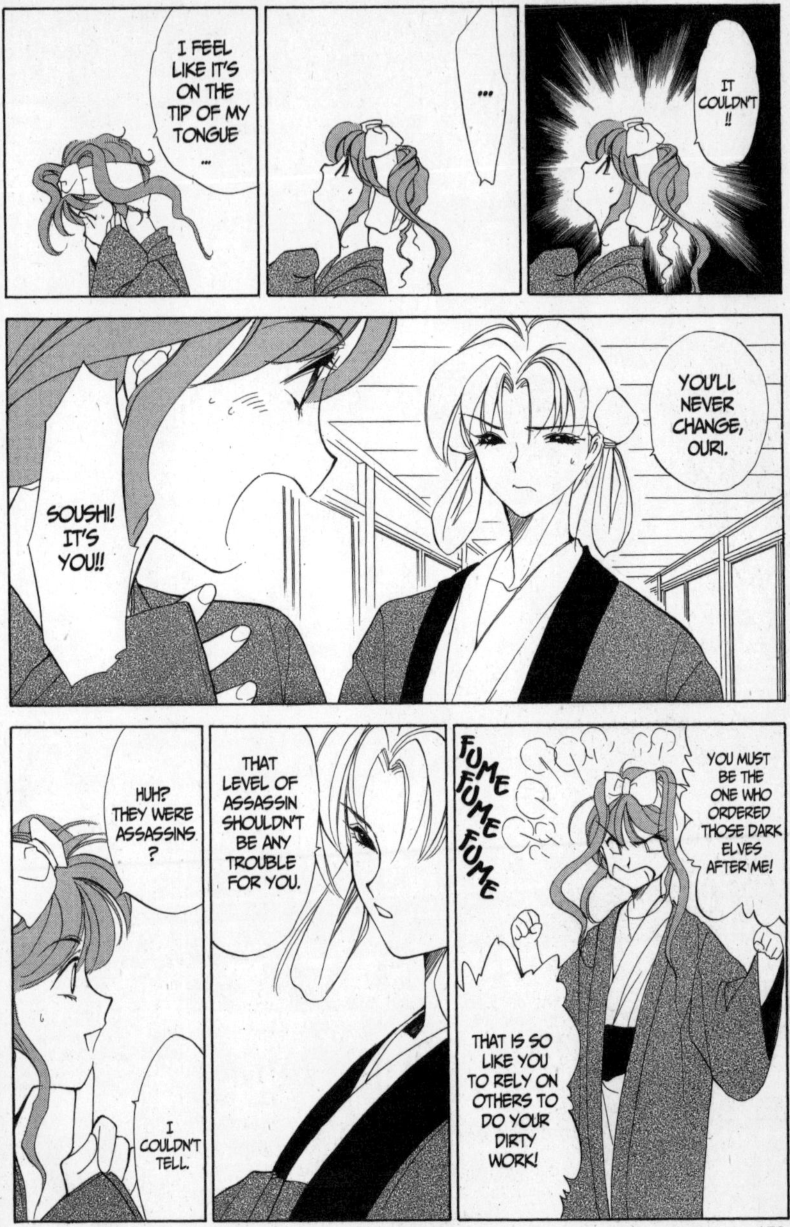
IT COULDN'T !!
...
I FEEL LIKE IT'S ON THE TIP OF MY TONGUE ...
YOU'LL NEVER CHANGE, OURI.
SOUSHI! IT'S YOU!!
YOU MUST BE THE ONE WHO ORDERED THOSE DARK ELVES AFTER ME!
FUME FUME FUME
THAT IS SO LIKE YOU TO RELY ON OTHERS TO DO YOUR DIRTY WORK!
THAT LEVEL OF ASSASSIN SHOULDN'T BE ANY TROUBLE FOR YOU.
HUH? THEY WERE ASSASSINS ?
I COULDN'T TELL.

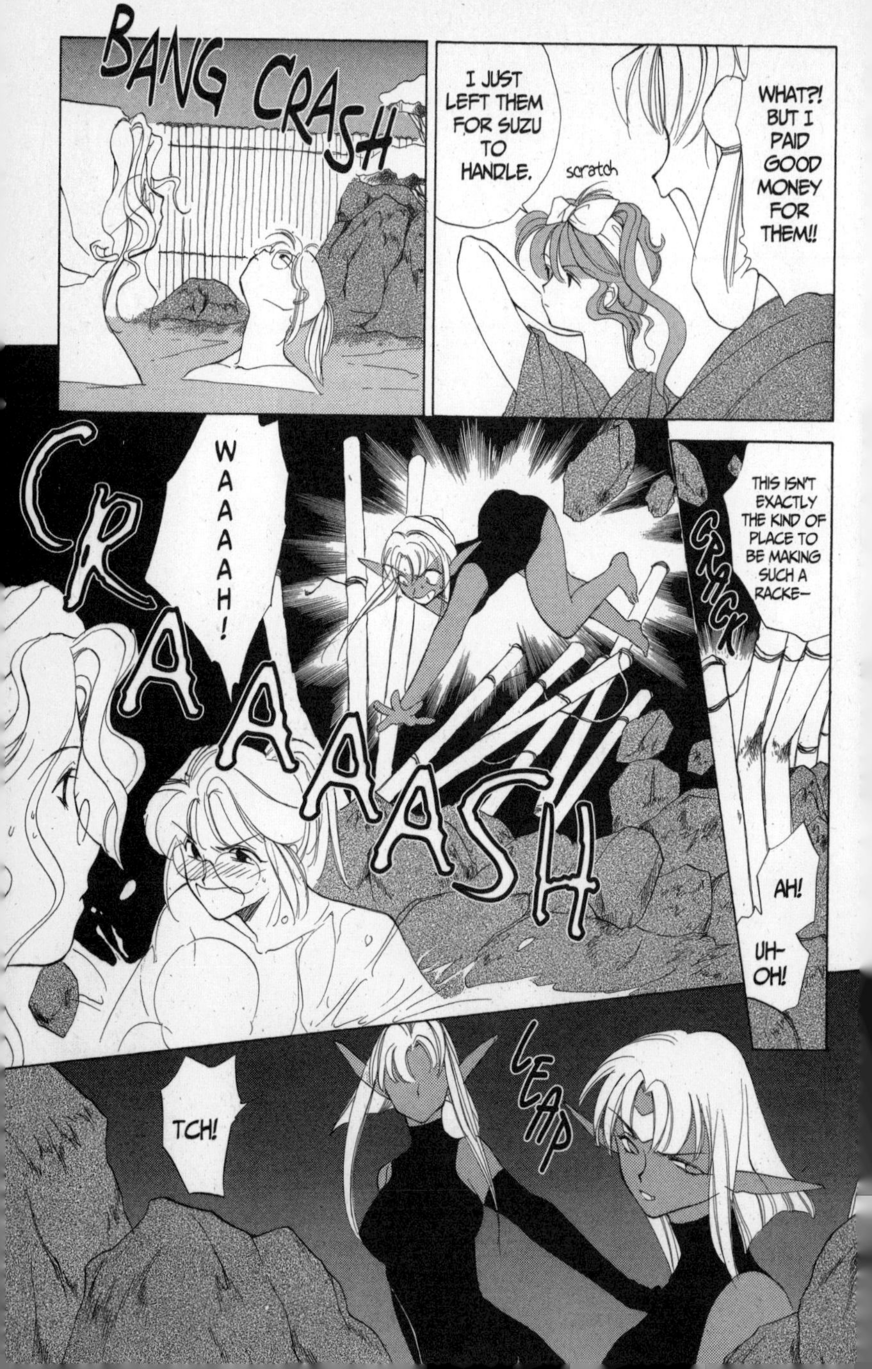
WHAT?! BUT I PAID GOOD MONEY FOR THEM!!
scratch
I JUST LEFT THEM FOR SUZU TO HANDLE.
BANG CRASH
THIS ISN'T EXACTLY THE KIND OF PLACE TO BE MAKING SUCH A RACKE—
CRACK
AH!
UH-OH!
WAAAAAH!
CRAAAASH
LEAP
TCH!

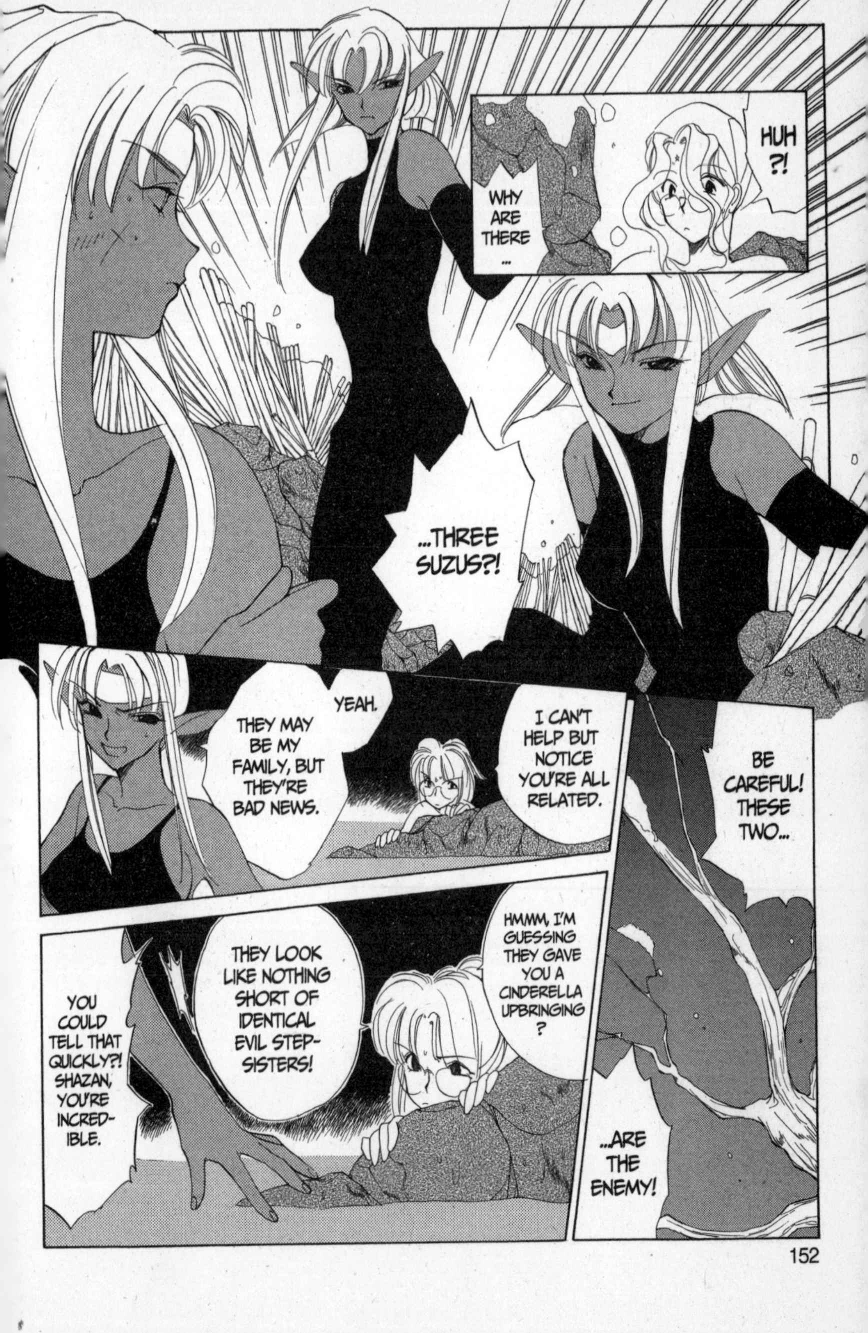
HUH ?!
WHY ARE THERE ...
...THREE SUZUS?!
BE CAREFUL! THESE TWO...
...ARE THE ENEMY!
I CAN'T HELP BUT NOTICE YOU'RE ALL RELATED.
YEAH.
THEY MAY BE MY FAMILY, BUT THEY'RE BAD NEWS.
HMMM, I'M GUESSING THEY GAVE YOU A CINDERELLA UPBRINGING ?
THEY LOOK LIKE NOTHING SHORT OF IDENTICAL EVIL STEP-SISTERS!
YOU COULD TELL THAT QUICKLY?! SHAZAN, YOU'RE INCRED-IBLE.

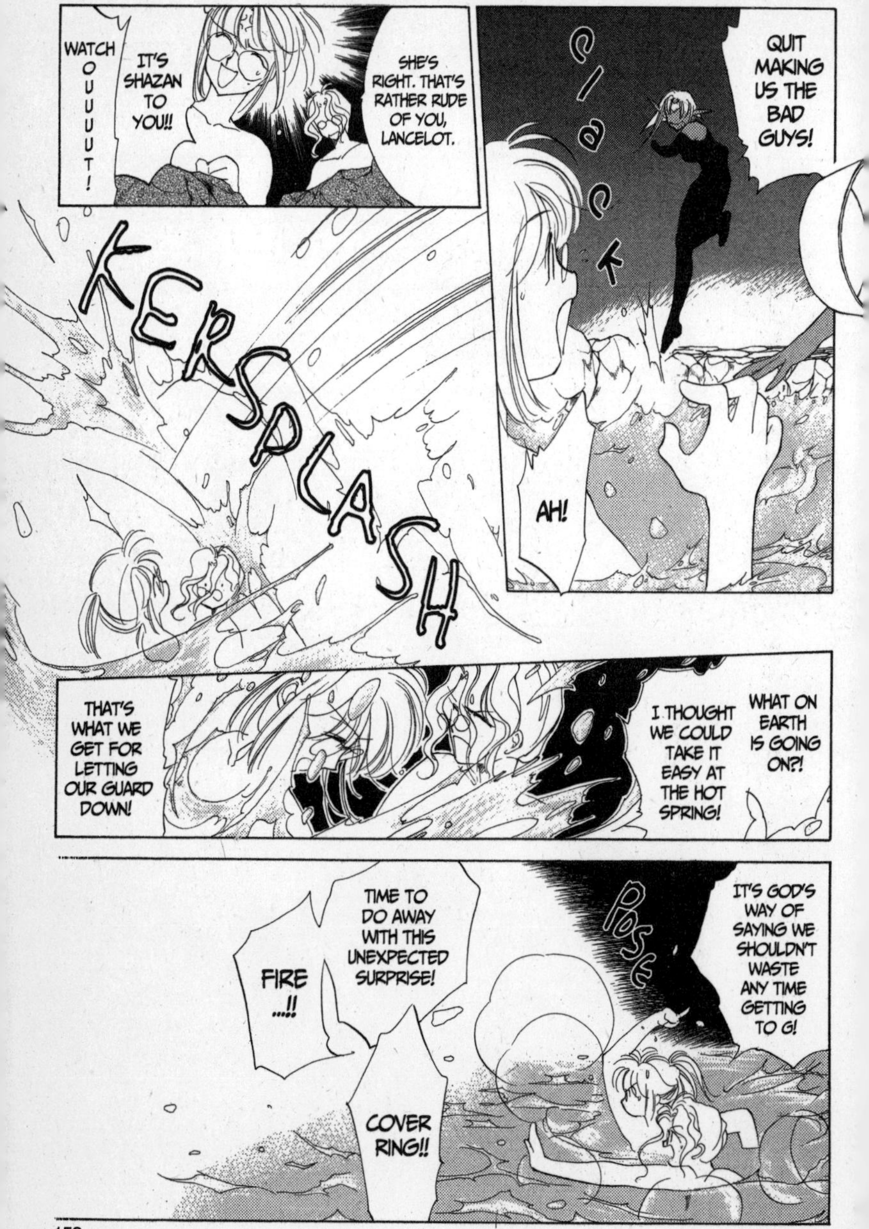
QUIT MAKING US THE BAD GUYS!
clack
AH!
SHE'S RIGHT. THAT'S RATHER RUDE OF YOU, LANCELOT.
IT'S SHAZAN TO YOU!!
WATCH OUUUUUT!
KERSPLASH
WHAT ON EARTH IS GOING ON?!
I THOUGHT WE COULD TAKE IT EASY AT THE HOT SPRING!
THAT'S WHAT WE GET FOR LETTING OUR GUARD DOWN!
IT'S GOD'S WAY OF SAYING WE SHOULDN'T WASTE ANY TIME GETTING TO G!
Pose
TIME TO DO AWAY WITH THIS UNEXPECTED SURPRISE!
FIRE ...!!
COVER RING!!

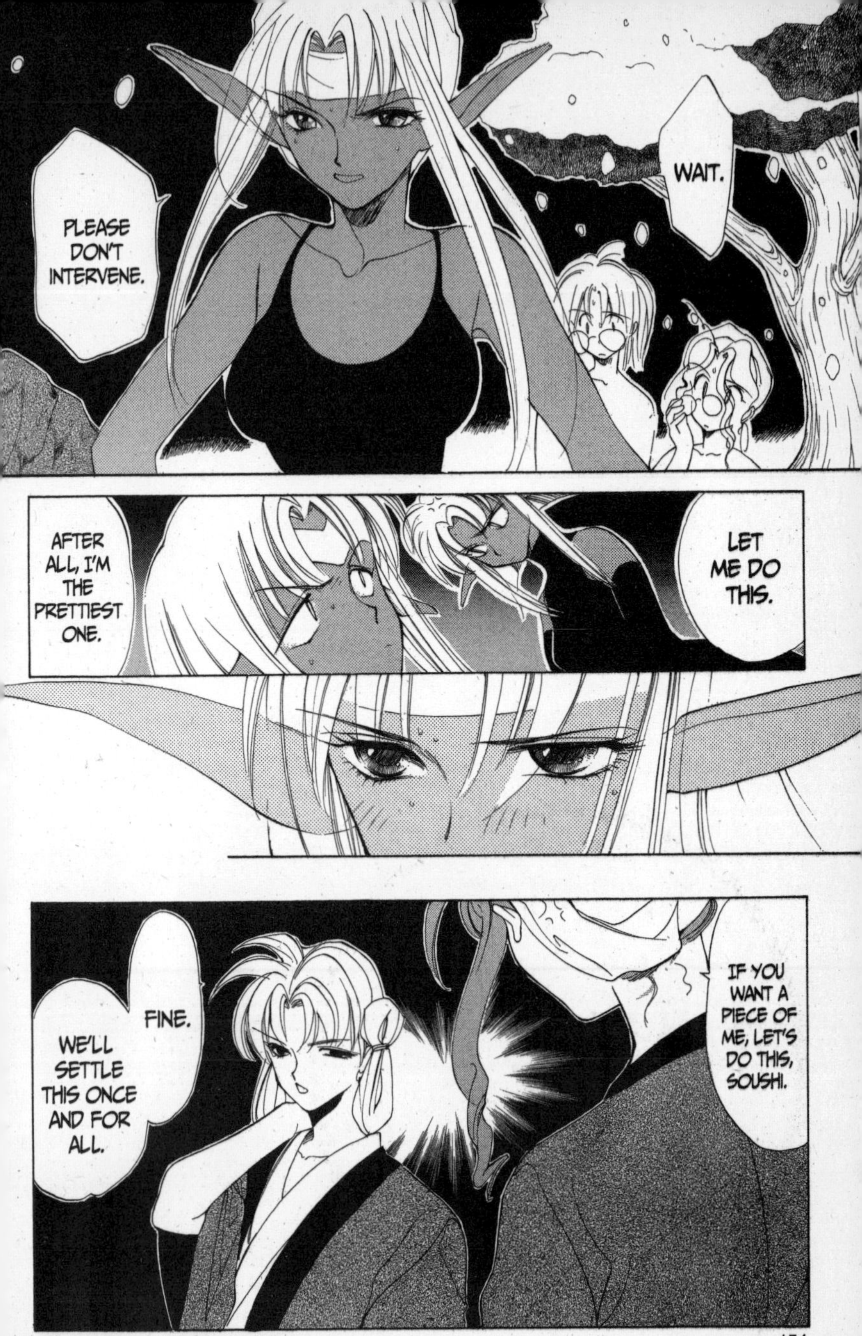
WAIT.
PLEASE DON'T INTERVENE.
LET ME DO THIS.
AFTER ALL, I'M THE PRETTIEST ONE.
IF YOU WANT A PIECE OF ME, LET'S DO THIS, SOUSHI.
FINE.
WE'LL SETTLE THIS ONCE AND FOR ALL.

Gestalt 2 / THE END

GESTALT

Character Designs

By any other names: Sketches

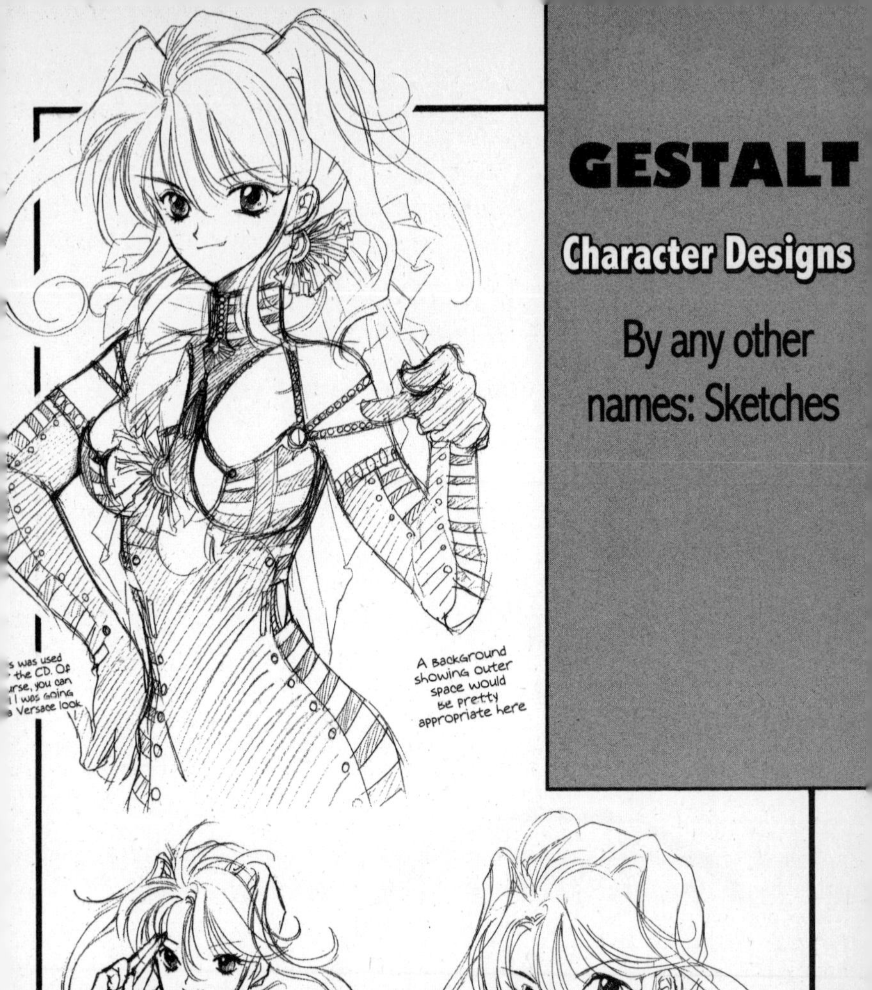

s was used
the CD. Of
urse, you can
l I was going
a Versace look
A background showing outer space would be pretty appropriate here

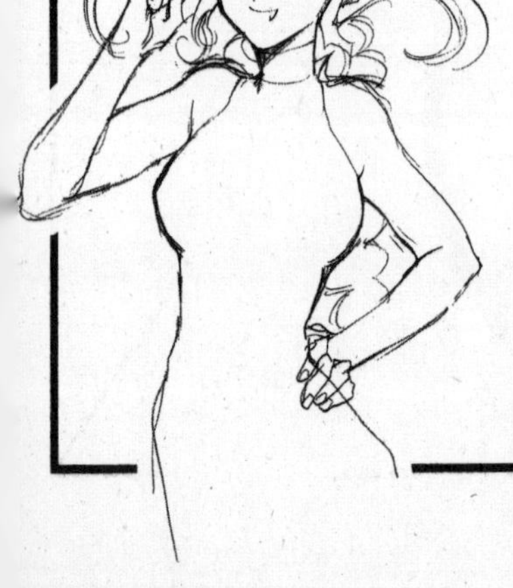

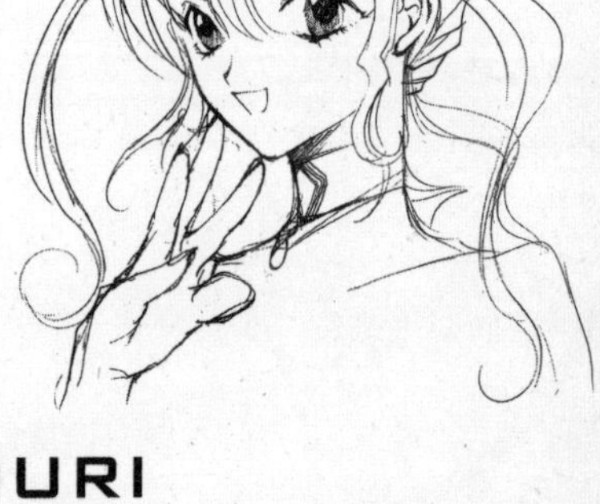

OURI

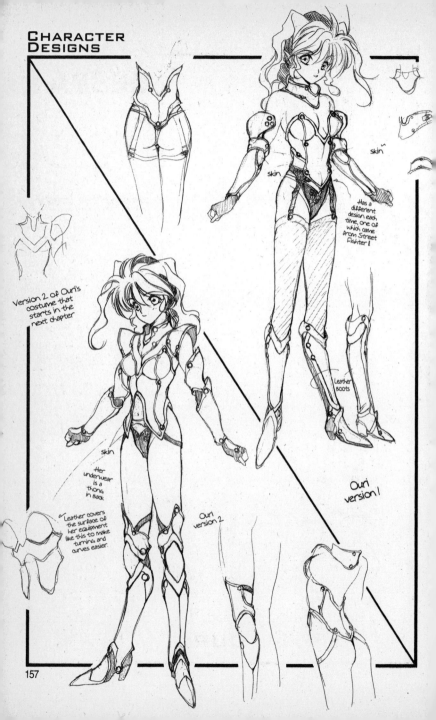

skin

skin

Has a different design each time, one of which came from Street Fighter!

Version 2 of Ouri's costume that starts in the next chapter

Leather Boots

skin

Her underwear is a thong in back.

Leather covers the surface of her equipment like this to make turning and curves easier.

Ouri version 2

Ouri version!

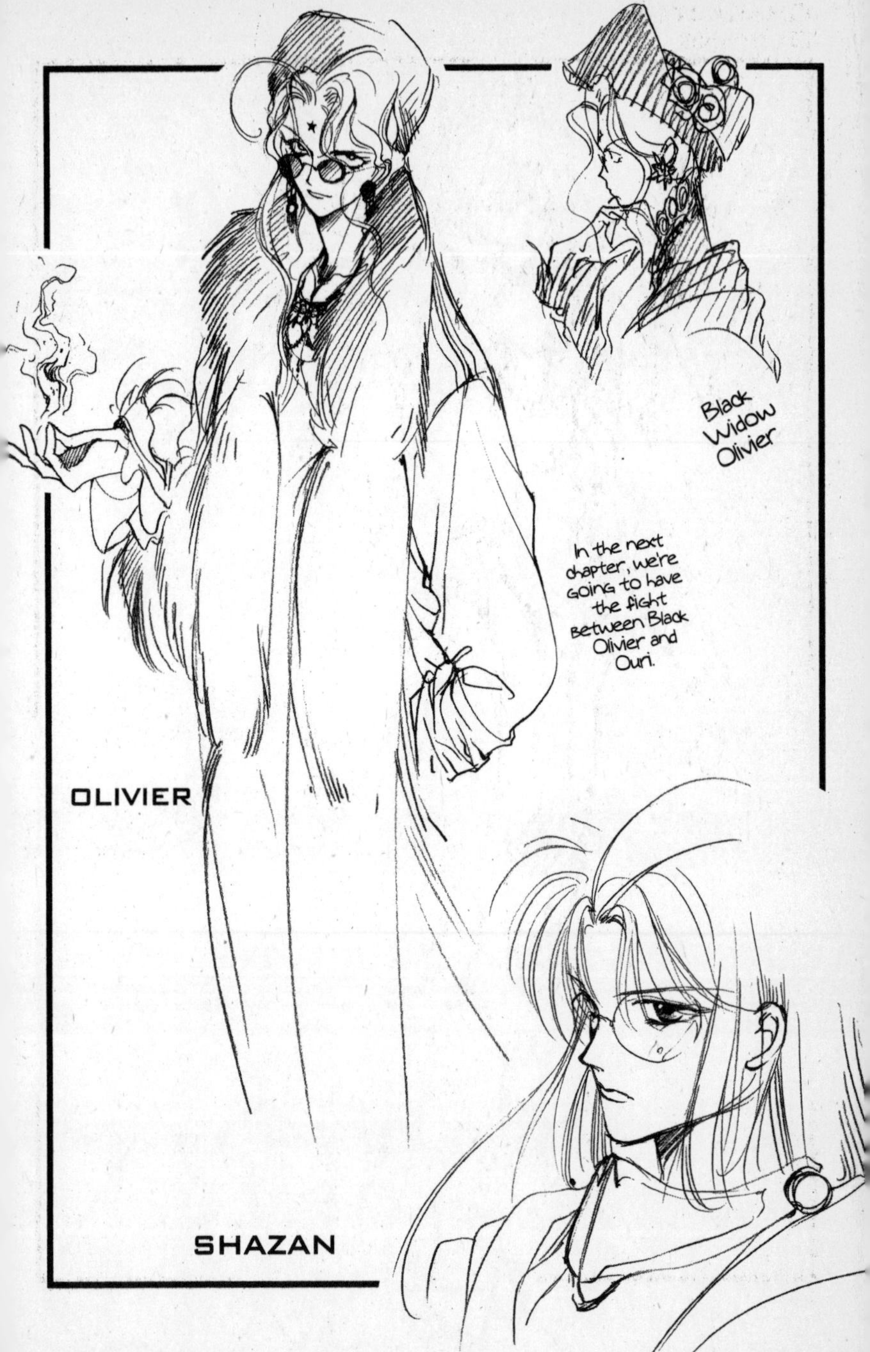
Black Widow Olivier
In the next chapter, we're going to have the fight between Black Olivier and Ouri.
OLIVIER
SHAZAN

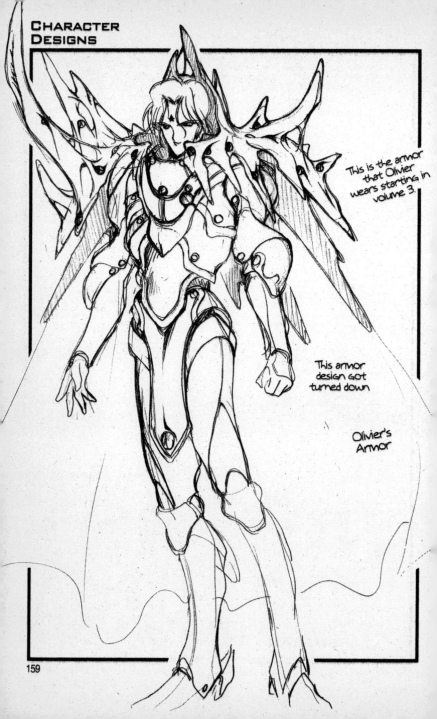

This is the armor that Olivier wears starting in volume 3.

This armor design got turned down

Olivier's Armor

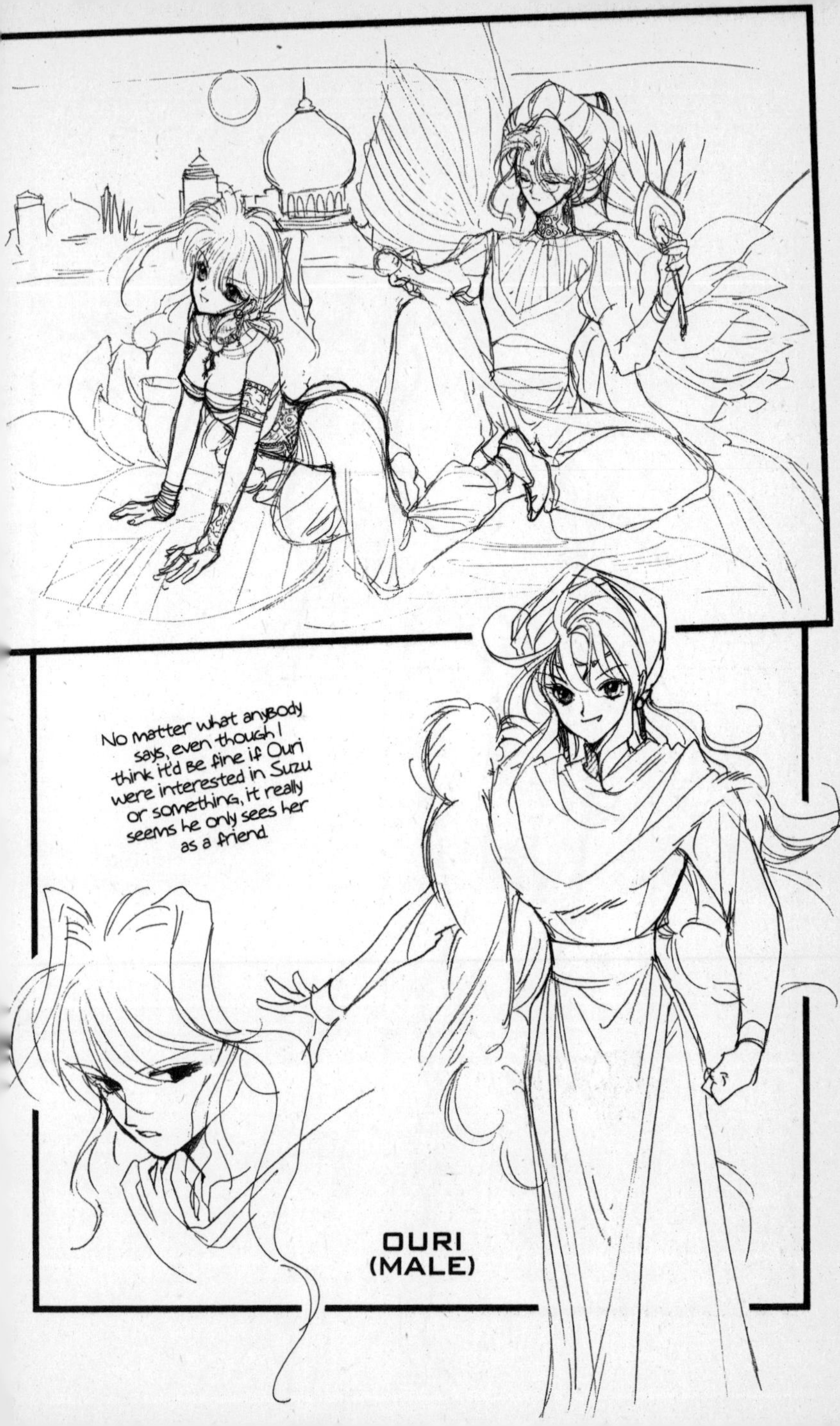
No matter what anybody says, even though I think it'd be fine if Ouri were interested in Suzu or something, it really seems he only sees her as a friend.
OURI (MALE)

We've more or less made it safely to publication!

Hello, it's me, Yun Kouga! I worked on volumes 1 and 2 simultaneously for this special edition, so the postscripts and covers were both done at the same time.

The editor who handled the script and colors was the same one who took care of the script for volume 1, so both hit home in a unique way for me.

Whenever I drew Olivier, I would think "Hottie! Gotta make him a hottie!" Like a small prayer to myself...

Olivier is right up Ouri's alley in terms of taste. One of my weaknesses is how much I like pretty people, so I always try to draw them as pretty as possible.

For being a hottie, he keeps getting bigger and bigger (throughout the manga). I guess I really have a thing for tall guys. He's probably about 6'3".

Time for a tangent.

So, we have Ouri who turns from a guy to a girl, but if I could go from a girl to a guy, I'd wanna be the kind of guy you'd see participating in K-1!! You know, a strong guy.

This kind of guy-to-girl (from a genderbending curse) plot point is one I've always been pretty fond of, but when I gave it a shot with Ouri, I knew from his personality that I wouldn't have any cause for worry nor a bit of trouble. (I wonder if I failed in a sense regarding that...)

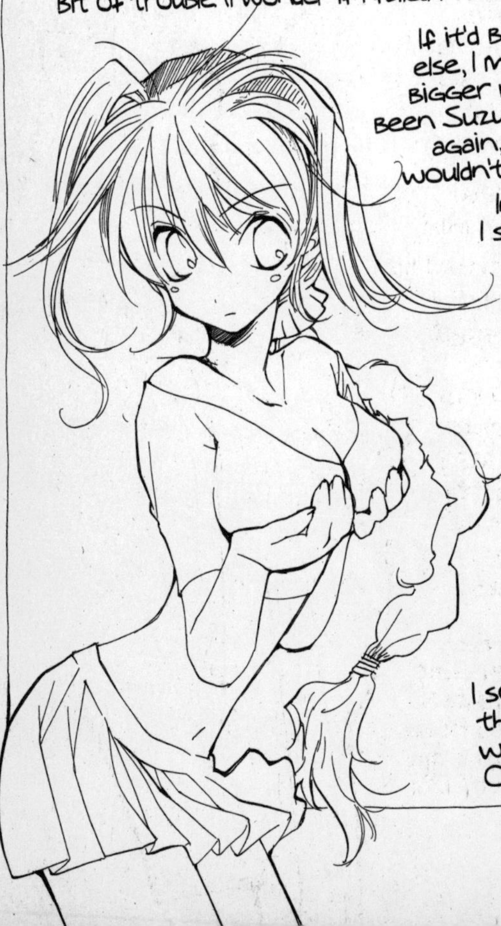

If it'd been with anybody else, I might've gotten a bigger reaction (like if it'd been Suzu or somebody). Then again, Shazan probably wouldn't have worked at all.

In any case, I guess I should mention that the image I always had for Ouri was the "Trickster".

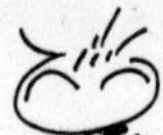

Well!!

I hope to see you again in volume 3!

Spring 2005
Yun Kouga

I sorta feel like this is the only way I ever draw Ouri. Wa ha ha!

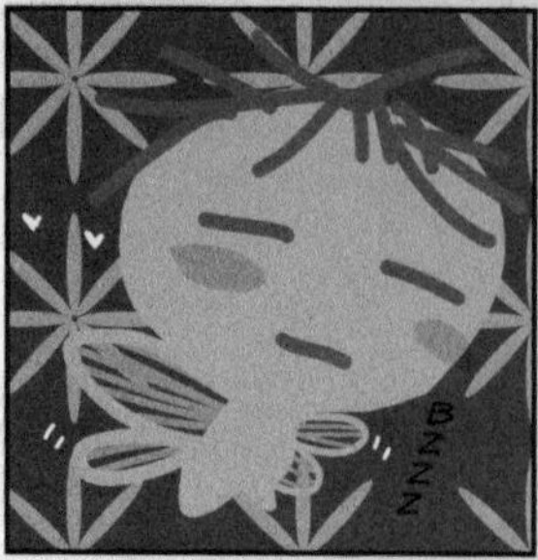
BNNN

Our favorite priest plans to mature into a wise sage some day. That priest is the character Olivier, who seems pretty dull and standard, and isn't usually the kind of character I'm into, but through the course of this manga, he's turned into a real favorite of mine. Priest types are the best! Like Angelo Kukule from *Dragon Quest VIII*.

Yun Kouga began her career as a doujinshi and debuted in 1986 with the original manga *Metal Heart*, serialized in *Comic VAL*. She is the creator of the popular series *Loveless* and *Earthian*, along with many manga and anime projects, including character design for *Gundam 00*.

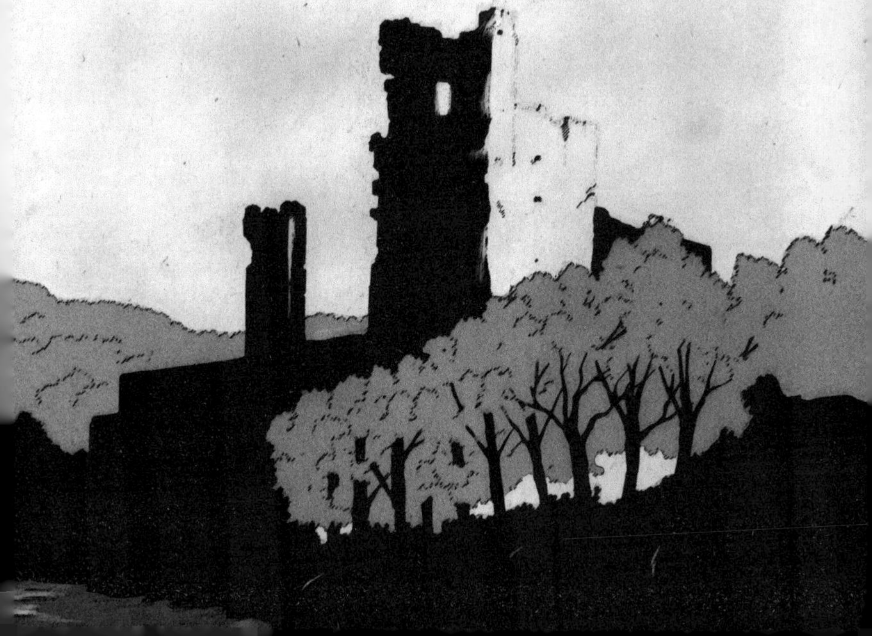

Gestalt
Vol. 2

Story and Art by Yun Kouga

Translation & English Adaptation/Christine Schilling
Touch-up Art & Lettering/Evan Waldinger
Design/Sean Lee
Editor/Chris Mackenzie

VP, Production/Alvin Lu
VP, Publishing Licensing/Rika Inouye
VP, Sales & Product Marketing/Gonzalo Ferreyra
VP, Creative/ Linda Espinosa
Publisher/Hyoe Narita

CHOUJUU DENSETSU GESTALT
© Yun Kouga / ICHIJINSHA

Printed in the U.S.A.

Published by VIZ Media, LLC
P.O. Box 77010
San Francisco, CA 94107

VIZ Media Edition
10 9 8 7 6 5 4 3 2 1
First printing, August 2009

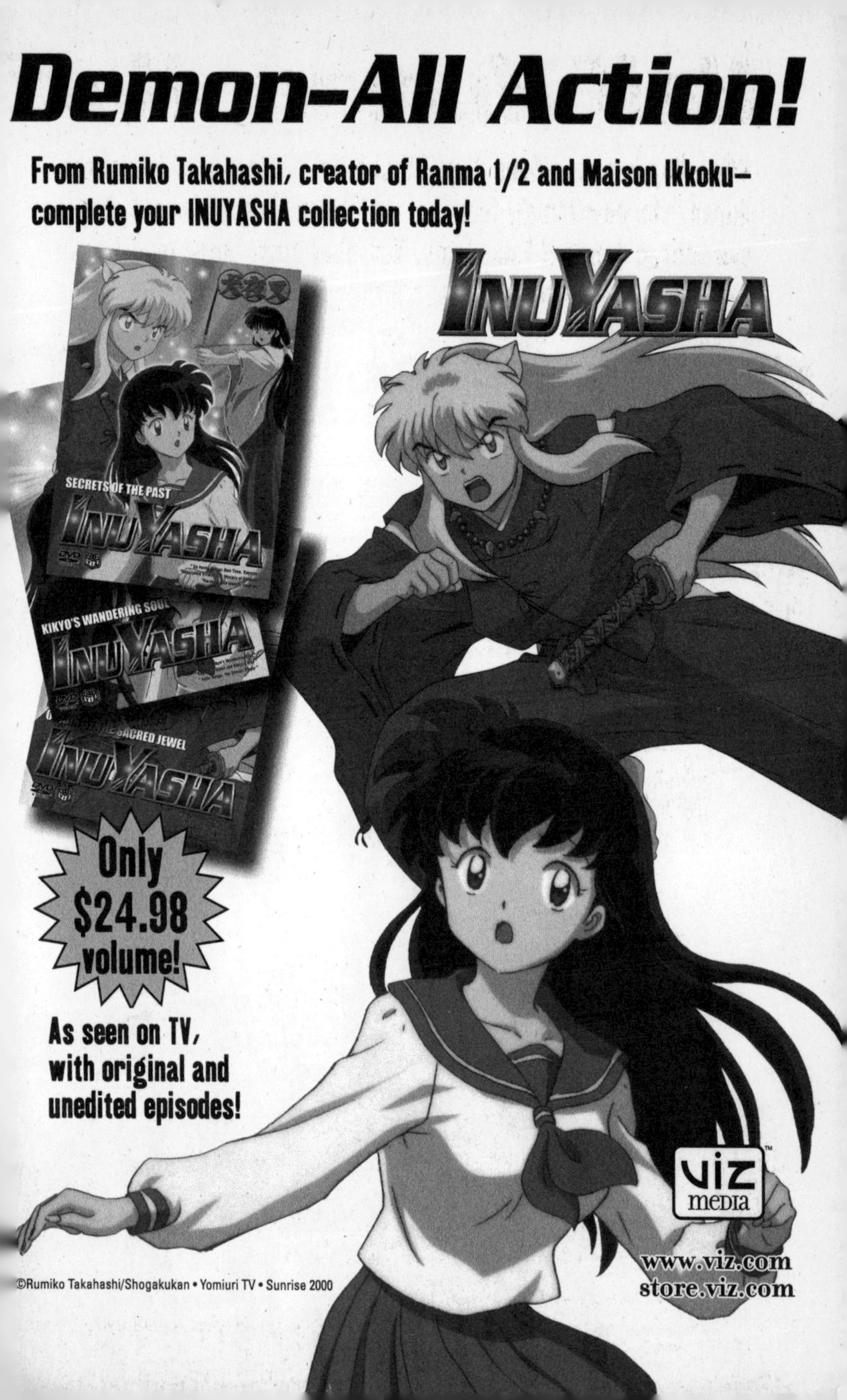
Demon-All Action!
From Rumiko Takahashi, creator of Ranma 1/2 and Maison Ikkoku–
complete your INUYASHA collection today!
INUYASHA
SECRETS OF THE PAST
INUYASHA
KIKYO'S WANDERING SOUL
INUYASHA
INUYASHA
Only $24.98 volume!
As seen on TV, with original and unedited episodes!
VIZ media
www.viz.com
store.viz.com
©Rumiko Takahashi/Shogakukan • Yomiuri TV • Sunrise 2000

Half Human, Half

When Kagome discovers a well that transports her to feudal era Japan, she unwittingly frees a half-demon, Inuyasha, and shatters the sacred Jewel of Four Souls. Now they must work together to restore the jewel before it falls into the wrong hands...

INUYASHA

The manga that inspired a phenomenon!

FULL COLOR adaptation of the TV series!

Only $9.95!

Only $11.95!